Christmas 101

Christmas 101

Celebrate the Holiday Season from Christmas to New Year's

Rick Rodgers

Photographs by Ben Fink

WM
WILLIAM MORROW
An Imprint of HarperCollins Publishers

FIRST WILLIAM MORROW EDITION

Designed by rlf design

Library of Congress Cataloging-in-Publication Data

Rodgers, Rick, 1953–
　Christmas 101 : celebrate the holiday season from Christmas to New Year's / Rick Rodgers.
　　p. cm.
　ISBN: 978-0-06-122734-9
　ISBN-10: 0-06-122734-X
　1. Christmas cookery.　I. Title.　II. Title: Christmas one hundred one.

TX739.2.C45R63 2007
641.5'686—dc22

2006041271

07 08 09 10 11　WBC/QWF　10 9 8 7 6 5 4 3 2 1

Contents

Acknowledgments

The holidays bring especially wonderful memories of my family. My parents, Dick and Eleanor Rodgers, play a big part in all of my books, because they taught my brothers and me how to cook in the first place. And in a holiday book where generosity and warmth of spirit are celebrated, this terrific couple deserves to be up front and center.

Diane Kniss, as always, stuck by me through countless dozens of cookies, mountains of candy, and yet another batch of turkey recipes. Celebrating Christmas outside of its season was fun, but even more so with Diane around.

Thanks to the friends who supplied recipes, Vicki Caparulo, Marie Intaschi, Ron Marten, Mary-Lynn Mondich, Grigg K. Murdoch, and Howard Shepherdson. A special note of gratitude is due to Kelly Polan for testing recipes.

When people ask me what I like most about my job, my answer is easy—teaching cooking classes. Nothing beats the interaction with my students, and traveling all over the country, I get a firsthand look at how people really like to cook and shop for groceries. I will always be grateful to the schools that gave me this invaluable opportunity: Sur La Table (headquartered in Seattle, WA), Adventures in Cooking (Wayne, NJ), Draeger's (Menlo Park and San Mateo, CA), The Silo (New Milford, CT), Classic Thyme (Westfield, NJ), Cook 'N' Tell (Colts Neck, NJ), Central Market (schools throughout Texas), Kroger's (Tampa and Sarasota, FL), In Good Taste (Portland, OR), and Let's Get Cookin' (Westlake Village, CA).

First, an extra serving of dessert to my old friend Harriet Bell, who originally saw the value in holiday cookbooks that taught the basics. Thanks to Gail Winston who took over the reins with grace, and was ably assisted by Sarah Whitman-Salkin. I am also happy for the support of Michael Morrison and David Sweeney at William Morrow/ HarperCollins. Production editor Ann Cahn kept the book on schedule, and I kept copy editor Leda Scheintaub busy. The original version of this book was improved by the work of Sonia Greenbaum. I lift a toast of Grand Marnier to Susan Ginsburg, my longtime agent and friend, and her assistant, Emily Scardino.

Finally, my deepest appreciation and admiration to Patrick Fisher, who has come home to goose dinners in the middle of July and kept his sense of humor throughout. And to his coworkers at *Newsweek* magazine, who gleefully helped eat all of those holiday cookies and candies.

Introduction

t's no secret. I love the holidays. Now, Thanksgiving is great, but I have to admit that there is one thing wrong with that holiday—it's only one day long. On the other hand, it makes up for this deficiency by being the start of the long Christmas and New Year's holiday season. The day after Thanksgiving, as soon as I set the turkey soup on to simmer, I inaugurate the next six weeks of partying. It's quite a whirlwind, but I revel in every second.

In my cooking classes, where many of my students are young people who want to start their own holiday traditions, I hear the same questions over and over again. How can I have a cocktail party that I will enjoy as much as my guests? How do I get my kitchen together to bake a big batch of cookies? What's a great Christmas dinner menu and how can it be organized to get all of the food on the table at once? But most of all, I hear a sad story: They never got that recipe for their favorite cookies from Grandma, and now they live a life of

regret. (They just might find the recipe in this collection.)

As in *Thanksgiving 101*, where I concentrated on how to deal with that holiday's demands and pleasure, I want to share my tips on how to have a hassle-free, fun, and delicious Christmas season. You can do it! It boils down to one word: organization.

When I was catering, we often had two or three parties on the same day. But as busy as I was, I never allowed business to get in the way of my own personal Christmas festivities. I always found the time to bake my own cookies, make food gifts, send out cards, and put up the tree. How? I baked cookies before the holiday rush and froze them. I made food gifts like flavored vinegars that improved with aging. I bought Christmas cards the first week they appeared in stores, and addressed them on lazy October afternoons or while trapped on long airplane flights between coast-to-coast cooking classes. And how did I put up the tree? I threw a tree-trimming party. I would much rather make a buffet meal of easy, never-fail recipes (that are included in this book) for friends than fret over hanging the ornaments.

Too many people think of these recipes as strictly holiday fare. OK—maybe you don't want to serve fruitcake at a Fourth of July bash, but there are plenty of other dishes here to use for year-round entertaining. Everyone should have a recipe for a great baked ham or roast tenderloin for buffets. The appetizers in this book would be welcome at any party. And the tips on how to turn out dozens of cookies without stress will come in handy whenever you have a cookie craving.

It is not the goal of this book to be a complete holiday cookbook—to include all of the traditional Christmas and New Year's foods cooked around the world would take volumes. These recipes are for my favorite holiday foods in time-tested versions that I have served to catering clients, cooking class students, and friends for years. Some recipes are labeled "101." These are basic recipes that I explain in depth, just as if you were taking one of my cooking classes. Also, I am fascinated with how our culinary traditions developed. In the sections entitled "It Wouldn't Be the Holidays Without . . ." you'll find out why we eat the things we do during the holidays.

This is a somewhat personal book, as I have been influenced by the recipes and traditions of my family and friends. If you have a family favorite that isn't included here, I hope it motivates you to get the recipe from your elders and start your own holiday collection. Don't be one of those people who regret not getting Aunt Zelda's cookie recipe. Ask her! That is the only way these wonderful traditions are passed along.

Making a List and Checking It Twice

Organization is a skill I developed as a caterer. The holiday season was our business time. We catered every kind of party, from corporate cocktail bashes to celebrity-studded open houses, to tree trimmings (once a hostess insisted that the children decorate cookies to hang on the tree—nice idea, but what a mess!), to elegant sit-down dinners. We often had two or three parties on the same day, so each one had to be organized to the last frilled toothpick. Lists saved the day.

No matter what kind of party you are giving, a series of lists will help you breeze through the process. Every time you mark a chore off the list, you will get a rewarding sense of accomplishment. And if you look at a list and feel overwhelmed, pick up the phone and get a friend to give you a hand. Here are the lists that I use again and again:

• **Guest List:** If you are having a large holiday party, send out invitations as early as possible, no later than three weeks beforehand. Very often guests will receive multiple invitations for the same evening, so get your claim in first. The most popular dates seem to fall on the second and third weekends of December. (On the weekend before Christmas, many prospective guests are already traveling to visit families.) We usually give our holiday party the week between Christmas and New Year's, or sometimes even up to Epiphany, on January 6. This avoids the usual holiday snafu, and we get a lot more acceptances. If necessary, send a map to the party along with the invitation so you don't have to spend time on the phone giving directions on the day of the event.

Plan on making follow-up calls to get an

accurate guest count. Lately, even with an RSVP, people just aren't very good about confirming invitations or even attending parties that they have accepted invitations to. You can go to a party invitation Web site, but I much prefer sending invitations in the mail. It is acceptable to include your Christmas card in the envelope, which accomplishes two mailing chores.

● **Grocery Lists:** For every large party, be it a buffet, cocktail gathering, or dinner party, make at least three grocery lists and a beverage list. This way you're not stuck doing a huge amount of shopping at the last minute. Also, try to shop during off hours. Especially during the last couple of holiday season weekends, it is usually less crowded at the supermarket on a Friday night than on a Saturday morning. When you write down your grocery items, organize them by category so you don't have to retrace your steps because you forgot something across the store.

The first grocery list is for nonperishable items that can be purchased two or three weeks ahead of the party. This includes candles, coffee filters, guest towels and soap, camera batteries, paper towels, aluminum foil, plastic wrap, and other incidentals. Buy coffee and freeze it. As I will be doing a lot of baking, I buy flour, sugar (granulated, brown, and confectioners'), eggs, vanilla, ground cinnamon, active dry yeast, and other common baking ingredients to have on hand. This way if I have some free time and the mood strikes, I don't have to go running out for the staples—I just preheat the oven and stir up some dough.

The second grocery list is for a few days before the party and is more specific. Buy all the produce that will keep for a week (like onions, potatoes, garlic, lemons, and

limes), dairy items (cheese, cream, milk, and more butter and eggs if you need them), and canned goods. If necessary, order special ingredients like Prime grade meat, fresh goose, seafood, or caviar. Call the bakery to reserve rolls, cookies, cakes, and pies (if you aren't baking them yourself).

The last grocery list is for the day before the party. Now is the time to get the meats, seafood, produce items, and ice that you'll need. I usually buy my produce at the greengrocer—it's less crowded and the quality is higher than most supermarkets.

Holiday recipes call for the very best ingredients. Baked goods in particular require high-quality candied fruits, nuts, and chocolate. If you need to mail-order ingredients or make a detour to a specialty shop, write a separate list for them. For example, I have a favorite shop that makes wonderful hard candies and sells great candied fruit and another that provides me with perfect walnut halves—the shops are out of my way, but if I anticipate what I need, I can stop by when I am in their neighborhoods.

The beverage list includes all drinks, alcoholic or not. If you live in a state that sells liquor in grocery stores, put it with the second list. Otherwise, don't forget nonalcoholic drinks and mixers on your first grocery list. And be sure to include drink garnishes like cinnamon sticks or whole nutmeg for grating.

● **Prep Lists:** There are a lot of cooking chores that can be done well ahead of time. Look at your menu for potential freezable items. I am not a big "freezer person," but I do freeze a few quarts of homemade stock.

Many cookie doughs need to be chilled for a few hours before rolling out, which can actually be a boon, as it allows a window of opportunity to bake other cookies that don't need prechilling.

Be realistic about how much time it will take for you to make something. Only you know how fast you can roll out and decorate cookie dough. And schedule in cleaning time. It is much easier to clean as you go along than to wait until the dishes are piled so high you can't stand it anymore.

Utensil Lists: When I was a beginning cook, I was pretty enthusiastic and very often jumped into a recipe before checking to be sure I had the right utensils or serving dishes. Sometimes the recipe turned out, and sometimes . . . not. The same thing happened when I designed an overly ambitious menu and found myself trying to make a sauce in a skillet because all of the saucepans were already filled.

Make a list of all the pots, pans, basters, roasting racks, coffeemakers, and baking dishes you'll need to make the food for your party. If you're baking cookies, take stock of your cookie cutters, decorating bags, and tips, as well as cookie sheets (you can never have too many of these during the holiday season). In the recipes here I've tried to use pots and pans found in typical kitchens, but if a recipe calls for something out of the ordinary, it will say so in the headnote. You may have to go to a kitchenware shop or mail-order source for a couple of items, but then you will have them for future holiday celebrations.

Purchase a healthy supply of large self-sealing plastic bags to store cookies and other baked goods. When I throw a party, I use them to store food in the refrigerator in place of bowls, which take up too much refrigerator space.

Tableware List: Check that you have all the serving dishes and utensils you need for your party. (I never had enough large serving forks and spoons until I finally went out and bought an extra pair as insurance.) Many items are stored away, so take them out and wash them. To keep all of these bowls and platters straight, list what food goes in what dish. If silver has to be polished or linens washed and pressed, schedule those jobs well ahead of time.

If you don't have enough china and silver, purchase high-quality disposable plates and utensils at a party-supply shop. Buy the good stuff—you really don't want your plate to collapse under the weight of the food. A few years ago, I bought inexpensive dishes and flatware at a restaurant supply shop (you can also find "buffet sets" at big-box stores), and they have paid for themselves many times over. Sure, you don't have to wash the disposable stuff, but my ecological conscience tells me that it's not so hard to wash plates and silverware. At a buffet, where you may be balancing food on your lap, a disposable plate can't hold a candle to a sturdy glass or china one.

In a pinch, I'll use plastic cups (or heatproof ones for drinks), but I still prefer my stash of cheap restaurant-quality glassware and coffee mugs. You can always borrow what you need from family or friends or rent them. Most rental companies have a minimum charge during the holidays. It might seem excessive, but if you factor in convenience, it may not seem so expensive after all. I admit that the number of guests and the amount of help you have in the kitchen to clean up will dictate the type of serveware used, but I much prefer the real thing to disposable at a special holiday affair.

For a multi-dish dinner party or buffet table, draw a "map" that shows where the serving dishes and centerpiece will go to make sure that everything will fit. If things are crowded, figure out where you will put the excess. At my house, I have found that I have more room if I put the plates on a sideboard, and the silverware (which has been rolled up inside the napkins) goes at the end of the buffet, so guests don't have to juggle it while filling their plates. If you are serving a crowd at a buffet, pull the table away from the wall if necessary, so guests can serve themselves from both sides, and put two utensils in each bowl for faster service.

- **The Bill of Fare:** Always write out the complete menu, including beverages, and tape it in a prominent space in the kitchen to be sure that everything is served. In the fray of a big party, it is easy to forget to put something out. For a large dinner party with dishes that require final preparations, I make a timetable (see the "Holiday Menu Planner" on page 159). I even put down "Make coffee and tea" on the timetable as a reminder.

I also have started a new tradition. A friend once gave me some blank engraved menu cards, so now in addition to the scribbled menu in the kitchen, I print out the complete menu in a nice font on the computer and place the menu card on a stand in the dining room. It's a nice touch, and my guests enjoy knowing the "official" names of the dishes. At sit-down dinners, I will even go so far as to print out a menu for each place setting.

When planning a menu, be realistic about what you can prepare and store. Don't become a victim of what I call "TV-itis." That's where someone who watches television cooking shows where the chefs prepare an elaborate dish thinks he or she can pull off the same dish with the same ease. What you don't see on these shows is the crew of helpers backstage chopping, mincing, and cleaning up!

A common holiday dinner party problem is having too many side dishes that need to be heated in the oven. Not everyone has a double oven, including yours truly, although I do have an auxiliary portable oven in my basement that is called into play to heat up casseroles and the like. To avoid an oven traffic jam, balance the baked side dishes with those that can be prepared on the stovetop. Also, for a buffet, it's easy to prepare too many dishes that require refrigeration. If necessary, plan to borrow refrigerator space from a neighbor. Occasionally, when the weather is cold, I turn my sun porch into a walk-in refrigerator and chill some food outside, but that's not for all climates, and if there's a warm spell, I'm in trouble. So be practical and design a menu that works for your kitchen and your cooking skills.

Decking the Halls

During the holidays, everyone wants his or her home to look like it came out the pages of a glossy lifestyle magazine. But my strengths lie in the kitchen. You won't find me making papier-mâché Nativity scenes or hot-gluing Styrofoam reindeer. But if you can fit crafts projects into your schedule, be my guest.

When it comes to holiday decorating, if it can't be done simply and quickly, I don't do it. One of my easiest and most effective centerpieces is a large glass bowl of red and green apples entwined with colorful French wired ribbon. The guests can eat the apples (I stick a small, sharp knife in an apple as a signal that it's OK to snack), and there are usually some left over to turn into apple pie or applesauce later. Clementines and persimmons, which are in season in December, look great in a bowl decorated with metallic gold ribbon.

A quick stop at the florist will give you lots of ideas. Take advantage of seasonal plants and greens: It's amazing what can be done with reasonably priced poinsettias, holly, mistletoe, and sprigs of pine. Please remember that the first three plants are poisonous, so don't use them to decorate food platters! To be safe, I don't put them anywhere near the food. And if you plan to use evergreen boughs anywhere near a lighted candle, spray the greens with fire retardant (available at hobby shops and nurseries). My florist also sells me large bowls of red ribbons (he calls them "church pew bows") that I wire to the stairway banister. Professionally tied and inexpensive, they look a lot better than anything I could come up with myself. If I store them properly, I can get a couple of years' use out of them.

When your friends walk into your home, don't they comment on the mouthwatering aroma of a roasting turkey or beef roast? Your house should smell delicious; it sets the scene for a good party. When I am having a cocktail buffet, a lot of the cooking has been done in advance, so there won't be enticing kitchen aromas. To compensate, I simmer a handful of spices (cinnamon sticks, allspice berries, cloves, and freshly sliced ginger) in a pot of water, allowing their scent to waft through the house. At the very least, I sprinkle room-scenting oil on a few lightbulbs (the heat of the bulb warms the oil and disperses the scent). Many of these oils are designed especially for the holidays and have evergreen or spice scents. My own taste runs to the spicy or herbaceous—I don't like anything too sweet or floral.

The lighting of your party location is important. Strings of twinkle lights are festive, but test the lights before you hang them and replace any bulbs as needed. Use candles to give the room a glow, but situate them properly (away from lamp shades or anyplace a guest could accidentally come into contact with the flame) to avoid any problems. Make sure to use dripless candles. I have seen plenty of furniture ruined by a lava flow of dyed hot wax. One of my catering clients always replaced a few of the lightbulbs in her lamps with soft-pink bulbs. She claimed it not only made the room more romantic but it made everyone look fabulous, too. She was right.

Even Santa Has Elves

The upside of having a big holiday party is enjoying the company of your friends in your festive, seasonably decorated home. The downside is cleaning the house and putting up the decorations. Make a list of all of the chores, from cleaning the windows to taking the Christmas boxes out of storage.

I also firmly believe in letting my friends help out. When I bake cookies, it is usually with my friend Diane at my side. With four hands and experience from our annual cookie fest, we can really crank them out. However, I have learned that potlucks don't work because my buddies don't always bring what they were assigned. ("I really tried to bake a cake, but when Santa came, he twisted his ankle coming down the chimney, and we had to take him to the emergency room, so I brought this wine instead.") What I really need is someone to come the night before a party and keep me company while I cook. Of course, they are asked to chop an onion or two or wash a few dishes during the visit, but it really helps me keep things under control.

But whenever I need serious help, I dig

into my pockets to pay for it. When I budget my holiday bash, I hire a maid service the day before to vacuum, dust, and do all the other mundane cleaning that I just can't find the time to do. If you don't want to call a maid service from the phone book, check with your local college to see if they have a temporary employment office, or hire a neighbor's kid.

If you are really pressed for time, remember the dictum I learned from Peg Bracken (the original "I Hate to Cook" lady) a long time ago: Clean the bathroom really well and be sure to shine the faucets. If the bathroom faucets sparkle, everyone will think you are a great housekeeper. If you use enough candles and turn the lights low enough, no one will ever notice the dust bunnies under the sofa.

If you're having a large party, budget for a waitstaff. For a party of thirty or fewer, you'll only need one person, but what a help that can be. Your waitperson can help answer the door, hang coats, pick up dirty glasses and dishes, warm things up, make drinks, keep the kitchen tidy, and do other little things that keep you from enjoying your guests. Make another list of duties that you expect them to perform. I live in the New York City area, where people are used to seeing waitstaff at parties. If you feel it is a little pretentious, why not hire someone familiar, like that neighbor's kid? Just be sure they are over drinking age if you expect them to handle alcohol. I hate having to face a dirty house after a party. My Christmas gift to myself is waking up after a bash to a clean home.

Rockin' Around the Christmas Tree

As any host or hostess will tell you, the right music is as important as the food and drink. At parties for other holidays, you can play whatever you like. (There is no Thanksgiving music, with the possible exception of "Alice's Restaurant," and no one will complain if you don't play "Stars and Stripes Forever" at your Fourth of July barbecue.) But Christmas carols are a huge part of the holiday experience, and should not be passed over just because a few of them are, well, not so bouncy.

Most traditional Christmas carols will slow a party down quicker than finding the family pet drinking out of the punch bowl. When I'm opening presents on Christmas morning, I'll put on "Messiah," but a good party needs music that swings. Here are my favorites, guaranteed to get the party moving. (P.S. These are also great albums to have around when you need some motivation to whip through your gift-wrapping.) It's a big variety, but different types of music will keep things interesting. There is hardly a slow song in the bunch—and if one shows up, just push "fast forward." So stack these babies up in the CD player, and push the "random play" button. Now, hang the mistletoe, and get down with Santa!

Identifying numbers refer to compact discs, unless stated otherwise.

A Christmas Gift for You from Phil Spector (Rhino; RNCD 70235). A classic album of Christmas pop tunes from the Ronettes, Darlene Love, the Crystals, and friends.

Christmas Jollies (Right Stuff; 7243-8-53714-2-4). Wanna disco around the Christmas tree? The Salsoul Orchestra will have the crowd putting down their cider to do the Hustle.

Ella Fitzgerald Wishes You a Swinging Christmas (Verve; ASIN B00000464M). Same to you, Ella. Upbeat versions of the favorites.

Christmas Cocktails Part One (Capitol; CDP 7243 8 52559 2 2). Before Brian Seltzer, there were great bands and singers recorded in fabulous high-fidelity sound. You're in Yulesville, baby!

Christmas Cocktails Part Two (Capitol; CDP 7243 8 21457 2 1). More of the same, even cooler.

A Broadway Christmas (Varese Sarabande; tape, VSC-5517). Various Broadway and cabaret artists croon their way through a jolly bunch of Yuletide songs from the Great White Way.

Appetizers, Snacks, and Beverages

t's the holiday season, and that means lots of parties—especially big cocktail parties. Be it the "let's have everyone in the office over for a drink" get-together to the New Year's Eve bash, I will throw a Yuletide cocktail party at the drop of a paper hat. As a caterer, I learned some pretty specific rules about what makes a good one. First of all, a good party is one that the host actually attends. To be specific, he is *not* buried in the kitchen, heating up little itty-bitty appetizers and artistically arranging them on platters.

In my catering days, I was handsomely paid to create intricate hors d'oeuvres, but my days of piping goat cheese into snow peas are over. If you hire a caterer with a full-service staff, then you can relax with your friends while they are working in the kitchen and passing those

doggone hors d'oeuvres. But if you're making and serving the food yourself, you'd better take a different approach.

Prepare lots of easy-to-make appetizers with bold flavors that go well with beverages, be they cocktails, beer, wine, or nonalcoholic drinks. Choose make-ahead recipes that can be multiplied into larger quantities. Banish any food that must be passed—especially hot appetizers that are only good if they are served warm from the oven. Serve big bowls of wonderfully tasty food to which people can help themselves: warm dips, savory spreads, spiced nuts, marinated olives, smooth-and-nutty cheese balls, crunchy snacks like my Santa Fe Crunch, flaky cheese straws, slow cookers filled with meatballs.

Fill out the menu with a baked ham or roast

turkey, an overflowing basket of fresh rolls, and condiments like honey mustard and mango chutney, so the guests can make sandwiches. Serve one or two salads, something substantial like Tortellini Antipasto Salad, and another salad on the light side, like The Original Ambrosia. To cut down on washing plates, make desserts that can be eaten out of hand, like homemade cookies or gingerbread. With this kind of a menu, all you need to do is fill up bowls and replenish platters every now and then.

Take a similar approach with the bar. You can be a bartender or a host, but rarely both. It's one thing to put out a few bottles of liquor and mixers and let your guests make their own drinks. It's another thing to pull out the blender, just in case someone wants a margarita. (Once they hear that blender going, you may be making margaritas all night.)

Holiday parties should have holiday drinks. Always serve at least one seasonal beverage, like ice-cold eggnog or warm mulled wine, and make that the evening's specialty of the house. (I love Christmastime beverages so much that I usually make one cold and one warm drink.) Because you are legally responsible to be aware of your guests' alcoholic intake, you should pay as much attention to your nonalcoholic beverages as the liquor. It is important that the designated drivers not feel left out. Make something like nonalcoholic Cider Wassail—guests can enjoy it plain, or with a little splash of brandy or rum. Or serve chilled sparkling cider in Champagne glasses. A lot of wine and champagne are poured during the holiday season. For a large party, it isn't easy to find someplace to chill a case or two. The worst place is in the refrigerator, because the bottles just take up too much room. In lieu of an ice chest, many kitchenware shops have attractive, large copper or galvanized tubs that will hold plenty of bottles. If you like to give parties, they are a very good investment, and can also be used in the summertime to hold the beers at your barbecues. In a pinch, I have lined the Champagne's cardboard cases with heavy-duty garbage bags, replaced the bottles in the cases, and filled them with ice. Place the ice-filled boxes someplace like an auxiliary sink or bathtub, where they can drip without causing a dangerous puddle. Don't forget to pick up or order plenty of ice.

There are a few cocktail party logistics that are commonly overlooked and should be addressed.

- Be sure you have enough space to hang coats. You may have to rent or borrow a coat rack.

- If parking might be a problem, talk to your neighbors before the party to see if you can work out a solution. (If you ask really nicely or bring them a box of your homemade cookies, they might let you use some of their parking area.)

- Remove all the furniture you can from the main gathering rooms, or at least rearrange it so the room can fit more people. Guests expect to stand at a cocktail party, and they can circulate more easily if they aren't tripping over the ottoman.

- Buy lots of cocktail napkins—you'll need some for the appetizers, and extra as coasters. Don't leave your guests to look all over for napkins, or you could end up with ring marks on your tables.

- Have the phone number of a taxi or car service handy, and use it to send any overindulgent driving friends home in style.

Caesar Dip with Crudités

Thick, cheesy Caesar salad dressing seemed a natural to turn into a dip. But when I was researching the original dressing recipe, I found out a fascinating fact. Caesar salad was originally served with whole romaine lettuce hearts because it was meant to be eaten with the fingers! And it's just as good with other vegetables. If you wish, serve the dip with Garlic Crostini, too. They'll be reminiscent of the croutons served on Caesar Salad.

Makes about 12 appetizer servings

Make Ahead: The dip can be made up to 3 days ahead; the vegetables can be prepared up to 1 day ahead.

DIP
1 cup mayonnaise
½ cup sour cream
½ cup freshly grated Parmesan or Pecorino Romano cheese
1 tablespoon fresh lemon juice
½ teaspoon anchovy paste
1 garlic clove, crushed through a press

Assorted fresh vegetables, such as romaine hearts separated into leaves, carrot, celery, and cucumber sticks, mushroom caps, cherry tomatoes, and Garlic Crostini (page 12), for dipping

1. To make the dip, mix together all the ingredients in a medium bowl. Cover and chill for at least 1 hour before serving.

2. To serve, transfer the dip to a serving bowl and serve with the vegetables.

Stilton and Walnut Balls

Cheese balls aren't supposed to be classy, just delicious, but this recipe has a very sophisticated combination of flavors. It goes well with plain water crackers, but it is also terrific spread on sliced pears.

Makes 12 to 16 appetizer servings

Make Ahead: The cheese balls can be made up to 5 days ahead.

8 ounces Stilton or other blue cheese, rind removed, at room temperature
One 8-ounce package cream cheese, at room temperature
2 tablespoons tawny port
¼ teaspoon freshly ground black pepper
1 cup walnuts, toasted and coarsely chopped
Water crackers, for serving
Cored, sliced, ripe Bosc pears, tossed with lemon juice to discourage browning, for serving

1. In a medium bowl, using a rubber spatula, mash the Stilton and cream cheese together until smooth. Work in the port and pepper. Place a piece of plastic wrap on the work surface, and scrape the cheese mixture into the center of the wrap. Use the plastic wrap to form the cheese mixture into a ball (it will be soft). Refrigerate until the ball is chilled and firm, at least 4 hours or overnight.

2. To serve, unwrap the ball and roll in the chopped nuts. Transfer to a platter and serve with the crackers and pears.

Sicilian Caponata
with Garlic Crostini

There are many ways to make caponata, a Sicilian vegetable spread, but the recipe should always include the capers that give the dish its name. It's as versatile as can be, effortlessly partnering with just about any cracker or bread you'd want to dunk. I make Garlic Crostini because I like the crunch, but untoasted bread is fine, too. Leftover caponata can be tossed with spaghetti for a quick supper, but bring the caponata to room temperature first so it doesn't cool the hot pasta.

Makes about 16 appetizer servings

Make Ahead: The caponata should be made 1 day ahead, but it can be stored for up to 5 days; the toasts can be made up to 8 hours ahead.

CAPONATA

1 large eggplant, cut into ¾-inch cubes
Salt
About ½ cup extra virgin olive oil
1 large onion, chopped
3 medium carrots, chopped into ½-inch pieces
3 medium celery ribs, chopped into ½-inch
    pieces
2 medium zucchini, cut into ½-inch pieces
1 large red bell pepper, cored, seeded, and cut
    into ½-inch pieces
3 garlic cloves, minced
One 28-ounce can tomatoes in juice, chopped,
    juices reserved
2 tablespoons red wine vinegar
2 tablespoons sugar
1 teaspoon dried basil
½ teaspoon dried oregano
½ teaspoon dried thyme
¼ teaspoon crushed hot red pepper
½ cup pitted, chopped Mediterranean black or
    green olives (or a combination of both)

3 tablespoons capers, drained, rinsed, and
    chopped, if large

GARLIC CROSTINI

⅓ cup extra virgin olive oil
2 garlic cloves, crushed under a knife and peeled
2 baguettes, sliced ¼ inch thick

⅓ cup pine nuts, toasted (optional)

1. To make the caponata, toss the eggplant with 1 tablespoon salt in a colander. Let stand in the sink to drain off the bitter juices, about 1 hour. Rinse very well, then pat dry with paper towels.

2. Meanwhile, in a large, heavy-bottomed pot, heat 3 tablespoons of the oil over medium heat. Add the onion, carrot, celery, zucchini, and bell pepper and cook, stirring often, until the vegetables are softened, about 10 minutes. Stir in the garlic and cook for 2 minutes. Add the tomatoes with their juice, the vinegar, sugar, basil, oregano, thyme, and crushed red pepper. Bring to a simmer and remove from the heat.

3. While the sauce is cooking, in a large nonstick skillet, heat the remaining 5 tablespoons oil over medium-high heat until very hot but not smoking. Add the eggplant and cook, turning occasionally, until browned, about 6 minutes, adding more oil if needed. Stir into the tomato sauce.

4. Bring the vegetables to a simmer over medium heat. Reduce the heat to medium-low and simmer, uncovered, stirring occasionally, until the vegetables are very tender, about 30 minutes. During the last 5 minutes, stir in the olives and capers. Remove from the heat and cool completely. Cover and refrigerate for at least 24 hours to marry the flavors. Remove from the refrigerator 1 hour before serving. Season with salt.

5. To make the crostini, position racks in the center and top third of the oven and preheat to 400°F. In a small saucepan, heat the oil and crushed garlic over low heat just until bubbles surround the garlic, about 5 minutes; do not brown the garlic. Remove from the heat and let stand for 10 minutes. Using a slotted spoon, discard the garlic.

6. Arrange the sliced bread on baking sheets. Brush the bread with the garlic oil. Bake until the toasts are golden brown, about 10 minutes. Cool on the baking sheets. (If making the toasts ahead, store in a paper bag. Do not store in a plastic bag, which will soften the toasts.)

7. To serve, transfer the caponata to a serving bowl and sprinkle with the pine nuts, if using. Serve with the crostini.

Santa Fe Crunch

You probably will recognize this as an updated version of that party mix everyone loves. It's everything a snack should be—sweet, spicy, salty, crunchy, nutty, and altogether addictive. I mean, this stuff disappears!

Makes about 18 cups; 20 appetizer servings

Make Ahead: The crunch can be made up to 3 days ahead.

4 tablespoons (½ stick) unsalted butter
¼ cup Worcestershire sauce
2 tablespoons light brown sugar
2 tablespoons chili powder
1 teaspoon salt
¼ teaspoon cayenne pepper
One 12-ounce box oven-toasted square corn
    cereal
4 cups (8 ounces) mini-pretzels
2 cups (8 ounces) dry-roasted peanuts
2 cups (8 ounces) pecans
2 cups (6 ounces) pumpkinseeds

1. Position a rack in the center of the oven and preheat to 300°F. In a small saucepan over medium-low heat, stir together the butter, Worcestershire sauce, brown sugar, chili powder, salt, and cayenne until the butter is melted.

2. In a large roasting pan (such as a turkey roaster), toss the cereal, pretzels, peanuts, pecans, and pumpkinseeds, drizzling with the butter mixture to coat.

3. Bake, stirring, every 15 minutes, until heated through, about 1 hour. Cool completely. (If making the crunch ahead, store in an airtight container.)

Spicy Cheese Straws

These elegant and flaky cheese straws are another fast-and-easy favorite. With the help of frozen puff pastry dough, you'll have beautiful appetizers in no time—at a fraction of the cost of what the local bakery charges for the same thing.

Makes 40 straws

Make Ahead: The straws can be made up to 2 days ahead.

One 17¼-ounce package frozen puff pastry
1½ cups (6 ounces) shredded extra-sharp
    cheddar cheese
½ cup freshly grated Parmesan cheese
2 teaspoons chili powder
1 teaspoon dried oregano
¼ teaspoon garlic powder
¼ teaspoon salt
¼ teaspoon cayenne pepper
1 large egg white, beaten until foamy

1. Thaw the puff pastry according to the package instructions. In a medium bowl, mix together the cheddar and Parmesan cheeses, the chili powder, oregano, garlic powder, salt, and cayenne. Set the cheese mixture aside.

2. Position racks in the center and top third of the oven and preheat to 375°F. Lightly grease two baking sheets or use ungreased nonstick sheets.

3. On a lightly floured work surface, unfold one sheet of pastry dough. Dust lightly with flour and roll into a 14 × 10-inch rectangle. Brush lightly but thoroughly with the egg white. Cut the dough in half to make two 10 × 7-inch rectangles. Sprinkle half of the cheese mixture evenly over one of the rectangles. Top with the second rectangle, egg white side down. Lightly roll the pin over the

dough to make the cheese adhere between the layers of dough. Repeat with the remaining ingredients. Place the dough rectangles on baking sheets and freeze until well chilled (this will help the twists hold their shape), about 15 minutes.

4. Working with one rectangle at a time, using a ruler and pizza wheel or a sharp knife and starting on a long side, cut the rectangle into twenty ½-inch-wide strips. Twist the strips into spirals and place ½ inch apart on the prepared baking sheets, pressing the ends of the strips onto the sheets so the spirals won't untwist during baking.

5. Bake, switching the position of the sheets halfway through baking from top to bottom and front to back, until the straws are golden brown, about 20 minutes. Let cool for about 1 minute on the sheets, then immediately transfer to wire racks. Cool completely. (If baking the straws ahead, store in an airtight container. Reheat and crisp, uncovered, for 5 minutes, in a preheated 350°F oven.)

Blue Cheese Straws: Omit the chili powder, oregano, garlic powder, and salt. Substitute 1½ cups (6 ounces) blue cheese, well crumbled, for the cheddar cheese. Substitute ½ teaspoon freshly ground black pepper for the cayenne.

Greek Mini-Meatballs

Do your friends like mini-meatballs as much as mine do? These have a slightly sweet sauce with a hint of cinnamon. If you have a good butcher who can provide you with lean ground lamb (ground lamb can be quite fatty, so ask to be sure), use it instead of the ground round. If you have any doubt about the lamb's fat content, ask the butcher to grind trimmed boneless leg of lamb. The fresh mint not only adds flavor, but color as well. If you aren't a mint fan (although it is especially delicious with lamb meatballs), use parsley or even basil.

Makes about 100 meatballs; 16 to 24 servings

Make Ahead: The meatballs can be made up to 2 days ahead.

SAUCE

3 tablespoons extra virgin olive oil
1 large onion, finely chopped
1 garlic clove, minced
One 28-ounce can crushed tomatoes in tomato purée
2 tablespoons light brown sugar
2 tablespoons red wine vinegar
1½ teaspoons dried oregano
¼ teaspoon ground cinnamon
¼ teaspoon crushed hot red pepper

MEATBALLS

3 pounds lean ground lamb or ground beef round (85 percent lean)
1 medium onion, grated through the large holes of a box grater
2 garlic cloves, crushed through a press
¾ cup dried bread crumbs
2 large eggs, beaten
1 tablespoon dried oregano
1 tablespoon salt
¾ teaspoon freshly ground black pepper
¼ cup chopped fresh mint or parsley (see Note)

1. To make the sauce, heat the oil in a large Dutch oven or saucepan over medium heat. Add the onion and cook, stirring often, until golden brown, about 8 minutes. (The onion should be cooked to golden brown to bring out its natural sugars, but do not scorch it.) Stir in the garlic and cook until fragrant, about 30 seconds. Stir in the tomatoes, brown sugar,

vinegar, oregano, cinnamon, and crushed red pepper. Bring to a boil, then reduce the heat to medium-low and simmer, stirring often, until slightly thickened, about 30 minutes. Set the sauce aside.

2. Meanwhile, make the meatballs. Position racks in the center and top third of the oven and preheat to 400°F. Lightly oil two rimmed baking sheets.

3. In a large bowl, combine all of the meatball ingredients until well mixed (your hands will do the best job). Occasionally rinsing your hands in water, roll level tablespoons of the meat mixture into balls. Place the meatballs on the baking sheets.

4. Bake until the meatballs are cooked through (cut into one to check), switching the position of the baking sheets from top to bottom and front to back halfway through baking, about 30 minutes. Stir the meatballs into the sauce. Stir in 2 tablespoons of the mint. (If making the meatballs and sauce ahead, cool, cover, and refrigerate. To reheat, stir ¼ cup water into the sauce. Cover and cook over low heat, stirring often, until heated through, about 20 minutes.)

5. Transfer the meatballs and sauce to a large chafing dish or electric slow cooker. Sprinkle with the remaining 2 tablespoons mint and serve with toothpicks and a small bowl to collect the used toothpicks.

Note: To chop herbs for garnish, prepare them as close as possible to serving time, or they may discolor. Wash the herbs in a bowl of cold water, spin dry in a salad spinner, then chop. If necessary, place the herbs in a small bowl, cover with a moist paper towel, and refrigerate until ready to use.

Pancetta, Leek, and Chèvre Tartlets

Individual savory tartlets are an elegant addition to any cocktail party menu. This filling dish, with its salty components of chèvre and pancetta, is especially tasty with those ever-popular holiday party beverages, wine and Champagne. The dough is a breeze to work with, and is simply pressed into nonstick mini-muffin tins without requiring rolling out.

Makes 24 tartlets

Make Ahead: The dough shells can be prepared up to 1 week ahead; the tartlets can be baked up to 1 day ahead.

DOUGH

1 cup all-purpose flour

¼ teaspoon salt

½ cup (1 stick) unsalted butter, chilled, cut into ½-inch cubes

One 3-ounce package cream cheese, chilled, cut into ½-inch cubes

FILLING

1 tablespoon unsalted butter

2 cups (about 3 large) chopped leeks, white and pale green part only, well rinsed

1 teaspoon vegetable oil

4 ounces thick-sliced pancetta, chopped into ½-inch dice

⅔ cup half-and-half

2 large egg yolks

¼ teaspoon salt

⅛ teaspoon freshly ground black pepper

2 ounces rindless goat cheese (chèvre), well crumbled

Fresh parsley leaves, for garnish

1. To make the dough, pulse the flour and salt in a food processor fitted with the metal blade to combine. Add the butter and cream cheese, and pulse about 10 times, until the mixture is crumbly, then process at a steady speed until the dough barely clumps together. Gather up the dough, press it into a thick disk, wrap in plastic, and refrigerate until just chilled, about 1 hour. The dough is easiest to handle when it is cold but not rock-hard.

2. Cut the dough into 24 equal pieces. Press 1 piece of dough evenly into each of 24 nonstick mini-muffin cups (2-tablespoon capacity) to make pastry shells. Freeze for 30 minutes. (If making the dough shells ahead, cover tightly with plastic wrap and freeze. Defrost at room temperature for 20 minutes before filling.)

3. To make the filling, heat the butter in a large skillet over medium heat. Add the leeks and cook, uncovered, stirring often, until tender and lightly browned, about 8 minutes. Cool.

4. Combine the oil and pancetta in a small nonstick skillet. Cook over medium-high heat, stirring often, until the pancetta is browned and crisp, about 6 minutes. Using a slotted spoon, transfer the pancetta to paper towels to drain.

5. Position a rack in the center of the oven and preheat to 350°F. In a medium bowl, whisk together the half-and-half, egg yolks, salt, and pepper. Stir in the leeks, pancetta, and chèvre. Spoon the filling into the shells. Bake until the filling is set and the edges of the pastry shells are lightly browned, about 30 minutes. Cool in the pans for 5 minutes, then remove the tartlets from the pans. (If preparing the tartlets ahead, reheat, arrange them on a baking sheet, and cover loosely with aluminum foil. Bake in a preheated 375°F oven until heated through, about 10 minutes.) Garnish with the parsley leaves and serve warm or at room temperature.

Chicken Liver, Pancetta, and Rosemary Rumaki

Here's a Tuscan twist on a cocktail party favorite. I admit that I was never a fan of rumaki—they were just a bit too pu-pu platter for me. But I was once challenged to make a special version for a catering client, and this is the savory result. One tip about serving: There are some very attractive skewers available, but they work best to impale cooked food, as they simply don't hold up under high heat. Even soaked, they can scorch in the broiler. Have another batch of fresh, unsoaked skewers ready to re-spear the cooked rumaki before serving, just in case yours burn during cooking.

Makes 24 rumaki; 6 to 8 servings

Make Ahead: The rumaki can be prepared up to 8 hours before grilling; the vinegar reduction can be made up to 4 hours ahead.

24 chicken livers (about 1 pound; see Note)
1 cup dry white wine
2 tablespoons finely chopped shallots
1 tablespoon finely chopped fresh rosemary
3 tablespoons extra virgin olive oil
¼ teaspoon salt
¼ teaspoon freshly ground black pepper
Twelve ¹⁄₁₆-inch-thick slices pancetta
24 bamboo skewers or wooden toothpicks, soaked in cold water for 30 minutes and drained
⅓ cup balsamic vinegar

1. Trim the livers of any connective tissue or green spots, leaving as whole as possible. Mix together the wine, shallots, rosemary, oil, salt, and pepper in a medium bowl. Add the livers and mix gently. Cover and refrigerate for at least 1 and up to 2 hours.

2. Drain the livers, leaving any shallots and rosemary clinging to them. Unroll each pancetta slice to make long strips; cut each in half crosswise to make 24 strips total. Wrap each liver with 1 pancetta strip; spear the pancetta through the liver with a soaked skewer to secure. (If preparing the rumaki ahead, cover loosely with plastic wrap and refrigerate.)

3. Boil the vinegar in a small nonreactive saucepan over high heat until it is thick and reduced to 2 tablespoons. Set aside. (The vinegar reduction can be prepared and kept at room temperature up to 4 hours ahead. Reheat gently until fluid.)

4. Position a broiler rack about 4 inches from the heat source and preheat the broiler. Arrange the rumaki on a lightly oiled broiler rack set over a drip pan. Just before serving, broil in batches until the pancetta is browned and the livers are slightly pink when pierced, about 4 minutes. Arrange on a serving platter and drizzle a few drops of balsamic reduction over each rumaki. Serve immediately.

Note: Chicken livers are often sold in 20-ounce containers. Buy the entire container to sort through and choose the plumpest livers; save the remaining livers for another use.

Spiced Caramelized Onion Dip with Cilantro-Garlic Pita Crisps

Whenever I serve homemade onion dip, the compliments come fast and furious. This one is extraordinary, made with sweet onions, warm spices, and crème fraîche. Garam masala, an Indian spice blend, used to be available only at Asian markets, but can now be found in the spice

rack of most supermarkets. This dip is also excellent with good old potato chips.

Makes 6 to 8 servings

Make Ahead: The dip can be made up to 3 days ahead; the pita crisps can be made up to 8 hours ahead.

DIP

2 tablespoons vegetable oil

3 cups chopped sweet onions, such as Vidalia or Maui

1½ teaspoons garam masala

One 8-ounce container (1 cup) crème fraîche or sour cream

Salt and freshly ground black pepper to taste

Chopped fresh chives, for garnish

PITA CRISPS

20 large fresh cilantro sprigs (about ½ bunch)

2 garlic cloves, crushed under a knife and peeled

¼ cup extra virgin olive oil

6 pocket pita breads

1. To make the dip, heat the oil in a medium skillet over medium heat. Add the onions and cook until softened, about 5 minutes. Reduce the heat to low and cook, uncovered, stirring often, until the onions are deeply browned, about 35 minutes. Add the garam masala and stir for 1 minute. Transfer to a medium bowl to cool.

2. Stir in the crème fraîche and season with salt and pepper. Cover and refrigerate until chilled, at least 2 hours. (If making the dip ahead, cover and refrigerate.)

3. To make the pita crisps, pull the leaves from the cilantro, reserving the stems. Finely chop the leaves (you should have 3 tablespoons) and set aside. Heat the garlic and oil in a small saucepan over medium-low heat until bubbles surround the garlic, about 5 minutes. Coarsely chop the cilantro stems and add to the hot oil. Remove from the heat and let stand for 10 minutes. Strain through a sieve and discard the solids.

4. Position racks in the center and top third of the oven and preheat to 350°F. Using a serrated knife, split each pita in half crosswise. Cut each pita round diagonally into 6 wedges. Arrange the pita wedges on rimmed baking sheets. Drizzle with the cilantro-garlic oil and toss gently to coat. Bake for 5 minutes. Sprinkle the wedges with the cilantro leaves and bake until lightly toasted, about 5 minutes longer. Cool. (If preparing the pita crisps ahead, store uncovered at room temperature.)

5. To serve, sprinkle the dip with the chives and serve chilled, with the pita crisps.

Coconut Shrimp with Sweet Chili Dip

Coconut shrimp have long been a popular cocktail snack, but this version has a few refinements that bring it into the twenty-first century. A dash of curry powder adds another layer of flavor, and Asian sweet chili sauce is the perfect dip. You'll find the latter in Asian markets and many supermarkets—it comes in tall bottles and looks a bit like apricot preserves with flecks of red chiles. As these are best served right after frying, set up the ingredients and necessary equipment beforehand so the cooking goes smoothly.

Makes 24 shrimp; 6 to 8 servings

Make Ahead: The dip can be prepared up to 1 day ahead.

DIP

¾ cup Asian sweet chili sauce (see Note)

3 tablespoons chopped fresh cilantro

2½ tablespoons fresh lime juice

BATTER

1 cup all-purpose flour

1¼ teaspoons Madras-style curry powder

1 teaspoon baking powder

¼ teaspoon salt

1 large egg, beaten

1 cup plus 2 tablespoons club soda

Vegetable oil, for deep-frying

1¼ cups unsweetened desiccated coconut

24 large shrimp, peeled and deveined, with tail segment left attached

1. To make the dip, mix together the chili sauce, cilantro, and lime juice in a small bowl. Cover and let stand until ready to serve. (If preparing the dip ahead, cover and refrigerate.)

2. To make the batter, whisk all of the batter ingredients together in a medium bowl until just combined; the batter should remain slightly lumpy. Set aside for 15 minutes.

3. Meanwhile, pour enough oil into a large, heavy saucepan to come halfway up the sides of the pan. Heat over high heat until the oil temperature reads 375°F on a deep-frying thermometer.

4. Spread the coconut on a plate. One at a time, hold a shrimp by the tail and dip into the batter, letting excess batter drip into the bowl. Roll the shrimp in the coconut to coat and place on a waxed paper–lined baking sheet.

5. Line a baking sheet with paper towels and set near the stove. Just before serving, deep-fry the shrimp in batches until golden brown, about 2½ minutes each. Using a mesh skimmer, transfer the shrimp to the paper towels to drain briefly. Serve hot, with the chili dip.

Note: If you can't find Asian sweet chili sauce, heat ¾ cup apricot preserves until melted. Strain through a wire sieve into a bowl and stir in 1 teaspoon crushed hot red pepper and 2 garlic cloves, crushed through a press.

White Four-Cheese Pizza with Basil and Garlic

Pizza without tomatoes? Sure—especially at a party where you don't want guests dripping tomato sauce down their fronts. Prepared pizza dough, fresh or frozen, is now available at many supermarkets. Use it to streamline the baking of an all-white pizza that goes great with drinks.

Makes 24 pieces; 6 to 8 servings

Make Ahead: The pizza can be made up to 4 hours ahead.

2 tablespoons extra virgin olive oil

1 garlic clove, finely chopped

One 16-ounce package fresh or thawed frozen pizza dough

6 ounces fresh mozzarella, sliced ¼ inch thick and coarsely chopped

3 ounces rindless goat cheese, crumbled

½ cup part-skim ricotta cheese

3 tablespoons freshly grated Parmesan cheese

3 tablespoons thinly shredded fresh basil

1. Position a rack in the center of the oven and preheat to 425°F. Lightly oil a 13 × 9-inch metal baking pan. Mix the oil and garlic together in a small bowl; set aside.

2. Roll out the dough on a very lightly floured work surface into a 14 × 10-inch rectangle. Fit into the pan. Top with the mozzarella, goat cheese, ricotta, and Parmesan, leaving a ½-inch-wide border around the sides.

Brush with some of the garlic oil, but leave the garlic solids in the bowl.

3. Bake until the crust is golden brown, 20 to 25 minutes. During the last 3 minutes, spoon the remaining garlic and oil over the pizza. Remove from the oven and let stand for 3 minutes. (If making the pizza ahead, store at room temperature. Reheat in a preheated 350°F oven until hot, about 10 minutes.)

4. Cut crosswise into 6 strips, then lengthwise into 4 pieces to make 24 pieces total. Sprinkle with the basil. Transfer to a platter and serve hot.

Chipotle Deviled Eggs

The smoky spiciness of chipotle chiles makes these deviled eggs truly devilish. While dried chipotles are available, look for the canned chipotles in adobo, which is a brick red chile sauce. Be very careful when handling the chiles— you may want to wear rubber gloves.

Makes 24 eggs; 6 to 8 servings

Make Ahead: The eggs can be made up to 1 day ahead.

12 large eggs
1/3 cup plus 2 tablespoons mayonnaise
2 to 3 teaspoons minced canned chipotle chiles
    in adobo, including sauce
Salt to taste
24 fresh cilantro leaves, for garnish

1. Place the eggs in a large saucepan and add cold water to cover. Bring to a simmer over high heat, then reduce the heat to low and simmer for 5 minutes. Remove from the heat, cover, and let stand for 10 minutes. Drain the eggs and place in a large bowl of ice water to cool completely.

2. Shell the eggs, then cut each egg in half lengthwise. Remove the yolks and reserve them separately from the whites.

3. Rub the yolks through a wire sieve into a bowl. Mix in the mayonnaise and 2 teaspoons of the minced chiles; add more chile for more heat, if desired. Season with salt. Transfer to a pastry bag fitted with a 1/2-inch-wide fluted tip. Pipe the egg yolk mixture into the egg white halves. Loosely cover with plastic wrap and refrigerate until chilled, at least 2 hours.

4. To serve, garnish each egg with a cilantro leaf, arrange on a platter, and serve chilled.

Old-fashioned Eggnog

Indulge in one of Yuletide's greatest pleasures, and make a batch of this heady, creamy, from-scratch eggnog. I can't imagine one of my Christmas parties without a big bowl of nog— and, according to the evidence, neither can my friends. One year, instead of entirely omitting it from the menu (because everyone had been moaning about their expanding waistlines), I compromised with a half batch, which disappeared quicker than an elephant at a magician's act in Las Vegas. Luckily, I had the ingredients handy to whip up more, and it evaporated, too. It's so easy to make, why buy the supermarket variety?

● To keep the eggnog cold, place a pint of vanilla ice cream in the punch bowl. It will melt slowly, and its flavor will complement the eggnog. For a break with tradition, try chocolate ice cream.

● This eggnog contains raw eggs, which have been known to contain harmful bacteria. When serving this recipe, take these precautions. Purchase fresh eggs without any signs of cracks, and wash the eggs before using them. Do not serve eggnog to people with compromised immune systems. If you prefer, serve the New Wave Eggnog (right), which is made with cooked eggs, a step that kills the dangerous bacteria.

Makes 2½ quarts; about 10 servings

Make Ahead: The eggnog should be chilled for at least 4 hours before serving, and served within 24 hours.

6 large eggs, separated
1¼ cups superfine sugar (see Note)
¾ cup dark rum
¾ cup brandy
¼ cup bourbon
1½ quarts heavy cream or half-and-half
1 pint high-quality vanilla ice cream, for serving
Freshly grated nutmeg, for serving

1. In a large bowl, using an electric mixer at high speed, beat the egg yolks and sugar until thick and pale yellow. Beat in the rum, brandy, and bourbon, then the cream.

2. In a large bowl, using an electric mixer at high speed, with clean beaters, beat the egg whites until soft peaks form. Fold into the eggnog. Cover tightly with plastic wrap and refrigerate until well chilled, at least 4 hours or overnight.

3. Transfer to a punch bowl. Using scissors, cut the container away from the ice cream, keeping the ice cream intact in one piece. Place the ice cream in the eggnog. Grate the nutmeg over the eggnog and serve immediately.

Amaretto Eggnog: Omit the bourbon. Substitute ¾ cup Amaretto for the brandy. Decrease the sugar to 1 cup. If desired, add ¼ teaspoon almond extract. When serving, substitute toasted almond ice cream for the vanilla ice cream.

Note: To make your own superfine sugar, process regular granulated sugar, about ½ cup at a time, in a food processor or blender until finely ground. It will take 1 to 2 minutes per batch.

New Wave Eggnog

This has an even creamier texture than the old-fashioned heady concoction. The cooked egg yolks make this the nog of choice for cooks who prefer to avoid raw eggs.

Makes 2½ quarts; about 10 servings

Make Ahead: The eggnog should be chilled at least 4 hours before serving, and served within 24 hours.

4 cups half-and-half or milk
1½ cups sugar
12 large egg yolks
½ cup dark rum
½ cup brandy
¼ cup bourbon
2 cups heavy cream
1 pint high-quality vanilla ice cream
Freshly grated nutmeg, for serving

1. In a medium saucepan over medium heat, stir the half-and-half with the sugar until the sugar dissolves and the mixture is hot. In a large bowl, whisk the egg yolks until thick and pale yellow. Gradually whisk in the hot half-and-half mixture. Rinse out the saucepan.

2. Return the egg yolk mixture to the saucepan and cook over low heat, stirring constantly with a wooden spatula, until the mixture is thick enough to coat the spatula (a thermometer will read 180°F), about 3 minutes. Strain through a wire sieve into another medium bowl. Place in a larger bowl of ice

water and let stand, stirring often, until completely cooled. Whisk in the rum, brandy, and bourbon. Cover and refrigerate until well chilled, at least 4 hours or overnight.

3. In a chilled, medium bowl, using an electric mixer at high speed, beat the heavy cream just until stiff. Fold into the chilled custard. Pour into the punch bowl. Using scissors, cut the container away from the ice cream, keeping the ice cream intact in one piece. Place the ice cream in the eggnog. Grate the nutmeg over the eggnog and serve immediately.

the butter, brown sugar, cinnamon, and nutmeg until light in color and texture, about 2 minutes. (If making the spiced butter ahead, transfer to a small container, cover, and refrigerate. Bring to room temperature before using.)

2. For each drink, place about 1½ tablespoons of the spiced butter into a mug. Add 2 tablespoons rum and enough boiling water (about ¾ cup) to almost fill the mug. If desired, garnish with a cinnamon stick. Using the cinnamon stick or a spoon, stir to dissolve the butter. Serve immediately.

Hot Buttered Rum

To take the chill off a cold winter's night, there is nothing like hot buttered rum. The drink is usually made with boiling hot water, but you can use cider, too. It's nice to have a batch of spiced butter ready in the refrigerator for when friends drop by. Although I have rarely had a guest say no to a hot buttered rum, if I have any butter left over at the end of the holiday season, it is just as delicious spread onto toast.

Makes 8 servings

Make Ahead: The spiced butter can be made up to 2 weeks ahead.

8 tablespoons (1 stick) unsalted butter, at room
     temperature
½ cup packed light brown sugar
½ teaspoon ground cinnamon
¼ teaspoon freshly grated nutmeg
1 cup dark rum
About 6 cups boiling water
Cinnamon sticks, for garnish (optional)

1. In a medium bowl, using a handheld electric mixer set at high speed, beat together

Grandma Perry's Tom and Jerry

This is my family's traditional holiday drink. The best way to serve Tom and Jerries is to make them one at a time. To warm the mugs, fill them with hot tap water and let stand for a minute, then toss out the water. You can have a heated pot of milk ready on the stove, but I usually heat the milk as needed in the microwave.

- **Tom and Jerries can also be served from a Tom and Jerry bowl (I have an antique one just like Grandma's) or a soup tureen as a hot punch. Tom and Jerry bowls are beautiful, but they don't keep the drink warm without some electrical help. Place the bowl on a flat-topped hot plate (not the coil burner–type) set on the lowest setting. Don't let the hot punch stand for more than two hours, or the heat may cause curdling. A slow cooker, even set on Low, is too hot and also could curdle the punch.**

Makes 10 servings

Make Ahead: The egg mixture can be made up to 4 hours ahead.

6 large eggs, separated, at room temperature

3 cups confectioners' sugar

2 quarts milk, heated until steaming hot

⅓ cup brandy

⅓ cup dark rum

Freshly grated nutmeg, for serving

1. In a large bowl, using an electric mixer at high speed, beat together the egg yolks and confectioners' sugar until very thick and light colored, about 2 minutes.

2. In a separate grease-free, large bowl, using an electric mixer at high speed, with clean beaters, beat the egg whites until soft peaks form. Stir about a quarter of the whites into the yolk mixture to lighten, then fold in the remaining whites, allowing some of the whites to stay fluffy. (If making the egg mixture ahead, cover and refrigerate. Remove from the refrigerator 1 hour before using so it

isn't ice cold; otherwise the drinks will be tepid.)

3. Heat the milk in a large saucepan over medium heat until small bubbles appear around the edges. Take care that the milk doesn't boil and bubble over.

4. To serve individually, place a heaping spoonful of the egg batter into a warm mug. Add about ½ tablespoon brandy and ½ tablespoon rum. Add enough hot milk to fill and stir gently. Grate nutmeg over the top and serve hot.

5. To serve as a punch, gradually whisk about half of the hot milk into the egg mixture. Whisk the egg mixture into the pot. Stir in the brandy and rum. Heat gently, stirring constantly, just to bring up the temperature a little bit from the addition of the liquor, about 1 minute. Do not heat too much or the eggs will start to cook and thicken the milk.

Tom and Jerries for Everyone

Proust had his madeleines, and I have my Tom and Jerries. This warm, soothing milk drink, really hot eggnog, has always been my favorite holiday drink, probably because it was served without fail at my Grandma Perry's Christmas Eve parties. (The children's drinks were spiked with a drop of brandy extract.) I remember one year my uncle mixed the egg batter so stiff that he burned out the electric hand mixer. My grandmother was pretty sore—it was not the first

Christmas Eve this had happened. When we opened presents, luckily Santa had thought ahead, and brought her a new mixer that year. This magic absolutely convinced me of Santa's omnipotence. Every year, I go through my own personal Christmas tradition: I mix up a small batch for myself, turn off all the lights except for the Christmas tree, and toast Grandma and the happy memories she helped create.

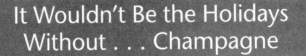

It Wouldn't Be the Holidays Without . . . Champagne

Champagne is practically a synonym for celebration. During the holidays, there are many opportunities to sip a glass of bubbly, from a special holiday meal to a New Year's Eve toast.

There are a few simple rules to buying Champagne. First, know where it comes from. Real Champagne, with its complex flavor and aroma, is only made in the Champagne region of France, not far from Paris. Even though we Americans use the word to describe any bubbling wine, the truth is, if it isn't *from* Champagne, it *isn't* real Champagne, and it must be labeled as sparkling wine. Some important names in the Champagne business include Moët-Chandon, Veuve-Clicquot, and Bollinger. These are top of the line, and are worth every penny they cost.

It is not just the grapes and the soil conditions that make Champagne special, but also its painstaking natural fermentation process. Called *methode Champenoise*, this is almost always indicated on the label. Sparkling wines made in other locations can still make their wine by the Champagne method. By contrast, cheap sparkling wines are injected with carbon dioxide to create the bubbles, and the results are dramatically different, to say the least.

There are less expensive, very good sparkling wines from France that are excellent bargains. (Not to be deceptive, but with their French labels, most guests will assume they are drinking the real thing.) Some of the French sparkling wines are called *blanc des blancs,* which means that they are made completely from white, not red grapes. *Blanc des noirs*, with a pink tinge, are made from red grapes. Some Spanish sparkling wines also are good values. California makes some fine sparkling wines, many made by American divisions of European Champagne families, like Domaine Chandon.

There is only one way to buy Champagne or sparkling wine, and that is according to your budget. For a small party, go all out and buy the best you can afford. But a larger event may call for some restraint. Consider the collective taste of your guest list, and if you think that a less expensive sparkling wine would be enjoyed as much as a pricey one, buy the cheaper variety. However, don't buy a very cheap sparkling wine just because you think you should have something bubbly. They just don't taste very good, and I don't care what anyone says, they can be responsible for some pretty nasty post-party hangovers.

If at all possible, serve your sparkling wine in glassware, not plastic. It makes a big difference in the tone of the party. If you don't feel like renting glasses, look in restaurant supply stores and price clubs and purchase a case or two. After a couple of annual parties, your initial investment will have paid off. I bought some at a post-holiday sale many years ago, and have never regretted it.

Immediately transfer to a warmed Tom and Jerry bowl or soup tureen. Grate nutmeg over the top and serve warm.

Small-Batch Tom and Jerry: In a small bowl, whisk ¼ cup confectioners' sugar with 1 egg yolk until thick. In another small bowl, using a clean whisk, whisk 1 egg white until soft peaks form. Fold the egg white into the yolk mixture, leaving some of the white fluffy. Heat 2 cups milk until hot, either on top of the stove or in a microwave. Divide the egg yolk mixture between two warmed large coffee mugs. Stir 1 tablespoon brandy or dark rum (or a splash of both) into each mug, fill with the hot milk, and stir gently. Grate nutmeg over the top and serve immediately. Makes 2 drinks.

Cider Wassail

Here's a wassail for today's tastes—this sherry-free version is sweeter and less bitter. The roasted apples are optional but add a touch of authenticity. And when you are looking for a delicious nonalcoholic hot cider, just replace the ale with more apple juice.

Makes 2½ quarts; 16 to 20 servings

Make Ahead: The wassail is best made just before serving.

2 Granny Smith apples, peeled, cored, and each cut into 8 wedges

2 lemons

4 quarter-size slices fresh ginger

12 allspice berries

6 whole cloves

Two 3-inch cinnamon sticks

Four 12-ounce bottles pale ale

1 quart fresh apple cider

½ cup packed light brown sugar

1. Position a rack in the center of the oven and preheat to 400°F. Lightly oil a large baking sheet.

2. Spread the apples on the baking sheet. Bake, turning the apple slices halfway during baking, until the apples are lightly browned and tender, about 30 minutes. Set aside.

3. Meanwhile, using a vegetable peeler, remove the zest from 1 lemon. Rinse and wring out a 12-inch-square piece of cheesecloth. Wrap the lemon zest, ginger, allspice, cloves, and cinnamon sticks in the cheesecloth and tie with a piece of kitchen string. Cut the lemons in half and squeeze the juice from the lemons. Set the juice aside.

4. In a large nonaluminum pot, combine the ale, cider, brown sugar, lemon juice, and the spice packet. Heat, stirring occasionally, over low heat until hot but not boiling, about 30 minutes. Transfer to a slow cooker set on Low and serve hot.

Nonalcoholic Wassail: Substitute an additional 1 quart apple juice for the ale.

Mulled Wine with Honey and Orange

There's mulled wine, and then there is this recipe. To be sure that the mulled wine is at its best, here are a few tips:

- **Use a fruity but full-bodied red wine. Merlot is my first choice, but Zinfandel or Cabernet Sauvignon also work. Beaujolais, while fruity, is too thin for my taste.**

- **Buy moderately priced wine, not cheap plonk. Your mulled wine will only be as good as your ingredients.**

- **Never let mulled wine come to a boil. Let it heat very slowly over low heat so the spices** and orange zest release their flavors. A slow cooker on the Low setting is the perfect serving utensil.

Makes 2 quarts; about 16 servings

Make Ahead: The wine is best made just before serving.

1 large seedless orange
12 whole cloves
12 allspice berries
Two 3-inch cinnamon sticks
3 cardamom pods, crushed (optional)
One 1½-liter bottle fruity red wine, such as
    Merlot
1 cup honey
⅔ cup orange-flavored liqueur, preferably Grand
    Marnier or Grand Gala

1. Using a vegetable peeler, remove the zest from the orange. Rinse and wring out a 12-inch-square piece of cheesecloth. Wrap the orange zest, cloves, allspice, cinnamon sticks, and cardamom, if using, in the cheesecloth and tie with a piece of kitchen string. Cut the orange in half and squeeze the juice from the orange. Set the juice aside.

2. In a large nonaluminum pot, combine the wine, honey, Grand Marnier, orange juice, and spice packet. Heat, stirring occasionally to dissolve the honey, over low heat until hot but not boiling, about 30 minutes. Transfer to a slow cooker set on Low and serve hot.

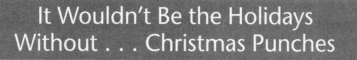

It Wouldn't Be the Holidays Without . . . Christmas Punches

Alcoholic holiday beverages have their roots in pagan winter solstice celebrations, which were never abstentious affairs. Those beverages packed a punch, and over the years their disorienting effect came to mean a heady, strong beverage.

The winter festivals lasted for a few weeks, and so did the partying. When Christianity overtook paganism, the old customs were applied to the new winter holiday, Christmas. But the pagans weren't about to trade a single-day holiday (and an alcohol-free "holy day," at that) for a monthlong party, so the tradition of the holiday season began. This came to mean the entire six-week period beginning with Advent Sunday (celebrating Christ's imminent birthday on the fourth Sunday before Christmas) and lasting until the Epiphany (also called Three Kings Day or Twelfth Night) on January 6. In fact, until the last 150 years or so, the Christmas season was abhorred by religious leaders because it was marked by heavy drinking and general misbehavior. The Puritan movement was practically all about establishing the non-celebration of Christmas. It was only through a hard-fought campaign to bring children into the holiday and the establishment of the kindly Santa Claus in American culture that the wild image of the holiday began to soften. But we still love our glass of punch.

The origin of the word *punch* is generally accepted as having derived from various Hindu, Sanskrit, and Persian words for the word *five*, as it was five ingredients (sweet, sour, bitter, sweet, and alcoholic) that supposedly created the beverage.

Eggnog is a close relative to the English sack posset, an egg and dairy drink that could be made from a dry Spanish wine called sack or from strong ale (also called *nog*). When the drink came over to America, the colonists substituted the more readily available rum and whiskey for the sack.

Practically every northern European country has a version of *mulled wine*, wine that is heated and flavored with spices. Most mulled wines are also fortified with liquor. For example, Swedish *glögg* is made with red wine and aquavit. (Talk about packing a punch!) *Mull* is an Old English word for dust, so mulled wine may mean "that which is dusted with spices."

The sugar trade was extremely important to the economy of the American colonies, and vast amounts of rum were distilled from molasses. *Hot buttered rum* became a favorite drink to chase away the winter chill.

Wassail is not just any old hot holiday beverage, but a very specific mixture of sherry and ale. The name comes from the Old Anglo-Saxon greeting *hale,* or "be hearty." It was originally topped with a garnish of toast, giving us the phrase "to drink a toast."

A number of bartenders claim the invention of the Tom and Jerry. In the 1820s,

a British boxing expert wrote an immensely popular book, *Life in London; or, the Days and Nights of Jerry Hawthorne and His Elegant Friend Corinthian Tom,* which many feel inspired the drink (that is not unlike a hot British posset). In America, Professor Jerry Thomas (who also lays disputed claim to the martini) says that he invented the Tom and Jerry during his tenure at the El Dorado bar in San Francisco during the 1850s. Being a San Franciscan who grew up on Tom and Jerries that were "spiked" with a drop of rum extract, I'm in the Professor Thomas camp.

Christmas at the Movies

Along with my ever-increasing collection of Christmas music, my accumulation of Christmas DVDs is growing. I play them during my parties to set a nostalgic mood. And animated movies keep the young set engrossed while the parents party.

And when it's an adults-only gathering, there is always a group of grown-ups in the TV room to cheer when Kris Kringle wins his courtroom battle against Macy's or sniffle when Jimmy Stewart gathers with his family around the Christmas tree. For my holiday films, I prefer the ones that I grew up with to flashy, special-effect-laden remakes. (But if your tastes run to *Elf, The Santa Clause, The Grinch,* or *The Nightmare Before Christmas,* don't let a die-hard traditionalist like me stop you.) Here are the movies that never fail to put me in the holiday spirit.

A Charlie Brown Christmas. A little cutesy, but the Vince Girauldi soundtrack is timeless.

A Christmas Carol. The British version, starring Alastair Sim, has authentic Dickens flavor. Forget the updated version (*Scrooged*) or the musical (*Scrooge*).

A Christmas Story. Just about everyone's favorite contemporary holiday movie, with a skewed sense of humor mixed with a good dose of nostalgia. I'm a sucker for the scene where the dogs eat the Christmas turkey and the subsequent episode in the Chinese restaurant.

Christmas in Connecticut. A sleeper from the mid-forties. Barbara Stanwyck plays a magazine food editor who can't boil water. As a publicity stunt, her unsuspecting editor invites a war hero to her country house to spend Christmas, and Barbara has to make like the perfect housemaker. Guess who falls in love with whom under the Christmas tree?

How the Grinch Stole Christmas. Boris Karloff narrates this Dr. Seuss classic for the baby boomers at the party.

It's a Wonderful Life. Before Tom Hanks, there was Jimmy Stewart to play Hollywood's Everyman. Have plenty of tissues handy when watching this heart-tugger.

Miracle on 34th Street. The original (with the young Natalie Wood playing the cynical little girl who doesn't believe in Santa Claus) is not only a great movie, but a lovely Christmas card to old New York.

The Nutcracker Ballet. The dancing is great, and the music isn't so bad, either. Look for the Mikhail Baryshnikov production.

Salads, Soups, and Other First Courses

It Came Upon a First Course Clear

Holiday dinner parties are sumptuous affairs, usually centered around a huge roast, be it meat or fowl. For that reason, the first course, be it soup or salad, should be on the light side; otherwise the guests will quickly get overstuffed.

Because few Christmas or New Year's main courses are seafood, I almost always use fish or shellfish in the first course to balance the menu. If your guests include seafoodphobes, cook one of the salads or vegetable soups in this chapter.

The most important thing about choosing a dinner party first course is ease of preparation and serving. A salad is always welcome, as it piques the appetite for heavier fare. When serving salad, have the greens washed and ready to toss with the premade dressing, and it will be on the table in no time. Also included in this chapter are salads that are at home on the buffet table—pasta salad, ambrosia, and the like.

Soup is an especially convenient first course, because it can be made a day or so ahead of time and heated up before serving—and it tastes so good as well. If possible, warm the soup tureen and soup bowls beforehand so the soup is served at its piping-hot best. It's easy to do: Just fill the tureen and bowls with hot tap water and let them stand for a few minutes. Pour out the water and dry the bowls. It's a little detail that can make the difference between hot and tepid food.

Crab Cakes on Baby Greens with Lemon Vinaigrette

The contrast of crunchy, warm crab cakes with cool, crisp salad is an appetite-teasing first course that is hard to surpass. The main rule for crab cakes is to remember that they should taste like crab, not bread crumbs. These delicious examples have just enough crumbs to hold them together. Try to find the best fresh lump crab available at the fish market, and use pasteurized or canned crab as a second choice.

Makes 10 servings

Make Ahead: The vinaigrette can be made up to 1 day ahead; the crab cakes can be made up to 4 hours ahead.

LEMON VINAIGRETTE

1/3 cup fresh lemon juice

1 tablespoon Dijon mustard

1 teaspoon sugar

1/2 teaspoon salt

1/4 teaspoon freshly ground black pepper

1 cup olive oil (not extra virgin)

2 tablespoons minced shallots

1 teaspoon grated lemon zest

CRAB CAKES

1 pound fresh lump crabmeat

1/4 cup mayonnaise

3/4 cup unseasoned dried bread crumbs

1 large egg, beaten

1 tablespoon Worcestershire sauce

1 tablespoon Dijon mustard

1 tablespoon chopped fresh chives

1/4 teaspoon hot red pepper sauce

1/4 cup vegetable oil

12 cups (about 10 ounces) mixed baby greens (mesclun)

Chopped fresh chives, for garnish (optional)

1. To make the vinaigrette, combine the lemon juice, mustard, sugar, salt, and pepper in a blender. With the machine running, gradually add the oil in a slow stream. Transfer to a bowl. Stir in the shallots and lemon zest. (If making the vinaigrette ahead, cover and refrigerate. Blend again before using to thicken.)

2. To make the crab cakes, pick through the crabmeat to remove any cartilage or shell bits. Place in a medium bowl. Add the mayonnaise, 1/4 cup of the bread crumbs, the egg, Worcestershire sauce, mustard, chives, and hot pepper sauce, and mix. Using a heaping tablespoon of crab mixture for each, form into 20 crab cakes. Place the remaining 1/2 cup bread crumbs in a shallow bowl. Coat each crab cake with bread crumbs, pressing to adhere. Place on a waxed paper–lined baking sheet. (If making the crab cakes ahead, cover tightly with plastic wrap and refrigerate.)

3. In a very large skillet (or in two medium skillets, using a bit more oil), heat the oil over medium heat until very hot but not smoking. Add the crab cakes and cook, turning once, until golden brown, about 5 minutes. The crab cakes should not crowd the skillet. Using a slotted spatula, transfer the crab cakes to paper towels to drain briefly.

4. Toss the greens with about 1 cup of the dressing. Divide the salad among large dinner plates, placing the salad to one side of the plate. Place 2 crab cakes on each plate opposite the greens. Drizzle the remaining dressing around the crab cakes. Sprinkle with the chives, if using. Serve immediately.

Scalloped Oysters with Mushrooms and Leeks

While this is neither soup nor salad, scalloped oysters are a first-course mainstay of the Yankee holiday table. Raw oysters and other shellfish on the half-shell show up at many Christmas dinners, but frankly, most of my friends prefer their bivalves cooked. Scalloped oysters are usually a very simple affair of creamed oysters layered with crumbled cracker crumbs, and not much else. This version is enhanced with mushrooms and leeks and buttery bread cubes. The dish should be assembled just before serving, but the components can be prepared ahead of time.

- **For this recipe, instead of shucking fresh oysters, I use containers of preshucked oysters. Buy large, plump "select"-size oysters. Smaller oysters will take less time to cook through, and may be overcooked by the time the cream comes to a boil in the oven.**

- **If you wish, bake the scalloped oysters in individual servings. Butter eight 1-cup ramekins or 1¼-cup (300-ml) large glass custard cups. Place a layer of the bread cubes in the ramekins. Divide the oysters and mushroom mixture evenly among the ramekins. Pour in the heavy cream–oyster juice mixture. Top with equal amounts of the bread cubes. Bake until the cream bubbles, about 15 minutes. Top with chopped parsley.**

- **When preparing the leeks, remember that they are usually very sandy and need to be well rinsed. Trim the leeks, and chop the white and pale green parts only, discarding the leafy dark green tops. Place the chopped leeks in a wire sieve and rinse well under cold running water, rubbing between your fingers to separate and expose the leek layers to the water. Drain well.**

Makes 8 servings

Make Ahead: The bread cubes can be made up to 1 day ahead; the vegetable mixture can be made up to 4 hours ahead.

6 tablespoons unsalted butter

10 slices firm white sandwich bread, cut into ¼-inch cubes

12 ounces white mushrooms, sliced

1 large leek, chopped, white and light green parts only (1 cup)

¼ teaspoon salt

¼ teaspoon freshly ground white pepper

1½ pints shucked "select" oysters

¾ cup heavy cream

Chopped fresh parsley, for garnish

1. Position a rack in the center of the oven and preheat to 375°F. Lightly butter an 11½ × 8-inch (2-quart) baking dish.

2. In a small saucepan over low heat, melt 4 tablespoons of the butter. In a rimmed baking sheet, toss the butter with the bread cubes. Bake, stirring occasionally, until the bread cubes are very lightly toasted and crisp, about 15 minutes. Set aside. (The bread cubes can be prepared, stored in an airtight container at room temperature, for up to 1 day.)

3. In a large skillet, melt the remaining 2 tablespoons butter over medium heat. Add the mushrooms and cook until they give off their liquid, about 4 minutes. Stir in the leek, salt, and pepper. Cook until the leeks soften and the mushroom liquid evaporates, about 4 minutes. Transfer to a bowl and set aside. (If preparing the vegetable mixture ahead, cool, cover, and keep at room temperature.)

4. In a large sieve or colander set over a bowl, drain the oysters, reserving the oyster liquid. In the same skillet, boil the oyster liquid over high heat until reduced to about ¼ cup, about 3 minutes. Stir in the heavy cream and set aside.

5. Layer half of the bread cubes in the bottom of the prepared baking dish. Top with the oysters, then the mushroom mixture. Pour over the heavy cream mixture. Top with the remaining bread cubes. Place the baking dish on a baking sheet.

6. Bake until the cream bubbles and the oysters turn opaque, about 25 minutes. If the cubes are browning too deeply, cover loosely with aluminum foil.

7. To serve, spoon the scalloped oysters onto salad plates and sprinkle with the parsley. Serve hot.

Marinated Shrimp with White Wine Beurre Blanc

Beurre blanc **means "white butter" in French, and it is nothing more than cold water whisked into a wine reduction to create an ivory-colored sauce. The secret is to warm the butter over low heat, so it softens to a creamy, pourable sauce without completely melting. Here it is served with marinated, broiled shrimp for a sophisticated first course. If the weather is cooperating, grill the shrimp outdoors.**

Makes 8 servings

Make Ahead: The shrimp need to marinate for 30 minutes to 1 hour; the sauce base can be made up to 4 hours ahead.

SHRIMP
1 cup dry white wine, such as Sauvignon Blanc or Pinot Grigio
¼ cup extra virgin olive oil
1 tablespoon finely chopped shallots
½ teaspoon freshly ground pepper

24 jumbo, colossal, or U-16 shrimp, peeled and deveined, with tail segment left attached
Nonstick vegetable oil spray

BEURRE BLANC
2 cups dry white wine, such as Sauvignon Blanc or Pinot Grigio
¼ cup coarsely chopped shallots
2 tablespoons white wine vinegar
¼ teaspoon whole black peppercorns
1 cup (2 sticks) unsalted butter, chilled, cut into 16 pieces
Salt and freshly ground white pepper to taste

1 tablespoon finely chopped fresh chives
1 tablespoon finely chopped fresh tarragon
1 tablespoon finely chopped fresh parsley

1. To prepare the shrimp, whisk together the wine, oil, shallots, and pepper in a small bowl. Pour into a self-sealing plastic bag. Add the shrimp and refrigerate, turning often, for at least 30 minutes but no longer than 1 hour.

2. To begin the sauce, bring the wine, shallots, vinegar, and peppercorns to a boil in a medium, heavy-bottomed saucepan over high heat. Boil until the liquid is reduced to ¼ cup, about 20 minutes. (If preparing the sauce base ahead, cool, cover, and keep at room temperature. Reheat to simmering before proceeding.)

3. Position the broiler rack 6 inches from the heat source and preheat the broiler.

4. To finish the sauce, reduce the heat under the saucepan with the sauce base to very low. One piece at a time, whisk the butter into the sauce base, allowing the butter to soften slowly into a creamy sauce, and letting each piece melt before adding another. If the butter heats too quickly, remove the saucepan from the heat and whisk briskly. Strain the sauce through a wire sieve into a small bowl. Season with salt and pepper. (The sauce can be made up to

15 minutes ahead, covered with aluminum foil, and kept in a warm place. Do not reheat. The sauce is not meant to be piping hot.)

5. Remove the shrimp from the marinade and discard the marinade. Spray the broiler rack with vegetable oil spray. Spread the shrimp on the broiler rack. Broil, turning once, until the shrimp are opaque, about 5 minutes.

6. Mix together the chives, tarragon, and parsley in a small bowl. For each serving, spoon equal amounts of the sauce in the centers of 8 warmed salad plates. Arrange 3 shrimp on each plate, interlocking the shrimp tails so the shrimp stand up. Sprinkle with the herbs and serve immediately.

Salmon and Spinach Terrine with Cucumber-Dill Sauce

Gorgeous and elegant, this is a first course for your finest dinner party. For a fancy appetizer, it comes together very quickly, and has the added attraction of being totally make ahead. It can also be served as a spread for a crowd at a cocktail party buffet.

Makes 12 servings

Make Ahead: The terrine must be chilled at least 4 hours or overnight; it can be made up to 2 days ahead of serving. The sauce can be made up to 1 day ahead.

TERRINE
  1 tablespoon unsalted butter
  3 tablespoons finely chopped shallots
  ½ cup dry vermouth
  20 ounces skinless salmon fillets, cut into pieces
  4 ounces sea or bay scallops

  ½ cup fresh bread crumbs (make in a food processor or blender)
  1 large egg
  1¼ teaspoons salt
  ¼ teaspoon freshly ground white pepper
  ⅛ teaspoon hot red pepper sauce
  1½ cups heavy cream
  One 10-ounce package frozen chopped spinach, thawed, squeezed well to remove liquid

CUCUMBER-DILL SAUCE
  1 medium cucumber, peeled, seeded, and cut into ¼-inch dice
  Salt
  ¾ cup sour cream
  2 tablespoons milk
  2 tablespoons chopped fresh dill
  ⅛ teaspoon freshly ground white pepper

  Fresh watercress or dill sprigs, for garnish

1. Preheat the oven to 325°F. Lightly oil an 8½ × 4½ × 2½-inch loaf pan. Line the bottom of the pan with waxed paper.

2. To make the terrine, in a small saucepan, melt the butter over medium-low heat. Add the shallots and cook until softened, about 2 minutes. Add the vermouth and cook until reduced to 1 tablespoon. Remove from the heat and cool.

3. In a food processor fitted with the metal blade, pulse the salmon and scallops until finely chopped. Add the shallot mixture, bread crumbs, egg, salt, white pepper, and hot pepper sauce. With the machine running, gradually add the heavy cream. Transfer 1 cup of the purée to a medium bowl and stir in the spinach.

4. Spread half of the salmon purée in the loaf pan, then spread the spinach purée over the salmon. Top with the remaining salmon purée. Cover with a piece of buttered waxed paper, buttered side down.

5. Place the loaf pan in a larger roasting pan and place in the oven. Add enough hot water to the roasting pan to come ½ inch up the sides of the loaf pan. Bake until an instant-read thermometer inserted in the center of the terrine registers 140°F, about 1 hour. Cool completely in the pan on a wire rack. Remove the waxed paper from the top of the terrine, then invert and unmold the terrine and remove the waxed paper from the bottom. Tightly wrap the terrine in plastic wrap. Refrigerate at least 4 hours or overnight.

6. Meanwhile, make the sauce: In a small bowl, toss the cucumber with ½ teaspoon salt. Let stand for 30 minutes. Place in a colander and rinse well. Pat dry with paper towels. Squeeze the cucumber to remove excess moisture.

7. In a medium bowl, mix together the cucumber, sour cream, milk, dill, and pepper. Season with salt to taste (you may not need very much, as the cucumber has already been salted). Cover with plastic wrap and refrigerate until chilled, at least 1 hour.

8. Cut the terrine into 12 slices. Divide slices among 12 dinner plates. Spoon equal amounts of the sauce alongside each slice. Garnish with the watercress. Serve immediately.

Salt-Roasted Yukon Gold Potatoes with Caviar and Crème Fraîche

When you bring out the caviar, your guests will know that you hold them in high regard. Good caviar is never inexpensive, so I reserve it for my best friends and very special occasions. The humble potato is somehow the perfect match for the elegant caviar. Here is one of the easiest, yet most satisfying, first courses around.

- Yukon gold potatoes are my first choice for this dish. They have a yellow-gold, buttery flesh that bakes beautifully. Small russet, Finn, or Maine potatoes are an alternative. Choose small-to-medium potatoes—this is supposed to be an appetizer, not a side dish to a steak.

- Baking the potatoes on a bed of kosher salt helps draw out the moisture from the potatoes, giving them an especially fluffy texture. If you can't find kosher salt, use large-crystal sea salt, available at natural food stores and many supermarkets. Table salt will work, but not as well.

- The amount of caviar you use is up to you. Caviar is rich. While you will need at least 1 ounce per person, more than 2 ounces will be excessive. Check your bank account, and take it from there.

- Crème fraîche is easiest to describe as French sour cream, but it is more buttery and less tangy, and it won't overpower the caviar like American sour cream might. It can be found in many supermarkets or specialty food stores with refrigerated food departments. It is easy to make your own, and I've included the recipe.

- Serve the crème fraîche or sour cream next to the potato, not dolloped on top. And sprinkle the chives around the potato and crème fraîche, not indiscriminately. That way each guest can decide how much to use—some people prefer to savor the clean, saline flavor of caviar with as few accoutrements as possible, but others like to gild the lily.

Makes 4 servings

It Wouldn't Be the Holidays Without . . . Caviar

Rare, costly, sublime—caviar is all of these. There are few foods that state elegance more implicitly. But with the recent United Nations ban on the exportation of caviar from the Caspian Sea (the traditional source of the finest caviar), those of us who love the little fish eggs learned to look elsewhere.

Caviar became a holiday luxury because of its traditional processing cycle, with one of the main two cycles occurring in October. Allowing a month for processing and shipping, the caviar would arrive just in time for Thanksgiving. Caspian caviar was processed from sturgeon eggs; the variety of sturgeon (beluga, osetra, or sevruga) designated the size, color, and flavor of the eggs.

Today's American caviar, obtained from sturgeon and other fish that are often farmed, is identified by the type of fish. At online caviar stores, you will find a few different kinds of American sturgeon caviar, each with its own flavor profile. I have more than one friend who swears by paddleback (a relative of sturgeon) caviar, comparing it to the best beluga. Whitefish caviar is golden, with crunchy, tiny eggs. Salmon caviar has large red "berries." When I am feeling flush, I serve a couple of different caviars so guests can compare. Lumpfish caviar is the dyed black stuff at supermarkets—it's not very good, and the dye can stain your lips. Don't use it for a special holiday dish.

When serving caviar, simplicity is the key. If you want to serve it as an hors d'oeuvre, perhaps the best way is to spoon the caviar onto toasts. (Cut rounds from firm, white sandwich bread and toast lightly for an attractive canapé.) Or serve the caviar in a traditional caviar *servoir*, which will keep the eggs ice-cold. You can simulate the servoir by nestling a glass bowl in a larger bowl of ice. Caviar aficionados insist that metal spoons never touch caviar, for fear that the metal will transfer its flavor to the delicate morsels. They recommend bone, wood, or ivory spoons, but I use a Bakelite espresso spoon. No matter how you serve caviar, don't overwhelm its saline flavor and pleasantly crunchy texture with lots of competing ingredients. If you want to extend it, offer small bowls of minced onion, crème fraîche or sour cream, separately chopped hard-boiled egg yolks and whites, and, of course, thin wedges of lemon. But do not encourage your guests to look at the caviar as an upscale salad bar.

Caviar is very delicate and requires very careful handling and constant refrigeration; otherwise the flavor and texture will suffer. Find a trustworthy local purveyor, preferably one with a large turnover of product, or use a reliable source from the Web, such as www. lapetitepearle.com.

About 2 cups kosher salt or coarse sea salt, for
baking
4 small Yukon gold potatoes (4 ounces each),
scrubbed but not peeled, pierced a few times
with a fork
4 to 8 ounces caviar, to taste
½ cup crème fraîche (see Note) or sour cream,
at room temperature
Chopped fresh chives, for garnish

1. Position a rack in the center of the oven
and preheat to 400°F. Spread enough salt over
an 8-inch square baking dish to make a thick
layer at least ½ inch deep. Nestle the potatoes
in the salt. Bake until the potatoes are tender,
about 45 minutes.

2. Brush the salt from the potatoes. Place
each potato on a salad plate. Cut the potatoes
lengthwise, then squeeze to open them up.
Spoon equal amounts of caviar on each potato.
Dollop crème fraîche alongside each potato.
Sprinkle the chives on each plate around the
potatoes and crème fraîche. Serve immediately.

Note: To make your own crème fraîche, start at
least 2 days before using. Fill a medium bowl
with boiling water, let stand for 5 minutes, then
drain and dry the bowl. Mix 1 cup heavy cream
(not ultra-pasteurized) with 2 tablespoons
buttermilk in the bowl. Cover loosely with
plastic wrap. Let stand in a warm place until
thickened, at least 12 hours and up to 24 hours,
depending on the temperature. Do not let the
crème fraîche get too thick, as it will thicken
further when refrigerated. Transfer to a jar or
airtight container and refrigerate at least
overnight. The crème fraîche can be kept,
refrigerated, for up to 2 weeks.

Roasted Beet
and Apple Salad

**This is one of my most popular dinner party
salads. Even people who think they don't like
beets love it, which is understandable because
roasted beets have it hands down over the
canned variety. The salad has many different
textures and flavors that meld together into a
beautiful crimson mélange.**

Makes 8 servings

Make Ahead: The beets can be prepared up to
1 day ahead.

3 large beets (about 2 pounds)
3 Granny Smith apples, peeled, cored, and
chopped into ½-inch dice
8 large red lettuce leaves
5 ounces Roquefort or blue cheese, crumbled
½ cup toasted, peeled, and coarsely chopped
hazelnuts

DRESSING
2 tablespoons balsamic vinegar
2 tablespoons cider vinegar
½ teaspoon sugar
½ teaspoon salt
¼ teaspoon freshly ground black pepper
⅔ cup vegetable oil

1. Preheat the oven to 400°F. If the beets
have their greens attached, trim the greens,
leaving about 1 inch of the stems attached to
the beets. Scrub the beets under cold running
water. Wrap each beet in aluminum foil and
place on a baking sheet. Bake until the beets are
tender when pierced with the tip of a long,
sharp knife, about 1½ hours, depending on the
size of the beets. Cool completely without
unwrapping the beets.

2. Unwrap the beets and peel them. Cut into ¾-inch cubes. Place in self-sealing plastic bags and refrigerate until chilled, at least 2 hours.

3. To make the dressing, in a large bowl, whisk together the balsamic and cider vinegars, the sugar, salt, and pepper. Gradually whisk in the oil. Add the beets and apples and mix.

4. To serve, place a lettuce leaf on each plate, and spoon the salad onto the lettuce. Top each salad with some of the cheese and hazelnuts. Serve chilled.

Cauliflower Salad with Red Pesto Dressing

Cauliflower is a very useful winter vegetable that is very often (and unfairly) demoted to the side-dish category, where it can be treated with apathy. It makes a terrific salad that lives up to my strict standards for a buffet dish: It looks great, tastes great, and holds up well at room temperature.

Makes 8 to 12 servings

Make Ahead: The salad can be made up to 1 day ahead.

RED PESTO DRESSING

1 cup (6 ounces) oil-packed sun-dried tomatoes, drained
¼ cup balsamic vinegar
1 garlic clove, crushed through a press
¼ teaspoon salt
¼ teaspoon crushed hot red pepper
1 cup extra virgin olive oil

2 medium heads cauliflower (3 pounds total)
Chopped fresh parsley, for garnish

1. To make the dressing, place the sun-dried tomatoes, vinegar, garlic, salt, and crushed red pepper in a food processor fitted with the metal blade. With the machine running, gradually add the oil in a thin stream, and process until the dressing has thickened. Set aside.

2. Trim the cauliflower and cut into bite-size florets. Bring a large pot of salted water to a boil over high heat. Add the cauliflower and cook until barely tender, 4 to 6 minutes. Drain, rinse under cold running water, and drain well.

3. Transfer the cauliflower to a large bowl and toss with the dressing. Cover and refrigerate until chilled, at least 2 hours. Sprinkle with the parsley before serving.

Mushroom and Parmesan Salad

Topped with curls of Parmesan cheese, this salad has a festive look especially suited for the holidays. For the best flavor, use only real Parmigiano-Reggiano cheese—look for the identifying stamp on the rind.

Makes 8 servings

Make Ahead: The dressing can be made up to 1 day ahead.

DRESSING

¼ cup fresh lemon juice
½ teaspoon salt
¼ teaspoon freshly ground black pepper
1 cup olive oil

2½ pounds fresh white mushrooms, thinly sliced
⅓ cup finely chopped shallots
2 tablespoons chopped fresh parsley

8 cups (about 7 ounces) mixed baby greens
   (mesclun)
One 4-ounce chunk Parmigiano-Reggiano cheese

1. To make the dressing, in a medium bowl, whisk together the lemon juice, salt, and pepper. Gradually whisk in the oil. (If making the dressing ahead, cover and refrigerate. Whisk well before using.)

2. Just before serving, in a medium bowl, toss ¾ cup of the dressing with the mushrooms, shallots, and parsley. In a large bowl, toss the greens with the remaining ½ cup dressing. On each of 8 large plates, place portions of the mushroom salad and greens side by side. Using a vegetable peeler, shave curls of Parmigiano-Reggiano over each salad. (You won't use all of the cheese, but you need a good-size piece to make the curls.) Serve immediately.

Orange and Red Onion Salad with Cranberry-Orange Vinaigrette

Cranberry balsamic vinegar is one of my favorite gifts from my kitchen. It takes no time to make, and can be multiplied as many times as you have room in your pot. And it's a great way to perk up a so-so bottle of inexpensive supermarket balsamic vinegar. (It is not intended to be made with a fine artisanal *balsamico*.) This is a light, refreshing opener, and very appropriate for a holiday meal that more than likely will be on the rich and heavy side. A short marinating period helps mellow the pungent red onion.

Makes 8 servings

Make Ahead: The Cranberry Balsamic Vinegar must be made 1 week ahead; the dressing

and oranges can be refrigerated up to 1 day ahead.

CRANBERRY-ORANGE VINAIGRETTE

¼ cup Cranberry Balsamic Vinegar (recipe
   follows) or regular balsamic vinegar
1 tablespoon light brown sugar (optional, if using
   regular balsamic vinegar)
Grated zest of 1 orange
½ teaspoon salt
¼ teaspoon freshly ground black pepper
¾ cup extra virgin olive oil

4 large oranges
1 small red onion, thinly sliced
2 heads Belgian endive, wiped with a moist paper
   towel (do not rinse)
1 large head red leaf lettuce, torn into bite-size
   pieces
1 medium head radicchio, torn into bite-size pieces
½ cup dried cranberries

1. To make the dressing, in a medium bowl, whisk together the vinegar, brown sugar, if using, the orange zest, salt, and pepper. Gradually whisk in the oil. (If making the dressing ahead, cover and refrigerate. Whisk well before serving.)

2. Using a serrated knife, cut off the top and bottom from each orange. Following the curve of each orange, cut off the thick skin, including the white pith, where it meets the orange flesh. Working over a bowl, cut between the membranes to remove the segments, letting them drop into the bowl.

3. About 30 minutes before serving, in a small bowl, toss the onion with 2 tablespoons of the dressing. Cover and set aside.

4. Using a sharp knife, cut the endive crosswise into ½-inch-wide pieces. Separate the endive pieces into strips, discarding any tough, solid center pieces.

5. When ready to serve, in a large bowl, toss the lettuce, radicchio, and endive with the dressing. Place an equal amount of salad onto each plate. Top with the orange segments and red onion, and sprinkle with the cranberries. Serve immediately.

Cranberry Balsamic Vinegar: In a medium, nonaluminum saucepan, combine 2 cups supermarket-quality balsamic vinegar, one 12-ounce bag rinsed and sorted cranberries, and ⅓ cup packed light brown sugar. Cook over medium-low heat, stirring occasionally, until the vinegar begins to simmer and the cranberries have collapsed, about 20 minutes. Strain through a wire sieve placed over a medium bowl, pressing gently on the cranberries to extract all of the juice and vinegar, but do not press any pulp through the sieve. Let drain for a few minutes. Transfer to glass bottles for gift giving. Makes about 2½ cups.

Tortellini Antipasto Salad

Of all the dishes you can put on a buffet, it is safe to say that pasta salad will be one of the first bowls you'll have to replenish. This one is loaded with the goodies you might find on an antipasti platter: Italian-style picked vegetables (*giardiniera*), salami, roasted peppers, and olives. Pasta salads have a tendency to soak up their dressings, and their flavor will change on standing. It's a good idea to reserve some of the dressing to perk up the salad just before serving.

Makes 8 to 12 servings

Make Ahead: The salad can be made up to 6 hours ahead.

DRESSING

¼ cup red wine vinegar
1 garlic clove, crushed through a press
½ teaspoon salt
¼ teaspoon freshly ground black pepper
1 cup extra virgin olive oil

2 pounds frozen cheese tortellini
One 24-ounce jar *giardiniera,* drained and coarsely chopped
6 ounces sliced (¼ inch thick) Genoa-style salami, cut into ½-inch-square pieces
1 cup pimento-stuffed green olives, coarsely chopped
1 large red bell pepper, roasted, cored, seeded, and cut into ½-inch-square pieces (see Note)
3 scallions, white and green parts, chopped
3 tablespoons chopped fresh basil, oregano, or parsley

1. To make the dressing, place the vinegar, garlic, salt, and pepper in a blender. With the machine running, gradually add the oil and process until thick and smooth. Set aside.

2. Cook the tortellini in a pot of boiling salted water according to the package instructions. Drain, rinse under cold running water, and drain well.

3. Transfer the pasta to a large bowl. Add the *giardiniera,* salami, olives, red pepper, scallions, and basil. Toss with a scant 1 cup of the dressing, covering and reserving the remaining dressing. Cover the pasta salad and refrigerate until chilled, at least 2 hours and up to 6 hours.

4. Just before serving, toss with the reserved dressing. Taste for seasoning, and add more salt and pepper, if needed. Serve chilled.

Note: There's more than one way to roast a pepper. Most methods ask the cook to turn the pepper over an open flame, but the following technique takes much less attention. Position the broiler rack about 6 inches from the heat source and preheat the broiler. Cut off the top of the pepper, just below and including the stem, then cut off ½ inch from the bottom of the pepper. Slit the pepper down the side, open it up, and cut out the ribs and seeds. Spread out the pepper, skin side up, and press on it to flatten. Broil, skin side up, until the skin is blackened and blistered, 5 to 10 minutes. Be careful not to burn a hole through the pepper—only the skin should blacken. (The flattened pepper can also be grilled, skin side down, over a hot charcoal fire or in a gas grill heated to the High setting.) Using kitchen tongs, transfer to a plate and let stand until cool enough to handle. Using a small knife, peel and scrape off the skin. Don't rinse the pepper under cold running water unless absolutely necessary.

The Original Ambrosia

What my grandma called ambrosia was really a matter of opinion. It was concocted entirely of canned fruits and mortared with sour cream and marshmallows. This recipe takes ambrosia back to its roots, using fresh fruit only to make a superior dish that works as a first course, buffet salad, or dessert. The liquor is totally optional but a nice touch.

- Preparing fresh coconut is a labor of love, but like so many other kitchen chores, it's easy to master once you get the hang of it. The coconut meat should be finely shredded—if it is too thick, it is unpleasant to eat. Unless you have a food processor with a fine shredding blade (which sometimes has to be special-ordered separately from the large shredding blade that comes with most machines), shred the coconut by hand on the medium-size holes of a box grater. Or shred chunks of the coconut in a handheld rotary grater.

- If desired, place regular sweetened flaked coconut in a wire sieve and rinse under hot water to remove the sugar coating. Drain and pat dry with paper towels.

Makes 12 servings

Make Ahead: The salad can be made up to 1 day ahead.

1 medium coconut
6 medium seedless oranges
1 ripe pineapple
¼ cup Grand Marnier, dark rum, or fresh orange juice

1. Position a rack in the center of the oven and preheat to 350°F. Pierce the eyes (the soft indentations on one end of the coconut) with a clean screwdriver and a hammer. Drain out the liquid. Place the coconut on a baking sheet. Bake for 30 minutes.

2. Using a hammer, rap the coconut around its equator to crack in half. Using a sturdy paring knife, pry the coconut in pieces from the shell. Using a vegetable peeler, remove the dark brown skin from the coconut. Shred the coconut. You should have 2 cups.

3. Using a serrated knife, cut off the top and bottom from each orange. Following the curve of each orange, cut off the thick skin, including the white pith, where it meets the orange flesh. Working over a bowl, cut between the membranes to remove the segments, letting them drop into the bowl.

4. Cut off the top of the pineapple, including the leafy crown. Cut the thick rind from the pineapple where it meets the flesh. Remove the dark eyes from the flesh. Quarter the pineapple lengthwise, and cut the hard core

from each quarter. Cut each quarter lengthwise again, then into bite-size pieces.

5. In a large glass bowl, toss together the pineapple, orange rounds, coconut, and Grand Marnier. Cover tightly with plastic wrap and refrigerate until well chilled, about 2 hours. (If preparing the salad ahead, cover tightly with plastic wrap and refrigerate.) Serve chilled.

Sangria Jell-O Mold

To many Americans, a holiday dinner means a molded Jell-O salad. My good friend Beth Hensperger, author of many cookbooks, told me that she always puts wine in her Jell-O mold to give it a little sophistication. While the salad can be served as a first course, I prefer it as a side dish or on a buffet with many other offerings. With this inspiration, here is a recipe that brings this old favorite into the new millennium.

- You will need a 6-cup mold for this salad. A metal ring mold will do, but Jell-O makes a beautifully designed plastic ring mold that I am very partial to. It is available in some supermarkets during the holidays or by mail order through the Jell-O Web site, www.jell-o.com (go to the "Corner Store," then the "Jell-O Molds" section).

- This recipe is easily halved again—fill a 9-cup mold (use three 3-ounce packages of Jell-O)—or doubled to fit a large mold. Just be sure that the gelatin mixture comes to the top of the mold; otherwise it will be difficult to unmold.

- As easy as it is to make, there are still some tips to make a good gelatin mold. First, be sure the gelatin is completely dissolved, which takes 2 minutes of constant stirring.

Don't cheat, or the mold won't set properly. Second, the gelatin must be partially set in order to support the weight of the added fruit or the chunks will sink to the bottom of the mold. You can chill it in the refrigerator for about 1½ hours, but chilling in an ice-water bath cuts the time and allows you to keep an eye on the progress.

- You should have 3 cups of combined orange segments, grape halves, and sliced strawberries for this salad. The exact proportion of each fruit doesn't matter, and you can add other fruit, such as peeled, cored, and diced apples or pears or sliced strawberries.

Makes 8 to 12 servings

Make Ahead: The mold can be made up to 2 days ahead.

1½ cups fruity red wine, such as Merlot
Two 3-ounce packages raspberry-flavored gelatin
1 tablespoon fresh lemon or lime juice
3 large seedless oranges
1 cup red or green seedless grapes (or a combination of both), cut into halves lengthwise
1 cup sliced raspberries
Nonstick vegetable spray, for the mold

1. In a small saucepan, bring the wine to a boil over high heat. In a stainless steel or glass (not plastic) bowl, using a rubber spatula, stir the gelatin with the hot wine until the gelatin is completely dissolved, occasionally scraping down the sides of the bowl, about 2 minutes. Stir in 1½ cups cold water and the lemon juice. Place the bowl in a larger bowl of iced water. Let stand, stirring occasionally, until the gelatin is partially set and a spoon briefly cuts a swath that allows you to see the bottom of the bowl, about 20 minutes.

2. Meanwhile, grate the zest from 1 orange and set aside. To cut all of the oranges into segments, use a serrated knife to cut the tops and bottoms from each orange. Following the curve of each orange, cut off the thick white pith where it meets the orange flesh. Working over a bowl, cut between the thin membranes to release the orange segments, letting them drop into the bowl. Drain the oranges before using.

3. Stir the orange segments, orange zest, grapes, and raspberries into the partially set gelatin. Lightly spray a 6-cup decorative mold with nonstick vegetable spray. Pour the gelatin into the mold and cover with plastic wrap. Refrigerate until set, at least 4 hours or overnight.

4. To unmold, run a knife around the inside edge of the mold to break the seal. Lightly moisten a serving platter (this will allow you to move the unmolded salad on the platter if you need to). Place the platter upside down over the top of the mold. Holding the mold and platter together, invert and shake firmly to unmold the salad. If the salad doesn't unmold, dip the outside of the mold briefly (less than 5 seconds) in a bowl of warm tap water. Dry the outside of the mold and try again. Serve chilled.

Parsnip and Leek Soup with Bacon

The sweet earthy flavors of parsnips and leeks create a smooth and elegant soup that will have your guests trying to guess the ingredients. A crisp topping of crumbled bacon is the perfect garnish.

Makes 8 servings

Make Ahead: The soup can be made up to 1 day ahead.

2 tablespoons unsalted butter

3 large leeks, chopped, white and pale green parts only (1½ cups)

1 pound parsnips, peeled and cut into 1-inch pieces

2 pounds baking potatoes, such as russet or Burbank, peeled and cut into 1-inch pieces

5 cups Homemade White Chicken Stock (page 46) or canned reduced-sodium chicken broth

¾ teaspoon salt

¼ teaspoon freshly ground white or black pepper

4 slices bacon

1. In a large pot, heat the butter over medium heat. Add the leeks and cook until softened, about 5 minutes. Add the parsnips and potatoes. Stir in the stock and bring to a simmer. Reduce the heat to low and cover. Cook until the vegetables are tender, about 25 minutes.

2. In batches, purée the soup in a blender or food processor. Return to the pot and add the salt and pepper. (If preparing the soup ahead, cool, cover, and refrigerate. Reheat over very low heat, stirring often. If the soup seems too thick, thin it with additional stock.)

3. Meanwhile, in a medium skillet over medium-high heat, cook the bacon, turning once, until crisp and browned, about 5 minutes. Transfer to paper towels to drain and cool. Crumble the bacon and set aside.

4. To serve, ladle the soup into soup bowls and top with the crumbled bacon. Serve hot.

Shrimp, Zucchini, and Red Pepper Bisque

This creamy bisque is an outstanding first course. The chunky, colorful sautéed shrimp-and-vegetable mixture not only provides the bulk of the flavor, it acts as a garnish, too. To avoid last-minute work, have all the sauté ingredients ready, then quickly cook them just before serving. The easiest serving procedure would be to stir the cooked shrimp and vegetables into the bisque. But I much prefer to bring a tureen of the soup to the table along with a bowl of the shrimp and vegetables and serve it from the head of the table, spooning the sautéed mixture into each bowl of soup—the splash of green, red, and pink in the creamy soup looks terrific.

Makes 8 servings

Make Ahead: The bisque can be made up to the point before adding the half-and-half up to 1 day ahead.

1 pound medium shrimp with shells
7 tablespoons unsalted butter
1 small onion, chopped
1 small celery rib with leaves, chopped
2 cups bottled clam juice
1 cup dry white wine
2 sprigs fresh parsley
⅛ teaspoon dried thyme
⅛ teaspoon black peppercorns
¼ cup all-purpose flour
2 tablespoons Madeira or dry sherry
1 tablespoon tomato paste
2 cups half-and-half
¼ teaspoon salt
¼ teaspoon freshly ground white pepper
1 medium zucchini, cut into ¼-inch dice
1 medium red bell pepper, cored, seeded, and
    cut into ¼-inch dice

1. Peel and devein the shrimp, reserving the shells. Coarsely chop the shrimp; cover and refrigerate.

2. In a medium saucepan, heat 1 tablespoon of the butter over medium heat. Add the onion and celery. Cover and cook until softened, about 5 minutes. Add the shrimp shells, 3 cups cold water, the clam juice, wine, parsley, thyme, and peppercorns. Raise the heat to high and bring to a boil. Reduce the heat to low and simmer for 30 minutes. Strain and reserve the stock (you should have 5 cups; add water as needed).

3. In a large, heavy-bottomed pot, melt 4 tablespoons of the butter over low heat. Whisk in the flour and let bubble, without browning, for 1 minute. Whisk in the sherry and tomato paste, then the reserved shrimp stock. Raise the heat to medium and bring to a simmer. Simmer until lightly thickened, about 3 minutes. (The bisque can be made to this point up to 1 day ahead, cooled, covered, and refrigerated. Reheat gently before proceeding.) Add the half-and-half and cook until very hot but not simmering. Season with ⅛ teaspoon of the salt and ⅛ teaspoon of the pepper.

4. In a large skillet, melt the remaining 2 tablespoons butter over medium-high heat. Add the zucchini and red pepper and sauté until just tender, about 7 minutes. Add the shrimp and cook until pink and firm, about 3 minutes. Season with the remaining ⅛ teaspoon salt and ⅛ teaspoon pepper. Transfer to a warmed bowl.

5. Pour the bisque into a warmed soup tureen. To serve, ladle the bisque into soup bowls, topping each serving with a spoonful of the shrimp and vegetable mixture.

Homemade Brown Stock 101

Nothing beats homemade stock. Just like most home cooks, I use canned broth (a good reduced-sodium brand, but never bouillon cubes, which are too salty and artificial tasting to me) for the majority of my cooking, but for a special holiday meal, I bring out the stockpot. Stock takes very little actual work and can be made well ahead of time and frozen. The only problem is that no matter how much you make and store, it always seems to disappear too quickly. This basic recipe can be altered to make different stocks by using different meaty bones.

- This basic recipe makes rich brown stock from roasted bones—the preferred stock for meat sauces and gravies. If you need stock for soups and white sauces, make Homemade White Chicken Stock (page 46), as its color is more neutral and the finished dish will look and taste lighter.

- What's the difference between a stock and a broth? A stock is generally made from bones, but a broth is the cooking liquid of braised meat or poultry. The biggest distinction, however, comes from the use of salt. Stock is unsalted, used in a recipe as an ingredient, and then the final dish is seasoned. Broth is usually seasoned and may be enjoyed on its own, like a soup.

- Never let stock come to a rolling boil, or it will become cloudy and have a less refined flavor. Cook the stock uncovered.

- Add the herbs to the stock after you've skimmed it. If you add them at the beginning, they will rise to the surface and be skimmed off with the foam. By the way, the foam isn't unwholesome—it's just the coagulating proteins from the bones. It is removed to make the stock clearer.

- The longer a stock simmers, the better, up to 12 hours. Replace the water as needed as it evaporates. While I trust my stove to simmer the stock overnight, some of my students are shocked at the idea. A great alternative is to make the stock in a 5½-quart slow cooker. Transfer the browned bones and cooked vegetable mixture to the crockery insert, add the herbs, and pour in enough cold water to cover well. Cover and cook on Low for 12 hours. This makes a clear, delicious stock. As a slow cooker holds less liquid than a stockpot, the stock will be very full-flavored. You may choose to use slightly fewer bones and vegetables (especially if you make the stock in a smaller 3½-quart pot), or dilute the finished stock with water, if you wish.

- If time is a factor, just simmer the stock for an hour or two—it still will be better than using water or canned broth. You may want to add a can of broth to boost the flavor, though. (It's cheating, but I won't tell.) Or make a pot well ahead of the holidays and freeze it.

- Make sure the stock is cooled before refrigerating or freezing. To speed the cooling, place the stockpot in a sink filled with ice water, adding ice as necessary to keep it as cold as possible. Stir occasionally until the stock is cool.

- Don't add salt to your stock. Stock is often reduced in recipes, so the final dish could end up too salty.

Makes about 2½ quarts

Make Ahead: The stock can be made up to 3 days ahead; it can also be frozen for up to 3 months.

3 pounds chicken wings, chopped into
   2- to 3-inch pieces
1 tablespoon vegetable oil
1 medium onion, chopped
1 medium carrot, chopped
1 medium celery rib, with leaves, chopped
6 sprigs fresh parsley
½ teaspoon dried thyme
¼ teaspoon whole black peppercorns
1 dried bay leaf

1. Position a rack in the upper third of the oven and preheat to 450°F. Spread the chicken wings in a large roasting pan. Roast, turning occasionally, until golden brown, about 45 minutes.

2. Meanwhile, in a large pot, heat the oil over medium-high heat. Add the onion, carrot, and celery to the pot and cook, stirring often, until softened, about 6 minutes.

3. Transfer the wings to the pot. Pour off all the fat from the pan. Place the pan over two burners on high heat. Add 1 cup water, scraping up the browned bits in the pan with a wooden spoon. Pour into the pot. Add enough cold water to cover the wings by 2 inches. Bring to a boil, skimming off the foam that rises to the surface. Add the parsley, thyme, peppercorns, and bay leaf. Reduce the heat to low. Cook at a bare simmer for at least 2 and up to 12 hours. Add more water to the pot as needed to keep the bones covered.

4. Strain the stock through a colander into a large bowl. Let stand for 5 minutes and skim off the clear yellow fat that rises to the surface. Cool the stock completely before refrigerating or freezing. (If making chicken stock ahead, cool completely, cover, and refrigerate. It can also be frozen in airtight containers for up to 3 months.)

Homemade Turkey Stock: Substitute 3 pounds turkey wings for the chicken wings. Using a heavy cleaver, chop the wings into 2- to 3-inch pieces (you may want to ask the butcher to do this, as turkey bones are often too heavy to chop at home). Add the turkey neck (chopped into 2- to 3-inch pieces), heart, and gizzard to the pot, but don't use the liver, as it would give the stock a bitter flavor.

Homemade Duck Stock: Substitute the carcasses, giblets (no liver), wing tips, and necks (chopped into 2- to 3-inch pieces) of 2 ducks for the chicken wings.

Homemade Goose Stock: You won't have enough bones from 1 goose to make a full-flavored stock, so use canned chicken broth to boost the flavor. Substitute the goose wing tips and neck (chopped into 1- to 2-inch pieces) and giblets (no liver) for the chicken wings. Substitute two 13¾-ounce cans reduced-sodium chicken broth for 3½ cups of water.

Homemade Beef Stock: Substitute 2 pounds beef bones and 1 pound beef shin for the chicken wings.

Homemade White Chicken Stock: Make the stock as directed, but do not roast the wings. Add the raw wings to the pot after the vegetables have softened.

Roasts, Birds, and Other Main Courses

The Groaning Board

The Christmas tradition of serving an extravagant array of victuals goes way back to Old England. The feudal lords were expected (nay, obligated) to feed their serfs throughout the holiday season. They literally opened their houses to the underlings—the beginning of today's "open house." The serfs didn't want a few canapés and a glass of wine, either. They expected, and got, a groaning board of food. If they didn't, they could find ways to make life pretty miserable for the lord.

Today's holiday dinners are centered around at least one roast or bird. I know many cooks who bake a ham, a turkey, and a few dishes of lasagna, just for starters. This can pose more than a few logistical problems for the cook. But the good news is that roasts are really easy to prepare. A lot of the guesswork is sidestepped simply by choosing a good cut of meat (see "Beefing Up" on page 51).

For my own Christmas dinner, I usually roast prime rib or crown roast of pork. Since each of these is delicious and has its own traditional side dishes, the final decision really comes down to the size of the guest list. If the meal is for eight, prime rib is just the thing. For groups of eight to twelve, I often prepare a crown roast. Roasts always need to stand for at least 15 minutes before carving, which gives me plenty of time to finish up the side dishes.

Not all holiday meals are sit-down affairs, of course, and buffets need main courses, too. You'll find many dishes here that will be perfect for an open house or cocktail party buffet.

Rib Roast *au Jus* 101

The verdict is in. My Christmas entree of choice is a gorgeous standing rib roast. Serving it is a surefire way to hear sighs of appreciation from guests. (At my house, we have to raffle off the roasted rib bones for post-supper gnawing.) With a rib roast, let the meat speak for itself. Keep the seasonings very simple and serve with a beef stock–based *au jus* sauce. I often offer horseradish sauce for those who must have it.

- If possible, buy a Prime-grade rib roast. While we use the term "prime rib" as a generic term to describe any rib roast, it is incorrect unless the meat is officially graded USDA Prime. This is the highest grade available, which virtually guarantees tender, well-aged, flavorful meat. It is expensive and only found at the finest butchers, but for Christmas dinner, get the best. Many supermarkets have Choice-grade beef, which can be excellent. But it is aged differently than Prime, and has less fat (and in beef, fat equals flavor). Choice beef will benefit from a 5-day aging period in your refrigerator. For details, see "Beefing Up" on page 51.

- The rib section of a steer has 12 ribs, but home cooks rarely serve a whole 12-rib roast. Try to buy a roast from the small end of the rib section, as it will have less fat and more meat to the pound. To serve 8 to 10 people, buy a 4-rib roast. For smaller or larger roasts, use the timing estimates below. If you are having a small crowd, still buy a 3-rib roast, as 2-rib roasts are hard to roast evenly.

- Some rib roasts are sold with the thick fat cap on top of the meat intact, and some are trimmed. I prefer to have most of the fat cap intact and trim it myself to a ⅛- to ¼-inch thickness if necessary. In any case, some meat will be exposed. If you trim away a good amount of fat, the purchased weight of the roast will be reduced, so adjust your cooking time as needed. While a kitchen scale is the best way to weigh the meat, you can simply estimate the difference.

- After the grade of the meat, timing is the next most important thing to keep in mind. Check the internal temperature with a good instant-read or digital thermometer. *Be sure to remove the roast from the oven 5°F before it reaches the desired internal temperature!* The residual heat in the roast will continue to cook the meat, even outside of the oven. So if you want medium-rare meat at 130°F, remove the roast when the thermometer reaches 125°F (or even a few degrees lower, if you are a rare meat fan). If you and your guests prefer medium meat, at 140°F, remove the roast when it reaches 135°F. It is a waste of money to cook a rib roast beyond 140°F because the rich, beefy flavor won't be there. If you have a "well-done" person at the table, serve them the end cuts, or place their sliced meat back in the oven for a few minutes (or microwave it until it looks the way they want it).

- My perfect roast beef has a tasty, crisply browned crust and a juicy interior. For a rib roast of any size, follow this roasting time estimate. Place the roast in a preheated 450°F oven and roast for 15 minutes. Reduce the heat to 350°F and continue roasting until done. Allow about 15 minutes per pound for medium-rare meat, and 17 minutes per pound for medium (calculate the time from when the roast goes in the oven, not from when the temperature is reduced). During the last 30 minutes of roasting time, be sure to check the roast's internal temperature occasionally to avoid overdone meat.

- Let the roast stand for at least 20 minutes before serving. If you are making Herbed Yorkshire Puddings (page 80) in the same oven, it will take about 35 minutes to heat the oven to 400°F and bake the puddings. As long as the roast is served within an hour, do not worry about the roast cooling off.

- *Au jus* sauce is nothing more than beef stock stirred into the degreased roasting pan and brought to a boil. It is not thick like a typical sauce or gravy. The *au jus* will only be as good as your stock, so I strongly recommend that you use Homemade Beef Stock (page 46). If you must use canned stock, buy the best you can find—some supermarkets and butchers sell store-made frozen stock.

Makes 8 to 10 servings

One 4-rib standing beef rib roast, preferably
    Prime grade (about 8 pounds)
2 large garlic cloves, peeled
1½ teaspoons salt
2 tablespoons olive oil
1 teaspoon dried thyme
1 teaspoon dried rosemary, crumbled
½ teaspoon freshly ground black pepper
3 cups Homemade Beef Stock (page 46) or
    canned reduced-sodium beef broth
Sour Cream–Horseradish Sauce (recipe follows;
    optional)

1. Position a rack in the lower third of the oven and *thoroughly* preheat to 450°F.

2. Using a sharp, thin knife, trim any fat on the top of the roast to a ¼-inch thickness. Using a large knife, finely chop the garlic on a work surface. Sprinkle with ½ teaspoon of the salt and mash and smear the garlic on the work surface to make a paste. Scrape into a small bowl. Add the remaining 1 teaspoon salt, the oil, thyme, rosemary, and pepper. Rub the seasoning mixture all over the roast, including the underside.

3. Place the rib roast, meaty side up, in a large roasting pan. (No need for a roasting rack, as the bones create a natural one.) Roast for 15 minutes. Reduce the oven temperature to 350°F. Do not open the oven door. Continue roasting until an instant-read thermometer inserted in the center of the roast reads 125°F, about 2 hours total roasting time for medium-rare meat. For an accurate reading, make sure the tip of the thermometer is positioned in the center of the meat. Transfer the roast to a carving board. Let stand for 20 minutes.

4. While the meat is standing, make the *au jus* sauce: Pour out all of the fat from the roasting pan and discard (or reserve if making Herbed Yorkshire Puddings, page 80). Place the roasting pan over two burners on medium heat. Add the beef stock and stir to release any browned bits in the pan. Bring to a boil and cook until the stock is slightly reduced, about 2 minutes. Transfer to a gravy boat.

5. To carve the roast, using a meat fork and a long, thin carving knife, stand the roast on the meaty end. Carve off the rib section in one piece and set aside. Slice the meat, cut the ribs into individual pieces, and serve immediately, with a spoonful of the *au jus* sauce poured over each serving. Pass the horseradish sauce on the side, if using.

Sour Cream–Horseradish Sauce: In a medium bowl, mix 1 pint sour cream, ½ cup well-drained prepared horseradish, ¼ cup chopped chives (optional), ½ teaspoon salt, and ¼ teaspoon freshly ground white pepper. If desired, add more drained horseradish to taste. Let stand at room temperature for 1 hour before serving. Makes 2½ cups. The sauce can be prepared up to 1 day ahead; bring to room temperature 1 hour before serving.

Marinated Beef Tenderloin

Marinated, roasted beef tenderloin is one of the most versatile dishes in a cook's repertoire. Served hot, it can be the main course of a holiday sit-down dinner. Cooled, then thinly sliced, it is often the centerpiece of an open-house buffet. The citrus–red wine–balsamic vinegar marinade used here is tasty but very strong—don't marinate the beef for too long, or the acids in the marinade could give the meat a mushy texture.

- This recipe assumes that you will be buying a whole, untrimmed beef tenderloin, which is available in vacuum-packed packages at large supermarkets and wholesale clubs. Even though you will trim the beef yourself, there still will be a fair amount of waste—a whole tenderolin weighing 6 pounds trims down to about 3½ pounds, plus about ¾ pound meat culled from the trimmings. Some cooks leave the disproportionately large clod of meat attached to the thinner main muscle, but I prefer to trim the clod off and save it for another meal (it's great chunked into kebabs or cut into strips for a stir-fry). You can also buy a 3½- to 4-pound trimmed tenderloin, if you prefer.

Makes 8 to 12 main-course servings, or 16 to 20 buffet servings

Make Ahead: The beef should marinate for 2 to 4 hours before roasting.

One 6-pound beef tenderloin, untrimmed

MARINADE
1 cup hearty red wine, such as Zinfandel
Grated zest and juice of 1 large orange
⅓ cup soy sauce
⅓ cup extra virgin olive oil
¼ cup balsamic vinegar
2 garlic cloves, crushed under a knife
1½ teaspoons dried rosemary
1½ teaspoons dried thyme
½ teaspoon whole black peppercorns

1 tablespoon extra virgin olive oil
½ teaspoon salt
½ teaspoon freshly ground black pepper

1. Drain the beef, rinse under cold running water, and pat dry with paper towels. (Do not be concerned about any odor—it will dissipate in a minute or so.) Using a sharp, thin-bladed knife, trim away any fat, including the large lump at the wide end, and discard. Pull and cut away the long, thin "chain" muscle that runs the length of the tenderloin. (If you wish, trim away the fat from the chain and reserve the meat for another use.) Following the natural muscle separation, cut away the large clod of meat at the wide end and reserve for another use. At one end of the meat, make an incision under the silver sinews covering the meat. Slip the knife under the sinew, and pull and trim it away. Work lengthwise down the tenderloin until it is completely free of sinew and fat.

2. Fold the thin ends of the tenderloin underneath so the tenderloin is the same thickness throughout its length, and tie with kitchen string. Tie the roast crosswise at 2- to 3-inch intervals.

3. To make the marinade, whisk together all of the ingredients in a large bowl to combine. Place the tenderloin in a jumbo-size self-sealing plastic bag, and pour in the marinade. Close the bag and refrigerate the tenderloin, turning it occasionally, for at least to 2 hours and up to 4 hours. Remove the tenderloin from the marinade and discard the marinade.

4. Position a rack in the center of the oven and preheat to 425°F. Rub the tenderloin with the oil and season with the salt and pepper.

Beefing Up

The perfect roast beef is tender, juicy, and full of meaty flavor. The USDA grades meat according to tenderness. Two main factors are the age of the steer (the older the beef, the tougher, but more flavorful, the meat), and the amount of fat marbled through its flesh (as this inner marbling moistens the meat as it cooks). The most common grades are Prime, Choice, and Standard. Beef has the most grades. Lamb and veal have fewer grades, and only the highest grades make it to market. Pork is so consistent that only one grade is sold directly to consumers.

Only about 2 percent of all beef is graded Prime. It is the very best meat you can buy and accordingly expensive. One of the reasons why it's so pricey is that it has gone through a special dry-aging process. All beef is aged after slaughter so the enzymes can break down and tenderize the flesh. Most beef is wet-aged in its juices in sealed plastic bags (like the ones for sale at wholesale clubs). But dry-aged beef is allowed to stand uncovered in special refrigerators for 3 weeks or more. This special aging process evaporates excess moisture from the meat. As the exposed surface must be trimmed away, dry-aged meat makes for a good amount of waste, so the price of the meat goes up.

By far, most of the meat in supermarkets is wet-aged and graded Choice. It's very good, but it lacks the depth of flavor that prime meat provides. If you roasted a Choice rib roast without any special treatment, it would be just fine but not great. But there is a way to simulate dry-aging for Choice meat at home, if you are willing to make space in your refrigerator for 5 days.

I have been doing this "quick" dry-aging method ever since I saw it outlined in Jane Frieman's *Dinner Parties*. Before you start, make sure your refrigerator is 40°F or below (use a refrigerator thermometer—don't just guess). Be aware that between the moisture evaporation and post-aging trimming, you will lose about 20 percent of the roast's purchased weight. The last time I aged a rib roast like this, I began with a 10-pound roast that cost $90. After aging and trimming, the roast weighed 8 pounds, so I "lost" $18 worth of meat. For my money, the improved flavor was worth every penny.

Purchase the roast 5 days before you plan to serve it. Unwrap the roast and place it on a wire rack positioned on a jelly-roll pan. Refrigerate for 5 days. The outside surface of the meat will dry out, but don't worry. When you are ready to roast the meat, use a sharp, thin-bladed knife to trim away all of the dried surfaces. The meat is ready to roast.

This method only works with very large pieces of beef or lamb, like a rib roast or leg of lamb. Don't try it with steaks or chops.

Place in a large roasting pan (no need to use a roasting rack). Roast until an instant-read thermometer inserted in the center of the roast reads 125°F for medium-rare meat (the internal temperature of the meat will continue to rise about 5°F outside of the oven).

5. If serving hot, let stand for 10 to 15 minutes before carving. If serving at a buffet, cool for at least 30 minutes, then carve and serve within 2 hours. Or cool completely, wrap tightly in foil, and refrigerate for up to 2 days before carving. Serve at room temperature.

Crown Roast of Pork with Apple Stuffing and Hard Cider Sauce

Truly one of the most magnificent of all holiday entrees, a crown roast of pork is surprisingly simple to prepare.

- Order your roast well ahead of time from the butcher. Be flexible with the actual size of the roast—the weight can vary quite a bit from roast to roast, even with the same amount of ribs. Allow about 20 minutes per pound, roasting until the meat is cooked to 155°F, and you'll be fine.

- Some butchers will grind the trimmings from the crown roast to supply some of the ground pork needed for the stuffing. Ask for additional ground pork to make up the 2 pounds total.

- Make the stuffing just before roasting so it is warmed slightly by the sautéed vegetables. A slightly warm stuffing will cook more quickly and evenly than a chilled one.

- The crown roast usually will come from the butcher on some kind of support to help

transfer the roast to the serving platter. If not, you can use the flat bottom of a springform or tart pan.

Makes 10 generous servings

Make Ahead: The seasoned pork roast must be refrigerated overnight.

One 8½-pound (12-rib) crown roast of pork
2 tablespoons vegetable oil
1 teaspoon salt
1 teaspoon sugar
½ teaspoon crumbled dried sage
½ teaspoon dried rosemary
½ teaspoon dried thyme
½ teaspoon freshly ground black pepper

APPLE STUFFING
2 tablespoons vegetable oil
2 medium celery ribs with leaves, chopped
⅓ cup chopped shallots
2 garlic cloves, minced
2 pounds ground pork
1 cup unflavored dried bread crumbs
3 large eggs, beaten
⅓ cup chopped fresh parsley
2 teaspoons dried sage
1 teaspoon dried rosemary
¼ teaspoon ground allspice
2 teaspoons salt
¾ teaspoon freshly ground black pepper
1 cup (4 ounces) packed coarsely chopped dried apples

HARD CIDER SAUCE
1½ cups Homemade Beef Stock (page 46) or canned reduced-sodium beef broth
1 cup dry hard apple cider
2 teaspoons cornstarch
3 tablespoons unsalted butter, cut into 3 slices, chilled
Salt and freshly ground black pepper to taste

1. The night before, brush the roast inside and out (including the underside) with the oil. Combine the salt, sugar, sage, rosemary, thyme, and pepper, and rub all over the roast. Place the roast in a roasting pan, cover loosely with plastic wrap, and refrigerate overnight. Remove the roast from the refrigerator 1 hour before roasting.

2. To make the stuffing, in a large skillet, heat the oil over medium heat. Add the celery and cook, stirring often, until softened, about 3 minutes. Add the shallots and garlic and cook, stirring often, until the shallots soften, about 2 minutes. Transfer to a large bowl. Add the ground pork, bread crumbs, eggs, parsley, sage, rosemary, allspice, salt, and pepper and mix well. Mix in the dried apples.

3. Position a rack in the bottom third of the oven and preheat to 450°F. Fill the center of the roast with stuffing. Cover the stuffing with aluminum foil. Cover each bone tip with a small piece of foil.

4. Roast for 10 minutes. Reduce the oven temperature to 325°F. Cook until a thermometer inserted in the thickest part of the roast, without touching a bone, reads 155°F, about 2 hours and 30 minutes. During the last 15 minutes of cooking time, remove the foil from the stuffing and bone tips to allow them to brown. Using a large spatula to help support the roast, transfer the roast to a serving platter. Let stand for 15 minutes before carving.

5. Meanwhile, pour off any drippings from the pan into a glass measuring cup. Skim off and discard any clear fat that rises to the surface. Reserve the dark juices in the cup. Place the roasting pan over two burners on high heat. Add the stock, cider, and reserved juices and bring to a boil, scraping up any browned bits from the bottom of the pan. In a small bowl, sprinkle the cornstarch over 2 tablespoons cold water and stir to dissolve the cornstarch. Whisk into the pan and cook until the sauce is slightly thickened. Remove from the heat and whisk in the butter, one slice at a time. Season with salt and pepper. Strain through a wire sieve into a small bowl. Pour the sauce into a warmed sauceboat.

6. Using a long, sharp knife, cut the roast into 1-rib servings. Serve with a spoonful of the stuffing, and pass the sauce on the side.

Baked Smoked Ham with Pineapple and Seeded Mustard Glaze

A sweet and tangy glazed smoked ham is another versatile holiday entree, equally at home on the dinner or buffet table. (Not to mention the bonus of leftover ham for post-party sandwiches and casseroles.) This recipe features the familiar flavors of glazed ham without resorting to the usual route of brown sugar, pineapple slices, and maraschino cherries. If you can't find pineapple preserves, substitute apricot preserves.

- In my opinion, a canned ham can't hold a candle to bone-in smoked ham. I have tried to appreciate spiral-cut hams, but the ones I have tried were too salty.

- This recipe uses an average-size 8-pound ham, but larger or smaller hams can be used to accommodate the amount of people you want to serve (and the leftovers you want to have!). Allow 15 minutes per pound at 325°F, glazing the ham during the last hour of baking, and make more or less glaze as needed.

- Sure, baked ham is delicious, but it also looks terrific on a buffet because it stands tall on the platter, and height adds visual interest to the display. I found a ham holder at a garage sale, a metal ring with prongs attached to a wooden handle that lifts the whole ham up and holds it securely for slicing. If you find one at a kitchenware or restaurant supply store (or garage sale or secondhand shop), grab it. More common are cone-shaped ham holders, made from metal tubing, which hold the ham straight up. Don't confuse either of these with a prosciutto holder.

- Common food safety requires that meat stand no longer than 2 hours at room temperature before serving. This isn't always easy to do. If necessary, serve sliced ham and replenish the platter as needed.

Makes 16 to 24 servings

One 8-pound bone-in smoked ham, preferably
    the shank end
1 cup pineapple preserves
2 tablespoons Dijon mustard
1½ teaspoons yellow mustard seeds

1. Position a rack in the center of the oven and preheat to 325°F. Line a roasting pan with aluminum foil.

2. Using a sharp knife, trim off all of the skin except for a 1- to 2-inch band around the shank. Trim off all of the fat, leaving a less than ¼-inch-thick layer.

3. In a small bowl, whisk together the preserves, mustard, and mustard seeds and set aside.

4. Place the ham on a roasting rack in the pan. Bake until a meat thermometer inserted in the thickest part of the ham (without touching a bone) registers 140°F, about 2 hours (allow 15 minutes per pound). During the last hour of roasting, spread with half of the glaze. After 30 minutes, spread with the remaining glaze.

5. Transfer the ham to a carving board or platter. Let stand for 15 to 30 minutes before carving.

Chicken Cassoulet

Cassoulet, the extravagant French version of pork and beans, is probably one of the most filling dishes on the planet, which makes it a good choice for an open house entree. The classic recipe can take days to create. It usually includes *confit* (duck or goose cooked and aged in fat), an essential ingredient if you live in the southwest of France . . . and I don't! Even my most discriminating foodie friends agree that my easy recipe is just as good as the time-consuming original. If you have guests who don't eat red meat, make the cassoulet with turkey sausage, and they can dig in.

- The cassoulet looks especially good when baked and served from a large 7- to 8-quart Dutch oven, preferably made of enameled cast iron. I have one left from my catering days, and it is one of my most used cooking utensils. If you don't own one, the bean mixture can be made in a standard Dutch oven, then divided between two 3½-quart casseroles. When ready to bake, stir 1 cup chicken broth or water into each casserole, and add the bread crumb topping.

Makes 12 to 16 servings

Make Ahead: The cassoulet can be made up to 1 day ahead (without the bread crumb topping).

3 tablespoons vegetable oil
3 pounds boneless, skinless chicken thighs, cut
    into 1-inch cubes (see Note)
1 teaspoon dried thyme
1 teaspoon dried rosemary
1 teaspoon dried sage
1 teaspoon dried oregano
¾ teaspoon salt
½ teaspoon freshly ground black pepper
1 cup dry vermouth or white wine

One 28-ounce can chopped tomatoes in juice,
  undrained
2 cups Homemade White Chicken Stock
  (page 46) or use canned reduced-sodium
  chicken broth
1 bay leaf
1½ pounds pork or turkey sweet Italian sausage,
  casings removed
2 medium onions, chopped
1 large red bell pepper, cored, seeded, and
  chopped
2 garlic cloves, chopped
Six 15- to 19-ounce cans cannellini (white kidney)
  beans, rinsed and drained
½ cup dried bread crumbs
¼ cup chopped fresh parsley

1. Position a rack in the center of the oven
and preheat to 350°F.

2. In a very large (7- to 8-quart) Dutch oven,
preferably enameled cast iron, heat 2
tablespoons of the oil over medium-high heat.
In batches without crowding, cook the chicken
thighs, turning occasionally, until browned
lightly on all sides, about 10 minutes. Using a
slotted spoon, transfer the browned chicken to
a platter. Return the browned chicken to the
Dutch oven. Season with the thyme, rosemary,
sage, oregano, salt, and pepper, and mix well.
Add the vermouth and bring to a boil, scraping
up any browned bits from the bottom of the
pan with a wooden spoon. Add the tomatoes
with their juices, the stock, and the bay leaf.
Bring to a simmer.

3. Meanwhile, in a large skillet, heat the
remaining 1 tablespoon oil over medium heat.
Add the sausage and cook, breaking it up into
bite-size pieces with the side of a large spoon
until it loses its pink color, about 8 minutes.
Add the onions, red pepper, and garlic. Cook,
stirring occasionally, until the onions are
softened, about 6 minutes. Stir into the chicken
mixture. Stir in the beans. (If preparing the

cassoulet to this point ahead, cool, cover, and
refrigerate. Stir 1 additional cup of chicken
stock or water into the cassoulet before
proceeding.)

4. In a small bowl, mix together the bread
crumbs and parsley. Sprinkle over the top of
the cassoulet. Bake for 30 minutes. Using a large
spoon, gently press the thin crust that has
formed on the cassoulet just under the surface.
Continue baking until the cassoulet is
simmering and a second thin crust has formed,
about 30 minutes. Let stand for 10 minutes.
Serve hot.

Note: Instead of paying a premium for
boneless, skinless chicken thighs, purchase
5 pounds chicken thighs with the skin and
bones, and remove the skin and bones yourself.
It's a quick and easy procedure.

Two-Way Duck with Pecan-Orange Wild Rice and Sautéed Spinach

Roast duck is a popular dish at my house, but a
single duck is really just enough for two people.
When I want to serve duck to friends, fitting two
birds into my oven just doesn't work. I devised
this solution, based on the way that many
restaurants serve their duck: Cut the duck into
parts, then cook each one so they are at their
best. Roast the leg quarters until crisp, cook the
boneless duck breast in a skillet until medium-
rare, turn the bony carcass and giblets into a
luscious classic demi-glace sauce, and render the
excess skin and fat. Each one of these steps is very
easy, so please do not be intimidated by the long
recipe. I've also included suggested side dishes
here, because they serve only four people, and
the other recipes in the book are for larger groups.

- Like goose, duck gives off a lot of fat. In France, where the word *cholesterol* is rarely uttered, rendered duck and goose fat are prized cooking ingredients. To play along with the American phobia for animal fats, you could certainly substitute butter or vegetable oil for the rendered fat in these recipes, but try the rendered fat, thinking of it as a special treat.

- Pecan-Orange Wild Rice is the perfect side dish to duck. Wild rice varies greatly from brand to brand and it is hard to gauge its cooking time and rate of liquid absorption. Hand-harvested wild rice is expensive, but it has an excellent, robust flavor and firm texture. It takes somewhat longer to cook than the less expensive, machine-harvested variety. If you have excess liquid in the pot when the rice is tender, simply drain it off. On the other hand, if the rice absorbs the liquid before it is done, add more stock (or water) as needed. Because of these variables, it may be best to make the rice ahead of serving and reheat it in a skillet or the microwave.

Makes 4 servings

Make Ahead: You can cut up the ducks, make the stock and sauce, and render the fat the day before serving. The duck quarters can be steamed up to 1½ hours before roasting.

Two 5½- to 6-pound Long Island (Peking) ducks
½ teaspoon salt
¼ teaspoon freshly ground black pepper
½ teaspoon dried thyme
2 quarts Homemade Duck Stock (page 46), made with reserved wings, giblets, necks, and carcass bones
Pecan-Orange Wild Rice (recipe follows)
Sautéed Spinach (recipe follows)

1. Prepare the ducks and stock the day before serving. Using a large, heavy knife, cut off the wings and reserve. Reserve the giblets (but not the livers, which you can save for another use or discard). Chop the necks and wings into 2- to 3-inch pieces. Set the wings, giblets, and necks aside for the stock. Pull out the clumps of fat inside the duck body cavity on either side of the tail, cover, and refrigerate.

2. Using a sharp, thin knife, cut off the leg quarters (thigh and drumstick together) at the thigh joints. Trim off excess skin from the perimeters of the duck pieces and reserve the skin pieces.

3. Make an incision down each side of the breastbone. With the knife tip pointing toward the rib bones, cut away the breast meat (with the skin still attached), pulling the meat away from the ribs as you cut. Cut off the breast section at the wing joint and the bottom of the rib cage. Pull the skin off the duck breasts and reserve. You will have 4 boneless breasts and 4 leg quarters. Season the duck with the salt, pepper, and thyme. Cover with plastic wrap and refrigerate.

4. To make the stock, using a heavy cleaver, chop the duck carcasses into manageable pieces to fit your stockpot, and use with the neck, wings, and giblets to make the duck stock according to the directions on page 46.

5. To render the duck fat, cut the reserved skin into thin strips and coarsely chop the reserved fat from the body cavity. Render according to the instructions in Roast Goose with Port Wine Gravy (page 58).

6. To make the sauce, place the duck stock in a large pot. Bring to a boil over high heat. Boil until the stock is reduced to about 1 quart, 1 to 1½ hours. Transfer to a medium saucepan and boil until dark brown and thick enough to coat a wooden spoon (about 1½ cups), about 30 minutes. (The sauce can be prepared up to 1 day ahead, cooled, covered, and refrigerated. Reheat before serving.)

7. Fit a large pot with a collapsible aluminum steamer rack and fill the pot with enough water to almost reach the rack. Add the duck leg quarters and bring to a boil over high heat. Cover tightly and reduce the heat to medium-low. Steam the duck leg quarters for 45 minutes. Remove the duck from the pot and transfer to a roasting pan. (The duck quarters can be prepared up to this point 1½ hours before roasting; set aside at room temperature.)

8. Position a rack in the top third of the oven and preheat to 450°F. Roast the steamed duck, turning occasionally, until crisp and golden brown, 30 to 40 minutes. Remove the duck breasts from the refrigerator and let stand at room temperature while the duck legs are roasting.

9. About 15 minutes before serving, heat 2 tablespoons of the rendered duck fat in a very large skillet over medium-high heat. Add the duck breasts and cook, turning once, until lightly browned and medium-rare, 6 to 8 minutes. (You can use a small, sharp knife to make an incision in the thickest part of the breast to check for doneness. Or press the duck with your finger—it should feel somewhat soft in the center. The firmer the meat feels, the more well-done it is.) Transfer the duck to a carving board and loosely cover with aluminum foil. Let stand for about 3 minutes for the juices to settle.

10. To serve, using a sharp carving knife, slice each breast into thin diagonal slices. Slip the knife under each breast and transfer to a dinner plate, fanning out the slices slightly. (If you wish, serve a whole breast, unsliced, on each plate.) Place a duck quarter on each plate. Divide the wild rice and spinach among the plates. Spoon some of the duck sauce around the duck, and serve immediately.

Pecan-Orange Wild Rice: In a medium saucepan, heat 2 tablespoons rendered duck fat over medium heat. Add 2 tablespoons finely chopped shallots and cook until softened, about 1 minute. Stir in 1 cup (6 ounces) rinsed and drained wild rice. Add 2⅔ cups Homemade Duck Stock (page 46) or canned reduced-sodium chicken broth, ⅓ cup fresh orange juice, the grated zest of ½ large orange, ¾ teaspoon salt, and ¼ teaspoon freshly ground black pepper. Bring to a boil over high heat. Reduce the heat to medium-low and cover tightly. Cook until the rice is tender and puffed, about 1 hour. Be flexible with the cooking time, as it will vary with the type of rice. Stir in ½ cup finely chopped pecans. Cover and let stand for 10 minutes. If necessary, drain any excess liquid from the wild rice before serving hot. (The rice can be made up to 2 hours ahead. If necessary, reheat in a covered large skillet over low heat, stirring often. Or place in a covered, microwave-safe bowl, and microwave on Medium-High or 70 percent power, stirring occasionally, until heated through, about 5 minutes.)

Sautéed Spinach: Fill a sink or very large bowl with cold water. Wash 2 pounds fresh spinach, tough stems removed. Shake the spinach to remove excess water, but do not dry completely. (The spinach can be cleaned up to 2 hours before cooking, stored at room temperature.) In a large saucepan, heat 2 tablespoons unsalted butter over medium-high heat. Add 1 small finely chopped garlic clove and cook until fragrant, about 1 minute. In batches, stir in the spinach, waiting for the first batch to wilt before adding another. Cook until the spinach is tender, about 5 minutes. Season with ½ teaspoon salt and ¼ teaspoon freshly ground black pepper. (The spinach can be made up to 1 hour ahead. Reheat over low heat, stirring often.) Serve hot, using a slotted spoon to leave excess liquid in the pot.

Roast Goose with Port Wine Gravy

There is a lot of romance about roast goose for Christmas, probably stemming from the Yuletide dinner scenes in British tales or from the German culinary tradition. Goose is a big bird, but first-time cooks should know that its size is deceiving— it doesn't yield a lot of meat. That said, the meat is dark, rich, and flavorful, reminiscent of both roast duck and well-done roast beef. In order to stretch the servings, offer lots of side dishes, like Red Cabbage with Apples and Bacon (page 73), Chestnut and Prune Stuffing (page 82), and Giant Potato and Leek Rösti (page 75).

- If possible, order a fresh goose from a specialty butcher. Frozen geese are also available and are quite good. For best results, thaw thoroughly in the refrigerator, allowing 2 to 3 days.

- Goose gives off a great amount of fat during cooking (about 3 cups!), which is a blessing in disguise. Goose fat is an excellent medium for frying and sautéing, especially in potato dishes like Giant Potato and Leek Rösti (page 75). There is plenty of visible fat to remove from the tail area and render in a saucepan. However, most of it is hidden in the skin, and it needs to be cooked out or the skin will be unappetizingly rubbery and greasy. My method uses two tricks to draw out the fat, culled from recipes for crisp-skinned Peking duck. First, leave the goose uncovered in the refrigerator for a day or two to dry and stretch the skin, which opens the pores and helps the fat run out of the skin during roasting. Second, steam the goose on a rack in a covered oval roasting pan (such as an old-fashioned turkey roaster) on top of the stove, a procedure that draws out the initial amount of fat better than roasting.

- Unlike turkey, you should be able to fit the entire batch of stuffing in the goose body cavity. Also, unlike turkey, the large opening to a stuffed goose needs to be sewn shut. Trussing needles are hard to find, even at professional restaurant supply stores. Mattress or canvas needles are easily purchased at sewing or hobby shops. They are long and sturdy, with large eyes that can thread cotton butcher's twine. I store my "goose needle" in my kitchen gadget drawer, taped to the inside of the drawer with a large piece of masking tape so it can't get lost.

- Make Homemade Goose Stock (page 46) to flavor the stuffing and make the gravy. The bony wing tips are always removed from the goose before roasting because they have a tendency to burn. Along with the goose neck and heart (the liver would make the stock bitter so it is used in the stuffing), the wing tips are the beginning of a great stock, but a bit of chicken broth boosts the poultry flavor. If you don't own a heavy cleaver that will cut through the strong bones, have the butcher remove the wing tips and chop them, along with the goose neck, before you bring the bird home.

- Goose should be cooked to 180°F, like a turkey, but don't expect the tenderness of the latter. The joints of a goose, especially at the hip, are very tight, and always take some work to pry them from the body. The skin is one of the best parts of the goose, and should be served in generous portions.

Makes 6 to 8 servings

Make Ahead: The goose must be refrigerated 1 to 2 days before serving. The rendered goose fat and stock can be made up to 2 days ahead.

One 10- to 12-pound goose, neck chopped into 2- to 3-inch pieces, and giblets reserved to make Homemade Goose Stock (page 46)

Chestnut and Prune Stuffing (page 82)

Salt

Freshly ground black pepper

4 tablespoons rendered goose fat or butter

¼ cup all-purpose flour

2⅔ cups Homemade Goose Stock (page 46)

⅓ cup tawny or ruby port

1. One to two days before roasting, rinse the goose and pat dry with paper towels. Pull out the clumps of pale yellow fat from around the tail cavity. Cut off any excess neck skin and reserve. Cut off the wings at the second joints, leaving only the last wing segment attached to the goose. Use the neck, giblets (no liver), and wing tips to make the stock, reserving the liver for the stuffing. Cover and refrigerate the fat, skin, wings, neck, wing tips, and liver until ready to use.

2. Place the goose on a rack in a roasting pan. Refrigerate at least overnight and up to 48 hours. The skin will dry out, but that's what you want.

3. Meanwhile, render the goose fat: Coarsely chop the goose fat and cut the skin into thin strips. Place in a medium saucepan and add ¼ cup warm water. Cook with the lid ajar over medium-low heat until the fat has rendered into a golden liquid and the skin strips are lightly browned, about 2 hours. Strain through a wire sieve into a bowl and let cool to room temperature. (You can discard the cracklings in the sieve or reserve them to serve sprinkled on a green salad.) Store the fat in small containers (1-cup deli containers work well), as you will most likely be using it in small amounts. It will make about 2 cups. (The rendered fat can be stored, covered and refrigerated, for up to 3 weeks or frozen for up to 3 months.)

4. When ready to roast the goose, fill the body cavity with the stuffing. Using a trussing needle and kitchen twine, sew up the opening.

Using the tip of the needle, prick the goose skin all over (without reaching into the meat), especially in the thigh area.

5. Place the goose on a rack in an oval roasting pan with a lid. Add 2 cups of water to the pan and bring to a boil on top of the stove over high heat. Cover tightly and reduce the heat to low. Steam the duck for 1 hour. Remove the goose on the rack from the pan and pour out the liquid in the pan. Return the goose and the rack to the pan and season the goose with 1 teaspoon salt and ¼ teaspoon pepper.

6. Place a rack in the center of the oven and preheat to 350°F. Roast the goose, uncovered, until an instant-read thermometer inserted in the thickest part of the thigh (without touching a bone) reads 180°F, about 1½ hours. During the last 15 minutes of roasting, increase the oven temperature to 400°F to crisp the skin. As the goose roasts and rendered fat accumulates in the pan, use a bulb baster to remove and add it to the rendered fat from step 3, if desired, or discard. Transfer the goose to a serving platter and let stand for 20 to 30 minutes before carving.

7. To make the gravy, pour all of the rendered fat out of the pan into the reserved fat. Set the roasting pan over two burners on medium-low heat. Add ¼ cup of the rendered goose fat to the pan. Sprinkle the flour into the pan, whisking constantly. Let the mixture bubble until it turns beige, about 1 minute. Whisk in the stock and port, scraping up the browned bits from the bottom of the pan. (Save the remaining stock for another use. It is an excellent substitute for chicken stock.) Simmer for about 5 minutes, whisking occasionally. Season the gravy with salt and pepper. If desired, strain the gravy. Transfer to a warmed sauceboat.

8. Carve the goose (see "Carving Up," page 61), and serve with a spoonful of the stuffing and a portion of the crisp skin. Pass the gravy on the side.

Roast Turkey with Bourbon Gravy

Some families think of turkey strictly as a Thanksgiving feast, but others wouldn't dream of having a Christmas meal without the bird making a return appearance. Turkey is a big bird, and a big subject. I have roasted hundreds of turkeys in just about every way possible. But this is my tried-and-true method that has given me my reputation as Mr. Turkey. For an in-depth discussion, pick up *Thanksgiving 101*. In the meantime, here are the most important things to remember:

- There is no flavor difference between a tom and a hen, only size. Toms weigh about 15 pounds and above and hens average between 8 and 15 pounds. Choose your turkey size by how many people you want to serve, figuring about 1 pound per person, which allows for seconds and leftovers. Toms are bred to have large breasts, so you will get more white meat for your money with a big bird. Use the roasting chart on page 62 to calculate the times for the turkey's weight.

- I prefer the flavor and moistness of a fresh turkey. If you must use a frozen turkey, defrost it properly in the refrigerator, never at room temperature. Allow a full 24 hours in the refrigerator to defrost each 5 pounds of turkey. A 25-pound bird will take a full 5 days to defrost. If you are a novice cook, buy a self-basting bird, which is injected with broth and fats to help keep the bird moist. Self-basting birds don't have a true turkey flavor, but they are practically failproof. But I guarantee that once you learn how to roast a beautiful, fresh, all-natural turkey, there is no turning back. Organic and free-range birds are excellent, but the added cost depends on your guests. Will they really appreciate the difference? My guests do.

- Invest in a few essential tools that you will use time and again to roast your holiday birds (and roasts). A *high-quality roasting pan* will make the best, beautifully browned gravy drippings, and, unlike those cheap disposable aluminum foil pans, you won't have to worry about the pan buckling under the weight of a heavy bird. My favorite pan is nonstick and measures 18 × 14 × 3 inches. Buy a *roasting rack* to fit the pan so the turkey doesn't stew in its own juices. Using a *meat thermometer*, preferably a digital probe model, is the best way to tell when the bird is cooked. Don't trust pop-up thermometers, as they often get glued shut from the turkey juices. A *bulb baster* will help distribute the cooking juices over the bird. And don't forget an *oven thermometer*—many oven thermostats are inaccurate. A *flat whisk* (buy a hard plastic one for a nonstick pan) will help you get into the corners of the pan to whisk the flour and butter into the drippings for the gravy.

- You will never be able to fit all of the stuffing into the bird, so plan on baking the leftover stuffing on the side. Fill the bird loosely with the stuffing, as it will expand during cooking.

- The trick with roast turkey is to have the white meat remain moist and succulent while the dark meat is thoroughly cooked and at its peak of flavor. White meat is cooked at 170°F, and after that point it begins to dry out. Unfortunately, dark meat needs to be cooked to 180°F in order for it to be tasty. Many cookbooks and cooking magazines instruct the cook to roast the bird to 170°F, or even less, which does give moist white meat but undercooked, red dark meat. It's not unhealthy to eat the dark meat—I just don't like the soft texture and underroasted flavor, and neither does anyone else I know. I correct the problem by wrapping—not tenting—the breast area with aluminum foil. This slows down the cooking in this crucial area. Baste under the foil (basting promotes a crisp, brown skin) whenever you like—every 45 minutes or so is plenty. During the last hour of roasting, remove the foil and allow the skin to brown.

- Use Homemade Turkey Stock (page 46) for the best gravy and stuffing. If you wish, make Quick Turkey Stock (page 63) from the

Carving Up

Here are step-by-step instructions for carving a roast turkey.

1. First, allow the bird to stand at room temperature for at least 20 minutes and up to 40 minutes before carving. This allows the juices to settle into the meat. If you carve it too soon, the juices will run out of the flesh, and you'll have dry turkey.

2. Remove the drumsticks to make the breast easier to reach and carve. Cut off each drumstick at the knee joint. If the turkey is properly cooked (that is, at least 180°F), they will pull away without any trouble, making the joints easy to sever. Do not remove the thighs at this point, or the bird will roll around the platter while you try to carve it. Transfer the drumsticks to a platter. To allow more people to enjoy the dark meat, tilt each drumstick, holding it from the foot end, and cut downward along the bone to slice the meat.

3. Hold the breast firmly with the meat fork. One side at a time, make a deep incision, cut parallel to the table down near the wing. Cut down along the side of the breast to carve it into thin slices. Every slice will stop at the parallel cut. Transfer the sliced breast to the platter. Turn the turkey around to carve the other side.

4. Pry the thighs away from the hips to reveal the ball joints, and sever at the joints. Transfer the thighs to the platter. To carve each thigh, hold the thigh with a meat fork, and carve the meat parallel to the bone.

5. Pry the wings away from the shoulder joints and sever at the joints. Transfer to the platter.

If you still feel nervous about carving in front of your guests, present the whole roast bird at the table in all its glory. Then, run back into the kitchen and carve the meat where no one is looking. Serve it carved on a platter, or use two platters, separating the dark and white meat. This actually works better, because the guests can serve themselves more easily. Here's a neat trick: If you have extra turkey stock, just before serving, pour a ladleful of the hot stock over each platter so the meat is steaming and looks especially juicy.

Carving a goose follows the same general idea, but the goose joints are very tight and will not sever as easily as the turkey, and a goose is all dark meat.

turkey neck and giblets. To make any amount of gravy, follow the recipe below, allowing 1½ tablespoons each of turkey fat and flour for every cup of stock and degreased turkey drippings.

Makes about 12 servings, plus leftovers

One l8-pound fresh turkey
Cornbread Succotash Stuffing (page 80) or your
    favorite stuffing recipe
6 tablespoons (¾ stick) unsalted butter, softened
Salt and freshly ground black pepper
About 8½ cups Homemade Turkey Stock (page
    46) or Quick Turkey Stock (recipe follows)
½ cup plus 1 tablespoon all-purpose flour
3 tablespoons bourbon

1. Preheat the oven to 325°F. Rinse the turkey well with cold water and pat dry. Remove the fat from the tail area and reserve it.

(If there isn't any fat, don't worry.) Turn the turkey on its breast. Loosely fill the neck cavity with the stuffing. Pin the neck skin to the back skin with a thin wooden or metal skewer. Fold the wings akimbo behind the back or tie to the body with kitchen string. Loosely fill the body cavity with stuffing. Place any remaining stuffing in a lightly buttered casserole, cover, and refrigerate to bake as a side dish. Secure the drumsticks at the tail with a clip or tie with kitchen string. Place the turkey, breast side up, on a rack in a large roasting pan. Rub the turkey with the softened butter. Season with salt and pepper. Place the reserved turkey fat in the pan. Tightly cover the breast area with aluminum foil. Pour 2 cups of stock in the bottom of the pan.

2. Roast, basting about every 45 minutes with the drippings in the pan (lift up the foil to reach the breast area), until an instant-read thermometer inserted in the thickest part of

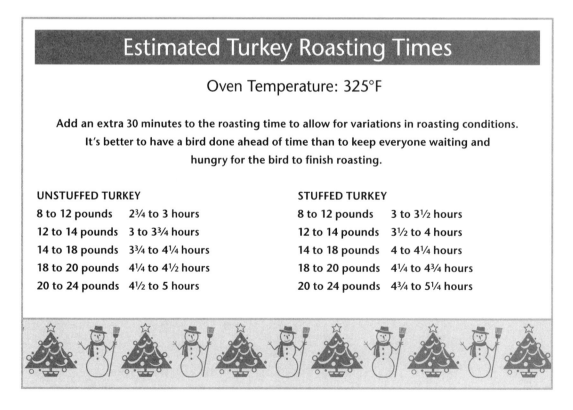

Estimated Turkey Roasting Times

Oven Temperature: 325°F

Add an extra 30 minutes to the roasting time to allow for variations in roasting conditions. It's better to have a bird done ahead of time than to keep everyone waiting and hungry for the bird to finish roasting.

UNSTUFFED TURKEY		STUFFED TURKEY	
8 to 12 pounds	2¾ to 3 hours	8 to 12 pounds	3 to 3½ hours
12 to 14 pounds	3 to 3¾ hours	12 to 14 pounds	3½ to 4 hours
14 to 18 pounds	3¾ to 4¼ hours	14 to 18 pounds	4 to 4¼ hours
18 to 20 pounds	4¼ to 4½ hours	18 to 20 pounds	4¼ to 4¾ hours
20 to 24 pounds	4½ to 5 hours	20 to 24 pounds	4¾ to 5¼ hours

the thigh (not touching a bone) reads 180°F to 185°F and the stuffing is at least 165°F, about 4½ hours. As the drippings in the pan evaporate, add 2 cups water. During the last hour, remove the foil to allow the skin to brown, making sure to baste a couple of times before the turkey is done to color the skin with the pan juices.

3. Transfer the turkey to a large serving platter. Let stand for 20 to 30 minutes before carving. Increase the oven temperature to 375°F. Drizzle the stuffing with ½ cup of turkey stock, cover, and bake until heated through, about 30 minutes.

4. Meanwhile, pour the drippings from the pan into a large glass bowl or gravy separator. Let stand for 5 minutes; skim off and reserve the clear yellow fat on the surface (or pour off the drippings and reserve both the drippings and fat in a separator). Add enough turkey stock to the skimmed drippings to make 6 cups total.

5. Place the roasting pan over two burners on medium heat. Add ½ cup plus 1 tablespoon of the reserved turkey fat (if necessary, add melted butter to make up any shortage). Whisk in the flour, scraping up the browned bits from the bottom of the pan, and let bubble until beige, 1 to 2 minutes. Whisk in the turkey liquid and bourbon. Reduce the heat to low and simmer for 5 minutes. (If the gravy seems too thick, add more stock or water.) Season with salt and pepper. Strain the gravy, if desired. Transfer to a warmed gravy boat. Carve the turkey (see "Carving Up," page 61), and serve the gravy and stuffing alongside.

Quick Turkey Stock: In a large saucepan, heat 1 tablespoon vegetable oil over medium-high heat. Add the turkey neck, chopped into 2- to 3-inch pieces, and the giblets (no liver). Cook, turning occasionally, until browned, about 8 minutes. Add 1 small chopped onion, 1 small chopped carrot, and 1 small chopped celery rib with leaves, and cook until softened, about

6 minutes. Add three 13¾-ounce cans reduced-sodium chicken broth and 1 quart water. Bring to a simmer, skimming off any foam that rises to the surface. Add 3 sprigs fresh parsley, ¼ teaspoon dried thyme, 8 peppercorns, and 1 bay leaf. Simmer for 1½ to 3 hours, the longer the better. Strain. Cool and skim off any clear yellow fat that rises to the surface. Makes about 8½ cups.

Baked Salmon Fillets with Salsa Verde

A chilled, whole poached salmon with herb mayonnaise has been the centerpiece of many a buffet. But, honestly, how many cooks have a salmon poacher? In this updated version boneless salmon fillets are slathered with an herbed sauce, then baked for a no-fuss, lovely main course for a serve-yourself feast. If you want a fish main course for a large dinner party, bake the salmon fillets but do not cool them.

Makes 16 to 20 buffet servings

Make Ahead: The salmon must be made at least 4 hours or up to 1 day ahead.

SALSA VERDE
½ cup coarsely chopped fresh parsley
½ cup packed fresh basil leaves
¼ cup sliced blanched almonds
2 tablespoons fresh lemon juice
1 tablespoon Dijon mustard
1 garlic clove, crushed through a press
½ teaspoon salt
¼ teaspoon freshly ground black pepper
½ cup extra virgin olive oil

Vegetable oil, for brushing
Two 3-pound salmon fillets, skin on
Lemon wedges, for serving

1. To make the salsa verde, in a food processor fitted with the metal blade, process all of the ingredients except the oil. With the machine running, gradually add the oil. Process, occasionally stopping the machine to scrape down the sides of the bowl, until the salsa is smooth, about 45 seconds. Set aside.

2. Position racks in the center and top third of the oven and preheat to 350°F. Brush a 2-foot-long sheet of extra-wide aluminum foil well with oil. Rub your fingers over the surface of one fillet and use tweezers to remove any stray bones. (Sterilize the tweezers first over an open flame.) Place the fillet, skin side down, on the foil and spread with half of the salsa. Bring the long sides of the foil up to meet over the fillet, and fold tightly to seal. Fold the short sides closed. Place on a large baking sheet. Repeat with the remaining fillet and salsa.

3. Bake for 20 minutes. Switch the positions of the fillets from top to bottom. Continue baking until the fish is done, about 20 minutes more. To check for doneness, open the foil and insert a knife between the flakes of meat in the center of the fillets—the flesh will be evenly opaque or have just a blush of pink in the center.

4. Open the foil and let the fillets stand until cooled to room temperature. Rewrap and refrigerate until well chilled, at least 4 hours or overnight. To serve, slide the fillets onto a platter. Cut the salmon on the platter into individual portions. Serve with the lemon wedges on the side.

Red and Green Lasagna

With a more delicate flavor than the typical beefy lasagna, this delicious chicken- and spinach-filled version is especially welcome at holiday time, where its green and red ingredients tie into the season's colors. In addition to the tomato sauce, it also has a creamy white sauce that gives the dish a northern Italian flair. Yes, it is a bit more complicated than other lasagnas, but the results are hard to beat.

● **Some cooks like to make and freeze lasagna 2 to 3 weeks before baking. The last time I baked a frozen batch of this dense lasagna, it took 2½ hours to cook through! In my opinion, the convenience of freezing isn't worth the lengthy baking time. (Of course, you could defrost the lasagna first.) I prefer to make and freeze the tomato sauce, chicken, and stock for up to 1 month. Then when I am ready to make the lasagna, I defrost them, make the filling and white sauce, and assemble.**

● **This lasagna is sublime with fresh pasta. If you have a pasta shop nearby, buy 1 pound fresh lasagna noodles. Cut the pasta into lengths to fit the dish. As you assemble the lasagna, boil the pasta as needed in batches in a large pot of lightly salted water over high heat until they are barely al dente and supple, about 3 minutes. Using a large skimmer, transfer the pasta to a colander, and rinse briefly under cold water to stop the cooking. Spread over kitchen towels and pat the tops dry with another towel. Working with one layer of lasagna noodles at a time keeps them from taking over your kitchen counter.**

Makes 12 servings

Make Ahead: The chicken, stock, and tomato sauce can be made up to 2 days before serving the lasagna, separately cooled, covered, and refrigerated. The lasagna can be prepared 1 day before baking.

CHICKEN AND STOCK

One 3½-pound chicken, cut into 8 pieces

1 medium onion, chopped

1 medium celery rib with leaves, chopped

1 medium carrot, chopped

2 sprigs fresh parsley

¼ teaspoon dried thyme

¼ teaspoon whole black peppercorns

1 bay leaf

TOMATO SAUCE

2 tablespoons olive oil

1 large onion, chopped

2 garlic cloves, minced

One 28-ounce can tomatoes in juice, chopped, juices reserved

One 6-ounce can tomato paste

1½ teaspoons dried basil

1½ teaspoons dried oregano

¼ teaspoon crushed hot red pepper

WHITE SAUCE

8 tablespoons (1 stick) unsalted butter

½ cup all-purpose flour

¼ cup heavy cream

¼ teaspoon salt

¼ teaspoon freshly ground white pepper

FILLING

Two 10-ounce packages frozen chopped spinach

1 cup fresh bread crumbs

½ cup heavy cream

1½ cups ricotta cheese

½ cup freshly grated Parmesan cheese

2 large eggs, beaten

⅓ cup chopped fresh parsley

¼ teaspoon freshly grated nutmeg

¼ teaspoon salt

¼ teaspoon freshly ground black pepper

1 pound dried lasagna noodles

3 cups (12 ounces) shredded mozzarella cheese

1. To prepare the chicken and stock, place the chicken, onion, celery, and carrot in a large pot and add enough cold water to barely cover the chicken (about 2 quarts). Bring to a boil over high heat, skimming off the foam that rises to the surface. Add the parsley, thyme, peppercorns, and bay leaf. Reduce the heat to medium-low and simmer, uncovered, for 30 minutes. Remove from the heat and cover tightly. Let stand for 30 minutes to allow the chicken to cook through.

2. Strain through a colander placed over a large bowl, reserving the chicken stock. Cool the chicken until easy to handle. Discard the skin and bones, coarsely chop the meat, and set aside. (The chicken and stock can be made up to 2 days ahead, separately cooled, covered, and refrigerated, or frozen for up to 1 month.)

3. To make the tomato sauce, heat the oil in a large saucepan over medium heat. Add the onion and cook until softened, about 5 minutes. Add the garlic and cook for 1 minute. Stir in the tomatoes with their juices, tomato paste, 1½ cups of the reserved chicken stock, the basil, oregano, and crushed red pepper, and bring to a boil, stirring to dissolve the tomato paste. Reduce the heat to low and simmer, uncovered, until thickened and reduced to about 6 cups, about 40 minutes. (The tomato sauce can be made up to 2 days ahead, cooled, covered, and refrigerated, or frozen for up to 1 month.)

4. To make the white sauce, in a medium, heavy-bottomed saucepan, melt the butter over medium-low heat. Whisk in the flour and let bubble, without browning, for 2 minutes. Whisk in 3½ cups of the reserved stock and bring to a simmer. (Reserve the remaining stock for another use.) Cook, stirring often, until thickened, about 3 minutes. Stir in the heavy cream and season with the salt and pepper. Transfer to a medium bowl. Cover with plastic wrap, pressing the wrap directly on to the surface of the sauce, and pierce a few holes in the wrap to allow the steam to escape (this prevents a skin from forming on the surface of the sauce). Set aside.

5. To make the filling, put the spinach in a wire sieve and rinse under warm water until thawed. A handful at a time, squeeze the moisture out of the spinach, and transfer the spinach to a large bowl.

6. In a small bowl, mix together the bread crumbs and heavy cream and let stand until the bread crumbs are softened, about 5 minutes. Scrape into the bowl with the spinach. Add the chopped chicken, ricotta and Parmesan cheeses, eggs, parsley, nutmeg, salt, and pepper. Set aside.

7. Bring a large pot of lightly salted water to a boil over high heat. One a time, stir the lasagna noodles into the water. Cover and bring the water back to a boil. Immediately uncover the pot, and cook the pasta until barely tender, about 7 minutes for dried. (The pasta will continue to cook in the oven, so it should still have some bite to it.) Drain and rinse under cold running water. Shake the colander well to remove excess water. (If not using immediately, toss the pasta with 1 tablespoon olive oil and set aside in the colander for up to 1 hour.)

8. Position a rack in the center of the oven and preheat to 350°F. Lightly oil a 15 × 10-inch baking dish.

9. Spread about ½ cup of the tomato sauce in the bottom of the dish. Arrange 5 lasagna noodles (4 horizontally and 1 vertically), slightly overlapping and cut to fit, in the dish. Spoon a third of the tomato sauce over the noodles. Scatter half of the chicken-spinach filling over the noodles, then spread half of the white sauce on top. Arrange another 5 noodles

in the dish. Top with half of the remaining tomato sauce, then the remaining filling, remaining white sauce, and 1 cup of mozzarella. Arrange a final layer of noodles, spread with the remaining tomato sauce, and sprinkle with the remaining mozzarella. Cover the lasagna tightly with aluminum foil. (The lasagna can be prepared up to 1 day ahead, covered tightly and refrigerated.)

10. Bake for 30 minutes. Remove the foil and continue baking until the sauce is bubbling throughout, about 30 minutes more. Let the lasagna stand for 10 minutes before serving.

Lasagna with Roasted Portobello Mushrooms

This luxurious lasagna has become a staple at my holiday parties because with a few minor adjustments, it can serve as a vegetarian main course. (I just make a second pan for my friends who don't eat meat, using all milk instead of the stock in the sauce, and leaving out the prosciutto in the mushroom mixture.) I can't encourage you enough to try this dish.

Makes 8 to 10 servings

Make Ahead: The mushrooms, prosciutto mixture, and sauce can be made up to 1 day before serving the lasagna, separately cooled, covered, and refrigerated. The finished lasagna can be prepared up to 8 hours ahead.

MUSHROOMS
10 medium (about 2½ pounds) portobello mushrooms

2 tablespoons plus 2 teaspoons extra virgin olive oil

Salt and freshly ground black pepper to taste

4 ounces prosciutto, cut into ¼-inch dice (about
   1 cup)

⅔ cup chopped shallots

1 teaspoon chopped fresh rosemary

1 teaspoon chopped fresh thyme

SAUCE

3½ cups milk

2 cups Homemade White Chicken Stock
   (page 46) or canned reduced-sodium
   chicken broth

1 bay leaf

½ cup (1 stick) unsalted butter

⅔ cup all-purpose flour

2 cups (8 ounces) shredded Gruyère cheese

⅓ cup freshly grated Parmesan cheese

⅛ teaspoon freshly grated nutmeg

Salt and freshly ground black pepper to taste

15 lasagna noodles

½ cup (2 ounces) freshly grated Parmesan cheese

2 tablespoons unsalted butter, cut into pieces

1. To prepare the mushrooms, preheat the oven to 400°F. Trim the dirty ends from the mushroom stems, but leave the stems attached to the caps. Rinse the mushrooms well under cold water to remove any grit. Toss the mushrooms with 2 tablespoons of the oil in a large bowl. Arrange on a large oiled baking sheet. Season with salt and pepper. Roast until tender, about 45 minutes. Remove from the oven and cool completely. Cut the mushrooms lengthwise into ⅓-inch-thick slices, including the stems.

2. Heat the remaining 2 teaspoons of the oil in a medium nonstick skillet over medium heat. Add the prosciutto and cook, stirring often, until browned, about 5 minutes. Add the shallots, rosemary, and thyme. Cook, stirring often, until the shallots are tender, about 4 minutes. Remove from the heat and set aside. (The mushrooms and prosciutto can be

prepared up to 1 day ahead, cooled, separately covered, and refrigerated.)

3. To make the sauce, bring the milk, stock, and bay leaf to simmer in a large saucepan or in a microwave. Let stand 10 minutes; discard the bay leaf.

4. Melt the butter in a medium, heavy-bottomed saucepan over medium-low heat. Whisk in the flour and let it bubble without browning, for 2 minutes. Whisk in the hot milk mixture, and bring to a simmer over high heat, whisking often. Reduce the heat to low and simmer until slightly thickened, about 5 minutes. Remove from the heat and stir in the Gruyère, Parmesan, and nutmeg. Season with salt and pepper. (The sauce can be made 1 day ahead. Transfer to a bowl and press a piece of plastic wrap directly on the surface of the sauce. Pierce a few slits in the wrap to allow steam to escape. Cool until tepid, then refrigerate. Reheat in a saucepan over low heat before using.)

5. Position a rack in the center of the oven and preheat to 350°F. Lightly butter a 13 × 9-inch glass baking dish.

6. Bring a large pot of lightly salted water to a boil over high heat. Add the lasagna noodles, one at a time, and cook until barely tender (they will continue to cook in the oven), about 7 minutes. Drain and rinse under cold running water. Pat the noodles dry on clean kitchen towels.

7. Spread 1 cup of the warm sauce in the baking dish. Arrange 4 slightly overlapping noodles lengthwise in the dish, then 1 noodle trimmed to fit crosswise. Spread with a third of the sauce. Arrange half of the mushrooms on top, then scatter with half of the prosciutto mixture. Layer with 5 more noodles, half of the remaining sauce, and the remaining mushrooms and prosciutto mixture. Finish with the remaining noodles and spread with the remaining sauce. Sprinkle the Parmesan evenly over top, and dot with the butter.

(The lasagna can be made 8 hours ahead, cooled, covered, and refrigerated.)

8. Bake until the top is golden brown and the sauce is bubbling, about 45 minutes (or 1 hour if refrigerated). Let stand 10 minutes. Cut into portions and serve.

Savory Sausage and Cheese Bread Pudding

Here's a carefree, delicious way to serve Christmas brunch. Layers of bread with sausage and vegetables, held together with a cheesy custard, this is sometimes called *strata* ("layers" in Italian). It can be made the night before, so when you are up to your neck in Christmas morning wrapping paper, all the pudding needs is a trip to the oven. Serve it with a winter fruit salad of sliced apples and pears, orange sections, and pomegranate seeds.

- Before assembling the pudding, remember to let the bread stand out at room temperature for at least 8 hours so it dries out a bit. If necessary, bake in a preheated 325°F until dried out but not toasted or crisp, 20 to 30 minutes—the bread will continue to firm up as it cools outside of the oven.

- The pudding can also be prepared right before it goes into the oven. To reduce the baking time, heat the milk in a medium saucepan until bubbles appear around the edges. Slowly whisk the hot milk into the eggs. Bake the pudding until a knife inserted in the center comes out clean, about 1 hour.

Makes 6 to 8 servings

Make Ahead: The pudding can be prepared the night before.

2 tablespoons extra virgin olive oil
1 large onion, chopped
1 medium red bell pepper, cored, seeded, and chopped
1 pound sweet Italian pork or turkey sausage, casings removed
6 large eggs
2 tablespoons Dijon mustard
1½ teaspoons Italian herb seasoning
½ teaspoon salt
¼ teaspoon freshly ground black pepper
1 quart milk
12 slices day-old, firm white sandwich bread, crusts trimmed
2 cups (8 ounces) shredded sharp cheddar cheese

1. In a large skillet, heat the oil over medium heat. Add the onion and red pepper. Cook, stirring occasionally, until softened, 5 to 7 minutes. Add the sausage and cook, breaking up the sausage with the side of a spoon, until the sausage loses its pink color, about 10 minutes. Drain off any liquid in the skillet and set the sausage mixture aside.

2. In a large bowl, whisk together the eggs, mustard, Italian seasoning, salt, and pepper. Gradually whisk in the milk. Set aside.

3. Lightly butter a 13 × 9-inch glass baking dish. Line the bottom of the prepared dish with the bread slices, trimming to fit if necessary. Sprinkle the bread with half of the cheese, then spread with all of the sausage mixture. Top with the remaining bread slices. Slowly pour the egg mixture over the bread, allowing it to soak in. Sprinkle the top with the remaining cheese. (The pudding can be prepared the night before, covered tightly with plastic wrap and referigerated.)

4. Position a rack in the center of the oven and preheat to 325°F. Uncover the pudding and bake until a knife inserted in the center of the pudding comes out clean, about 1½ hours. Let stand for 10 minutes before serving.

It Wouldn't Be the Holidays Without . . . Roasts

There are many reasons why you'll usually find a big roast on a Christmas dinner table. Of course, roast meat is delicious, and it is a pretty easy way to feed a crowd. However, serving a large cut of meat during the biggest winter holiday goes way back to Roman times.

We take refrigeration for granted. If we want fresh meat, no problem. But until about a hundred years ago, most meat was preserved by salting, corning, or smoking. The main butchering took place in the winter, when it was cold and the meat could be refrigerated naturally. Winter was about the only time that the average person could enjoy fresh meat.

In Roman times, the main winter holiday occurred on December 25, the "Birthday of the Invincible Sun God," Mithras. Mithraism was the main religion of the Roman Empire, and Mithras's birthday was a big feast day.

It made sense to use up as much of the freshly butchered meat possible before it went bad, and when better than during one of those big Roman feasts that you see in the movies?

When Christianity established itself, the Church fathers usurped Mithras, and declared December 25 as Christ's birthday. In order to persuade former pagans to commemorate Christ's birth, the Church had to change its former position on celebrating the day. (The early Christians did not want to celebrate Christ's birthday, as they thought that kind of natal day was the province of Pharaohs and other false gods.) Mithraists were allowed to keep the winter festival, as long as Mithras had nothing to do with it. Many of the old pagan traditions took centuries to die, and some of them, like serving big roasts on the most important winter holiday, never went away.

Side Dishes and Stuffings

From Cranberries to Black-Eyed Peas

What would roast beef be without potatoes or Yorkshire pudding served alongside? Roast goose without red cabbage and potato pancakes? Or the ultimate in holiday unthinkables—turkey without cranberry sauce? Never underestimate the importance of side dishes. In my family, we look forward to Mom's cheesy scalloped potatoes just as much as we do her delicious ham.

To serve your side dishes at their best, follow these tips:

- Unless you plan accordingly, you could easily have a traffic jam in the oven trying to reheat all those sides. Be sure that at least one dish is prepared on top of the stove to lessen the load.

- Many side dishes can be prepared ahead and stored in the refrigerator until ready to serve. Increase the baking time by 10 to 15 minutes if the dishes have been chilled.

- Allow at least 20 minutes for the food to heat through in the oven. In most cases, cover dishes with their lids or aluminum foil.

- Warm the serving dishes (in a preheated 200°F oven for a few minutes or by filling with hot water) before adding the food.

- If a hot dish is going to be served in the casserole or baking dish it was cooked in, have trivets and clean pot holders at the table to make serving easier.

Black-Eyed Pea Stew (Hoppin' John)

Another southern holiday tradition, black-eyed peas are always served at New Year's celebrations because they represent the countless coins that we hope to accumulate during the upcoming prosperous year. Hoppin' John is a black-eyed pea and rice stew that is hearty enough to serve as a main course, but I serve it as a side dish with baked ham. There are many ideas on how it got its unusual name, but one seems to make the most sense. The dish arrived in our country via the African slaves from French Caribbean islands, where a rice and pigeon pea stew was cooked. "Hoppin' John" is an Americanization of *pois à pigeon*, French for "pigeon peas," which are related to black-eyed peas.

- Black-eyed peas have a distinctively earthy flavor. Because they have thin skins, they don't have to be soaked like many other dried legumes. However, it is difficult to gauge their cooking time (some beans are just drier than others). So keep an eye on the pot, and check often for tenderness.

- There are many, many ways to make Hoppin' John, but this version uses a ham hock stock. This step takes little effort, just a bit of patience. Reserve the ham for another use, and do not add it to the peas (unless you want a very filling side dish).

- To serve Hoppin' John at a buffet, serve it from the Dutch oven on a hot plate, or transfer to a chafing dish or slow cooker.

Makes 12 to 16 servings

Make Ahead: The black-eyed peas can be made up to 1 day ahead and reheated. Add the cooked rice just before serving.

3 ham hocks, about 2¼ pounds total (see Note)
2 medium onions, chopped
3 medium celery ribs, chopped
2 tablespoons vegetable oil
1 medium red bell pepper, cored, seeded, and chopped
2 garlic cloves, minced
1½ tablespoons Cajun Seasoning (recipe follows) or a salt-free, store-bought blend
1 pound black-eyed peas, picked over to remove stones, rinsed, and drained
1 cup long-grain rice
Salt
Hot red pepper sauce to taste

1. Place the ham hocks, 1 onion, and 1 celery rib in a large pot and add 3 quarts cold water. Bring to a boil over high heat. Reduce the heat to medium-low and partially cover. Simmer until the ham hocks are tender, about 1½ hours. Strain through a colander placed over a large bowl, reserving the liquid. You should have about 2 quarts stock; add water, if necessary. If desired, remove the meat from the bones and reserve it for another use.

2. In a Dutch oven, heat the oil over medium heat. Add the remaining onion and 2 celery ribs and the red pepper. Cook, stirring often, until softened, about 5 minutes. Add the garlic and Cajun seasoning and stir until fragrant, about 30 seconds. Add the black-eyed peas and enough of the ham stock to cover the peas by 1 inch, about 2 quarts. Increase the heat to high and bring to a boil.

3. Reduce the heat to medium-low and partially cover the pot. Cook, stirring occasionally, until the peas are tender, about 1 hour. The mixture will be somewhat soupy. (The black-eyed peas can be prepared to this point up to 1 day ahead, cooled, covered, and refrigerated. Reheat gently over medium-low heat, adding about 2 cups water to return it to its former soupy consistency.)

4. Meanwhile, in a medium saucepan, bring the rice, 2 cups of the remaining ham stock, and ½ teaspoon salt to a boil over medium heat. Reduce the heat to low and cover tightly. Cook until the rice is tender and has absorbed the liquid, 15 to 17 minutes. Remove the pan from the heat and let stand, covered, for at least 5 minutes. (The rice will stay hot for at least 30 minutes.)

5. To serve, fluff the rice with a fork and stir into the black-eyed peas. Season with salt and hot pepper sauce. Serve immediately.

Note: Ham hocks are the traditional seasoning meat in southern cooking. With attention to reduced-fat cooking, most of my southern and African American friends substitute smoked turkey wings for ham hocks—it's an excellent alternative. Substitute two 1-pound smoked turkey wings, cut into 2-inch pieces, for the ham hocks.

Cajun Seasoning: Mix together 2 tablespoons sweet paprika (preferably Hungarian), 1 tablespoon each dried thyme and dried basil, 1 teaspoon each garlic powder and onion powder, ½ teaspoon freshly ground black pepper, and ⅛ teaspoon cayenne pepper. Store leftover seasoning tightly covered in a cool, dark place. Use to season grilled poultry, fish, or pork, or to sprinkle on popcorn. Makes about ⅓ cup.

Brussels Sprouts with Pancetta

While Brussels sprouts are popular on winter menus, they often need a bit of gussying up to make them appropriate for a holiday meal. Pancetta, a peppered, unsmoked, and rolled bacon available at Italian delicatessens and many supermarkets, gives a boost to the humble Brussels sprouts. If you want to substitute regular bacon, blanch it first to remove the smoky taste: Place the bacon strips in a skillet, add cold water to cover, and bring to a simmer over low heat. Drain, rinse, pat dry with paper towels, and chop coarsely.

Makes 8 to 10 servings

4 ounces sliced (¼-inch-thick) pancetta, coarsely
    chopped
1 tablespoon extra virgin olive oil
⅓ cup chopped shallots
Three 10-ounce containers Brussels sprouts,
    trimmed and cut lengthwise into ½-inch-thick
    slices
1 cup Homemade Brown Stock 101 (page 45),
    Homemade Turkey Stock (page 46), or
    canned reduced-sodium chicken broth
¼ teaspoon salt
¼ teaspoon freshly ground black pepper

1. In a large skillet, cook the pancetta in the oil over medium heat, turning occasionally, until crisp and brown, about 5 minutes. Add the shallots and stir until softened, about 1 minute. Stir in the Brussels sprouts. Add the stock and season with the salt and pepper.

2. Cover and reduce the heat to medium-low. Simmer until the Brussels sprouts are tender when pierced with the tip of a small, sharp knife, about 20 minutes. If any stock remains in the skillet, increase the heat to medium-high and cook until it evaporates. Serve hot.

Maple-Glazed Butternut Squash

Sautéed cubes of butternut squash with a simple maple syrup glaze is an excellent side dish, and much easier to prepare than winter squash recipes that require long baking. Butternut squash has a thinner skin than other types of winter squash, which is easy to remove with a vegetable peeler (some of the other varieties need a machete to peel and chop). If you use real maple syrup, the flavor will be subtly sweet; if you want a more maple taste, use pancake syrup, which gets its punch from artificial flavorings. Instead of finely ground black pepper, try a coarse grind—it works well to accent the sweet glaze.

Makes 8 servings

Make Ahead: The squash can be peeled and cubed up to 8 hours before cooking.

4 pounds butternut squash
3 tablespoons unsalted butter
6 tablespoons maple syrup, preferably Grade B
1 teaspoon salt
½ teaspoon coarsely cracked black pepper (crush in a mortar or under a heavy saucepan)

1. Peel the squash with a sturdy vegetable peeler. Using a large knife, cut into 1-inch pieces, discarding the seeds. (The squash can be prepared, covered and refrigerated, for up to 8 hours.)

2. In a very large skillet, heat the butter over medium-high heat. Add the squash and cover. Cook, stirring occasionally, until the squash is lightly browned and almost tender, about 12 minutes.

3. Stir in the maple syrup and season with the salt and pepper. Cook, uncovered, stirring occasionally, until the cooking liquid has reduced to a glaze and the squash is tender, about 5 minutes. Serve immediately.

Red Cabbage with Apples and Bacon

This sweet-and-sour dish only gets better if made a day ahead. It's equally at home with roast goose or pork. When not gracing the holiday table, this dish is excellent alongside grilled pork chops.

Makes 8 to 12 servings

Make Ahead: The cabbage can be made up to 1 day ahead.

6 slices bacon
1 tablespoon vegetable oil
1 medium onion, thinly sliced
2 Granny Smith apples, peeled, cored, and thinly sliced
6 tablespoons cider vinegar
⅓ cup packed light brown sugar
1 medium red cabbage (2½ pounds), quartered, cored, and thinly sliced crosswise
1 cup Homemade Beef Stock (page 46) or canned reduced-sodium beef broth
1 teaspoon dried thyme
1 bay leaf
½ teaspoon salt
¼ teaspoon freshly ground black pepper

1. Cook the bacon with the oil in a Dutch oven over medium heat, turning the bacon once, until crisp and browned, about 6 minutes. Using a slotted spatula, transfer the bacon to paper towels to drain, leaving the bacon fat in the pot.

2. Add the onion to the pot and cook, stirring often, until golden brown, about 8 minutes. Add the apples and stir for 1 minute. Stir in the vinegar and brown sugar. Gradually stir in the red cabbage, then the beef stock, thyme, bay leaf, salt, and pepper. Cover and reduce the heat to medium-low. Simmer until the cabbage is very tender, about 45 minutes.

(The cabbage can be made up to 1 day ahead, cooled, covered, and refrigerated. Reheat gently over medium-low heat.) Chop the bacon and stir it into the cabbage. Serve hot.

Baby Carrots and Green Beans in Tarragon Butter

When the main course calls for a brightly colored, crisp-tender side dish, this is the technique to use. The night before, blanch the vegetables, rinse under cold running water, and pat dry. They now can be refrigerated overnight. When it's time for dinner, just give them a quick sauté in butter with the shallots to heat them up. *Voilà!* Baby carrots and green beans are featured here, but other vegetables and herbs work, too. Broccoli and cauliflower florets, sprinkled with fresh thyme, are a nice winter combination, too.

Makes 8 servings

Make Ahead: The carrots and green beans can be parcooked up to 1 day ahead.

12 ounces trimmed baby carrots
12 ounces trimmed green beans, preferably
    haricots verts
2 tablespoons unsalted butter
2 tablespoons finely chopped shallots
1 tablespoon chopped fresh tarragon or
    1 teaspoon dried tarragon
¼ teaspoon salt
¼ teaspoon freshly ground black pepper

1. Bring a large pot of lightly salted water to a boil over high heat. Add the carrots and cook until barely tender, about 5 minutes. Remove from the water with a skimmer and place in a colander. Rinse under cold water. Pat dry with paper towels.

2. In the same pot of boiling water, cook the green beans until barely tender, about 3 minutes. Drain and rinse under cold water. Pat dry. (The vegetables can be prepared up to 1 day ahead, wrapped in paper towels, stored in self-sealing plastic bags, and refrigerated.)

3. In a very large skillet, melt the butter over medium heat. Add the shallots and cook for 1 minute. Add the carrots and green beans and cook, stirring occasionally, until heated through, about 6 minutes. Stir in the tarragon and season with the salt and pepper. Transfer to a warmed serving dish and serve hot.

Long-Simmered Greens

Just as southern cooks make Hoppin' John on New Year's because the black-eyed peas represent coins, simmered greens are another must-have because they resemble the loads of greenback bills we hope to gather in the coming year. Long-cooked greens are a perfect accompaniment to baked ham, too, which graces many a holiday buffet or dinner. Some cooks serve quickly sautéed greens, but in my opinion, those cooks are very misguided—the assertive flavor of the greens needs plenty of cooking time to mellow.

- There are many varieties of greens that are appropriate for long simmering: Kale, curly kale, collards, mustard greens, turnip greens, and dandelions are the most popular. They have distinctive tastes, from the relatively mild collards to the peppery mustard greens. If you don't have a preference, I suggest collards. You can also mix the greens to come up with a personal blend.

- Old-fashioned recipes for greens call for cooking them in a ham stock. Many African American cooks use turkey wings instead of ham hocks in traditional soul-food fare.

Turkey wings are less fatty than ham hocks, but there is still plenty of fat in the turkey skin. At any rate, they're less expensive and have a good smoky flavor all their own. You can use a ham hock here if you wish.

● Savvy cooks sip the cooking liquor, colloquially known as "pot likker," from the greens—it's especially good as a dunk for cornbread. To make be sure that the pot likker is as full-flavored and delicious as it can be, use chicken stock as part of the cooking liquid. Southern restaurants often serve greens and likker in individual serving dishes so you have plenty of likker for dunking (and the juices won't run all over the plate).

Makes 8 to 12 servings

Make Ahead: The greens can be made up to 1 day ahead.

5 pounds dark, strong-flavored greens (see suggestions above)

2 tablespoons vegetable oil

1 large onion, chopped

2 garlic cloves, finely chopped

1 cup Homemade White Chicken Stock (page 46) or canned reduced-sodium chicken broth (optional)

¼ teaspoon crushed hot red pepper

One 1-pound smoked turkey wing, cut into 2-inch pieces

1 teaspoon salt

1 tablespoon cider vinegar

1. Remove the thick stalks from the greens and discard. Stack the leaves and cut crosswise into 1-inch-wide strips. Fill a sink with tepid water (lukewarm water helps loosen any grit better than ice-cold water). Add the greens, swish them in the water, and let stand for 1 minute. Lift the greens from the water, trying not to disturb the grit that sinks to the bottom of the sink, and place the greens in a large bowl. Do not drain the greens.

2. In a large pot, heat the oil over medium heat. Add the onion and cook until softened, about 4 minutes. Stir in the garlic and cook for 1 minute. Add 2 cups of water (or 1 cup water and the chicken stock). In batches, stir in the greens with any water clinging to them, covering the pot and letting the first batch wilt before adding the next batch. Stir in the crushed red pepper. Bury the turkey wing in the greens.

3. Cover the pot and reduce the heat to low. Simmer, stirring occasionally, until the greens are very tender, about 45 minutes. Remove the turkey wings, discard the skin and bones, and chop the meat. Stir the turkey meat back into the greens. Season with the salt, then stir in the vinegar. (The greens can be made up to 1 day ahead, cooled, covered, and refrigerated. Reheat before serving.) Transfer the greens and cooking liquid to a warmed serving dish. Serve hot, using a slotted spoon.

Giant Potato and Leek Rösti

Rösti, a big potato pancake, is a specialty of Switzerland. This is a great side dish for roast goose, as it uses some of the copious amounts of tasty goose fat that the bird gives off. The pancake turns out crispy and golden brown with a surprise filling of tender leeks. You'll find other uses for it as well. Try it for brunch with a dollop of sour cream, poached eggs, and slices of bacon or ham.

Makes 6 to 8 servings

Make Ahead: The potatoes must be chilled, so prepare them at least 4 hours or the day before. The leeks can be cooked up to 1 day ahead.

6 large baking potatoes, such as russet or
    Burbank, scrubbed but unpeeled (3 pounds)
2 tablespoons unsalted butter
3 medium leeks, white and green parts only,
    chopped
1 teaspoon salt
½ teaspoon freshly ground black pepper
6 tablespoons rendered goose or duck fat
    (see pages 58 and 56) or vegetable oil
Chopped fresh chives, for garnish (optional)

1. Place the potatoes in a large pot of lightly salted water and bring to a boil over high heat. Reduce the heat to medium and cook, uncovered, until the potatoes are tender when pierced with a knife, 25 to 35 minutes. Drain and rinse under cold water. Cool completely. Cover and refrigerate until chilled, at least 4 hours or preferably overnight.

2. Position a rack in the center of the oven and preheat to 400°F. In a very large (12-inch) nonstick skillet, heat the butter over medium heat. Add the leeks and cook until tender, stirring often, about 4 minutes. In a small bowl, combine the salt and pepper. Season the leeks with ¼ teaspoon of the salt-and-pepper mixture. Transfer to a small bowl and set aside. (The leeks can be prepared up to 1 day ahead, cooled, covered, and refrigerated.)

3. Peel the potatoes and shred on the large holes of a box grater. In the skillet, heat 3 tablespoons of the goose fat over medium-high heat until very hot but not smoking. Spread half of the potatoes in the skillet in one layer. Season with half of the remaining salt-and-pepper mixture. Spread with the leeks, leaving a 1-inch border around the edges. Top with the remaining potatoes, and season with the remaining salt-and-pepper mixture.

4. Cook until the underside of the pancake is golden brown, about 7 minutes. Hold a flat, round skillet top or pizza pan on top of the skillet. Invert the skillet and the skillet top

together so the pancake falls, upside down, onto the skillet top. (If this seems too heavy to handle, slide the pancake carefully out of the skillet onto a plate. Place a second plate on top, and invert.) Return the skillet to the stove and heat the remaining 3 tablespoons goose fat until very hot. Slide the pancake back into the skillet, browned side up. Cook until the other side is browned, 5 to 7 minutes.

5. Bake for 10 minutes. Turn the pancake as above, and bake until crisp, about 10 minutes more.

6. Transfer to a warmed round platter and sprinkle with the chives, if using. Serve hot, cut into wedges.

Sour Cream and Chive Mashed Potatoes

These incredible mashed potatoes are based on the ones I learned to make while working with chef Alfred Portale on his *Gotham Bar and Grill Cookbook*. When Alfred makes them, he adds yet another 4 tablespoons of butter, but I am satisfied with a mere 16. It is the sinful, over-the-top use of butter and sour cream that puts these mashed potatoes into the *luxe* category.

Makes 8 to 12 servings

Make Ahead: The potatoes can be peeled and cut up to 4 hours ahead.

5 pounds baking potatoes (such as russet,
    Burbank, or Eastern)
Salt
1 cup (2 sticks) unsalted butter, at room
    temperature
1 cup sour cream, at room temperature
¼ cup chopped fresh chives
½ teaspoon freshly ground white pepper

1. Fill a large pot (5 quarts or larger) halfway with cold water. Peel the potatoes, cut into chunks about 1½ inches square, and drop them into the pot. Add more cold water to completely cover the potatoes by 1 to 2 inches. (The potatoes can be prepared to this point up to 4 hours ahead and stored at cool room temperature.)

2. Stir in enough salt until the water tastes mildly salty. Cover tightly, raise the heat to high, and bring to a boil.

3. Reduce the heat to medium-low and set the lid askew. Cook at a moderate boil until the potatoes are tender when pierced with the tip of a small, sharp knife, about 20 minutes; add more boiling water if needed to keep the potatoes covered. Do not overcook the potatoes.

4. Drain the potatoes well and return to the warm cooking pot. Add the butter. Using a handheld electric mixer set at medium speed, mash the potatoes, incorporating the butter. Mix in the sour cream and chives. Season with 1 teaspoon salt and the pepper. Transfer to a warmed serving dish and serve immediately.

Scalloped Potatoes 101

Good old-fashioned scalloped potatoes, layered with milk and sharp cheddar cheese, have a special place in the hearts of American cooks. French-style gratins, made with heavy cream and sometimes no cheese at all, have their own admirable qualities. But when you want a piece of hot, cheesy, down-home goodness to go alongside your glazed ham, it's got to be scalloped potatoes! Here's a classic derived from my mom's recipe.

- Many a holiday dinner has been delayed because the scalloped potatoes aren't done yet. To speed things along, cut the potatoes evenly and on the thin side (a mandoline or plastic V-slicer helps), and heat the milk. Scalloped potatoes made with cold milk take forever to bake through.

- Use starchy baking potatoes, such as russet Burbank. They will give off their starch and, along with the flour, help thicken the milk. You may store peeled, unsliced potatoes in cold water to cover for a few hours before slicing. This also works for chunked pieces for mashed potatoes. But do not store sliced potatoes in water, or you will wash off the valuable starch.

- Scalloped potatoes are best served immediately after baking, as they can develop a reheated flavor if refrigerated overnight. If you must reheat them, make them as close as possible to serving time: Bake 2 to 3 hours ahead of serving, and let stand at room temperature. Cover with aluminum foil and reheat in a preheated 350°F oven until heated through, 20 to 30 minutes. Or cover with plastic wrap and reheat in a microwave on Medium for about 10 minutes.

Makes 12 servings

Make Ahead: The potatoes are best served immediately after baking. They can be made up to 2 hours ahead.

3 cups whole milk

1¼ teaspoons salt

½ teaspoon freshly ground black pepper

8 medium (4 pounds) baking potatoes, such as russet, peeled and sliced into ⅛- to ¼-inch-thick rounds

4 tablespoons unsalted butter, cut into small pieces

1½ cups (12 ounces) shredded extra-sharp cheddar cheese

3 tablespoons minced onion

3 tablespoons all-purpose flour

1. Position a rack in the center of the oven and preheat to 400°F. Lightly butter a 13 × 9-inch glass baking dish.

2. In a medium saucepan over medium-high heat, heat the milk until small bubbles appear around the edges. In a small bowl, mix the salt and pepper together.

3. Layer half of the potatoes over the prepared dish. Season with half the salt-and-pepper mixture and dot with 2 tablespoons of the butter. Sprinkle with 1 cup of the cheese, the onions, and the flour. Spread the remaining potatoes on top. Season with the remaining salt-and-pepper mixture and dot with the remaining 2 tablespoons butter. Pour the hot milk over all. Cover tightly with aluminum foil. Place the dish on a baking sheet.

4. Bake for 45 minutes. Uncover and sprinkle with the remaining ½ cup cheese. Continue baking, uncovered, until the potatoes are tender, about 45 minutes. (The scalloped potatoes can be made 2 hours ahead of serving. Let stand at room temperature. Cover loosely with aluminum foil and reheat in a preheated 350°F oven until heated through, about 20 minutes. Or cover with plastic wrap and reheat in a microwave on Medium for about 10 minutes.) Let stand for 10 minutes before serving. Serve hot.

Potato, Mushroom, and Roquefort Gratin

A gratin is the French way of making scalloped potatoes. There are quite a few differences between the two, though. The main difference is that a gratin uses heavy cream, and lots of it. The high butterfat content in cream allows it to be baked for a long time without curdling, so a gratin can be prepared without the butter and flour that are needed to thicken the milk in scalloped potatoes. The result is rich and luxurious. Try this gratin with roast beef or tenderloin.

Makes 8 to 12 servings

Make Ahead: The gratin can be made up to 2 hours ahead.

2 tablespoons unsalted butter
1 pound shiitake mushrooms, stemmed and cut into ½-inch-thick slices
⅓ cup chopped shallots
2 cups heavy cream
1 cup Homemade White Chicken Stock (page 46) or canned reduced-sodium chicken broth
6 ounces Roquefort or other blue cheese, crumbled
5 large (about 3¼ pounds) baking potatoes, such as russet or Burbank, peeled and thinly sliced
½ teaspoon salt
¼ teaspoon freshly ground black pepper

1. Position a rack in the top third of the oven and preheat to 350°F. Lightly butter a 13 × 9-inch baking dish.

2. In a large skillet, heat the butter over medium heat. Add the mushrooms and cook, stirring often, until tender, about 10 minutes. Stir in the shallots and cook until softened, about 1 minute. Set aside.

3. In a medium saucepan, bring the cream and stock just to a simmer over medium heat. Remove from the heat and stir in the cheese until melted.

4. Spread half of the potatoes over the prepared dish and sprinkle with half of the salt and half of the pepper. Top with the mushrooms, followed by the remaining potatoes. Season with the remaining salt and pepper. Pour the hot cream mixture over all. Cover tightly with foil.

5. Bake for 40 minutes. Remove the foil and continue baking until the potatoes are tender and the top is golden, about 40 minutes more. (The gratin can be made up to 2 hours ahead of serving. Let stand at room temperature. Cover loosely with aluminum foil and reheat in a preheated 350°F oven until heated through, about 20 minutes. Or cover with plastic wrap and reheat in a microwave on Medium for about 10 minutes.) Let stand for 10 minutes before serving.

Yam and Pineapple Pudding

I used to say that I didn't like yams. (Yams are the orange-fleshed tubers that many people call sweet potatoes, but, in fact, sweet potatoes are yellow-fleshed and not very sweet at all.) But I found out that what I didn't like was ooey-gooey, sweet-enough-to-set-your-teeth-on-edge yam recipes. This one is just sweet enough. If your family is a "marshmallows-or-perish" group, sprinkle 2 cups of tiny marshmallows over the top of the baked pudding and broil in a preheated broiler just until the marshmallows are lightly toasted.

Makes 8 servings

Make Ahead: The pudding, before adding the egg whites, can be prepared up to 2 hours ahead.

PUDDING

4 pounds orange-fleshed (Louisiana or jewel) yams (about 5 large yams), scrubbed
4 tablespoons (½ stick) unsalted butter
½ cup heavy cream
½ cup packed light brown sugar
One 20-ounce can crushed pineapple, drained well
4 large eggs, at room temperature, separated
½ teaspoon ground cinnamon

½ teaspoon ground cloves
Grated zest of 1 lemon

TOPPING

¼ cup packed light brown sugar
2 tablespoons all-purpose flour
2 tablespoons unsalted butter, at room temperature
½ cup coarsely chopped pecans

1. To make the pudding, place the yams in a large pot and add enough water, lightly salted, to cover. Bring to a boil over high heat. Reduce the heat to medium and partially cover. Cook at a brisk simmer until the yams are tender when pierced with the tip of a knife, 30 to 40 minutes. Drain and rinse under cold water until cool enough to handle. Peel and place in a large bowl.

2. Position a rack in the center of the oven and preheat to 350°F. Lightly butter a deep 2½-quart casserole.

3. In a large bowl, using an electric mixer on low speed, mash the yams with the butter. Add the heavy cream and brown sugar, beating to dissolve the sugar. Add the crushed pineapple. One at a time, add the yolks, beating well after each addition, then mix in the cinnamon, cloves, and lemon zest. (The pudding can be prepared to this point up to 2 hours ahead, loosely covered with plastic wrap and stored at room temperature.)

4. In a medium bowl, using clean beaters, beat the egg whites at high speed until soft peaks form. Stir about a quarter of the whites into the pudding, then fold in the rest. Transfer to the prepared dish and spread evenly.

5. To make the topping, in a small bowl, using your fingers, work together the brown sugar, flour, and butter until combined, then work in the pecans. Sprinkle over the pudding.

6. Bake until the pudding is slightly puffed and lightly browned, about 1 hour. Serve immediately.

Herbed Yorkshire Puddings

These light, puffy popovers are irresistibly crisp on the outside and tender within. They are a classic accompaniment to roast beef (see page 48), as they use the rendered beef fat from the roasting pan. Some cooks make a big rectangular pudding, but I like to make individual puddings in a muffin pan. Vary the herbs to go with your menu, or leave the puddings plain.

● Don't trim the fat cap on the rib roast too closely before roasting, or you may not have enough fat in the pan to make the puddings. Some butchers trim the fat cap to a fare-thee-well, so you may not have a choice. To gather the rendered beef fat from a beef rib roast, pour the clear light brown drippings out of the roasting pan, leaving the brown bits in the pan. Make up any shortage of beef drippings with melted butter.

● The puddings are baked in a hot oven while the roast is standing during its precarving wait. Heat the oven thoroughly to 400°F before baking the puddings—most ovens will take 10 minutes to climb up from 325°F. Do not be concerned that the roast might cool down while the puddings bake. Just store the roast, loosely tented with foil, in a warm place near the stove. The internal temperature of the roast will actually rise 5°F to 10°F before it starts to cool.

● It is important to place the muffin tins on a baking sheet because the fat in the tins may overflow as the puddings bake and rise.

Makes 12 puddings

9 tablespoons rendered beef fat from the beef roasting pan (see instructions above)
1½ cups all-purpose flour
½ teaspoon dried thyme
½ teaspoon dried rosemary
¾ teaspoon salt
Generous ¼ teaspoon freshly ground black pepper
1½ cups milk
3 large eggs, beaten

1. Position a rack in the top third of the oven and preheat to 400°F. Measure 3 tablespoons of the beef fat and set aside. Spoon about ½ tablespoon of the remaining fat into each of 12 nonstick muffin tins.

2. In a medium bowl, whisk together the flour, thyme, rosemary, salt, and pepper to combine. Make a well in the center of the flour mixture and pour in the milk, eggs, and beef fat. Using a whisk, mix the liquid ingredients a bit to combine, then whisk them into the flour mixture just until smooth. Do not overbeat.

3. Pour or ladle equal amounts of the batter into the prepared muffin tins, filling them about three-quarters full. Place the muffin tins on a rimmed baking sheet. Bake until the puddings are puffed, golden brown, and crisp, about 30 minutes. Serve immediately.

Cornbread Succotash Stuffing

I can never decide what kind of stuffing to make for the turkey, but cornbread stuffing continues to be a strong annual contender. (Truth be known, I usually break down and make two stuffings, including one old-fashioned bread-and-herb stuffing to keep traditionalists happy.) This one is filled with colorful vegetables and flavor packed.

● For the best cornbread stuffing, you must make your own cornbread. Cornbread mixes are usually oversweetened. The recipe below is easy as can be, and makes a firm, unsweetened cornbread that can be turned into a very fine stuffing. (Call it dressing if you prefer—it still tastes the same.)

- It is safe to stuff a turkey if you take some simple precautions. Stuff the bird with warm, freshly prepared stuffing. Never stuff a bird with ice-cold stuffing. And absolutely never stuff the turkey the night before, even if you plan to refrigerate it.

- Insert an instant-read thermometer deep into the stuffing to make sure it has cooked to 165°F. If the turkey is done but the stuffing isn't hot enough, remove the stuffing, transfer to a casserole, and bake until heated through.

Makes 12 generous servings

Make Ahead: The cornbread should be made 1 day ahead.

CORNBREAD

1¼ cups yellow cornmeal, preferably stone-ground
¾ cup all-purpose flour
2 teaspoons baking powder
½ teaspoon salt
1 cup milk
3 tablespoons unsalted butter, melted
1 large egg, beaten

STUFFING

½ cup (1 stick) unsalted butter
2 medium onions, chopped
2 medium red bell peppers, cored, seeded, and chopped
2 medium celery ribs with leaves, chopped
One 10-ounce package frozen lima beans, thawed
2 cups frozen corn kernels, thawed
⅓ cup chopped fresh parsley

1 tablespoon dried sage
1 tablespoon dried thyme
2 teaspoons crumbled dried rosemary
1 large egg, beaten
About ½ cup Homemade Turkey Stock (page 46) or canned reduced-sodium chicken broth, as needed
1 teaspoon salt
½ teaspoon freshly ground black pepper

1. The day before preparing the stuffing, bake the cornbread: Position a rack in the center of the oven heated to 375°F. Lightly butter an 8-inch square baking pan.

2. In a medium bowl, whisk together the cornmeal, flour, baking powder, and salt. Make a well in the center and pour in the milk, melted butter, and egg. Using a wooden spoon, stir just until smooth. Spread the batter in the prepared pan.

3. Bake the cornbread until the top springs back when gently pressed in the center, about 20 minutes. Cool in the pan on a wire rack. Coarsely crumble and spread onto a rimmed baking sheet. Let stand overnight, uncovered, at room temperature.

4. To make the stuffing, in a large skillet, melt the butter over medium heat. Add the onions, red peppers, and celery and cover. Cook, stirring occasionally, until softened, about 10 minutes. Transfer to a large bowl.

5. Add the cornbread, lima beans, corn, parsley, sage, thyme, and rosemary. Stir in the egg and enough stock to thoroughly moisten the stuffing without making it soggy. Season with the salt and pepper. Use immediately to stuff the turkey—do not pack the stuffing into the bird. Place any remaining stuffing in a buttered baking dish, cool, cover, and refrigerate. To reheat, drizzle with about ¼ cup additional stock and bake, covered, in a preheated 350°F oven until heated through, 20 to 30 minutes.

Chestnut and Prune Stuffing

A very rich stuffing that was created to accompany roast goose, this is also delicious with the holiday perennial roast turkey. In either case, reserve the liver from the bird to use in the stuffing. The stuffing is also excellent baked in a shallow casserole as a side dish to roast pork (just leave out the liver).

- Chestnuts are a popular winter food, but preparing them can be trying—you always discover a few inedible ones during peeling. It's hard to judge the freshness of the nuts, because they are always imported, usually from Italy. Always buy a few more chestnuts than you need, just to be sure. You can also use one 15-ounce jar vacuum-packed chestnuts, available at specialty food stores. Avoid canned chestnuts, which don't have much flavor.

Makes 8 to 12 servings

¾ cup (½-inch dice) pitted prunes

½ cup tawny port

5 tablespoons rendered goose fat (see page 58) or unsalted butter

1 goose or turkey liver, trimmed of membranes

1 large onion, chopped

2 medium celery ribs with leaves, chopped

1 pound chestnuts, roasted, peeled, and chopped (see Note)

⅓ cup chopped fresh parsley

2 tablespoons chopped fresh sage or 1 tablespoon dried sage

12 ounces day-old, firm white sandwich bread, cut into ½-inch cubes (6 cups)

3 tablespoons unsalted butter, melted

About ¾ cup Homemade Goose Stock (page 46) or canned reduced-sodium chicken broth, as needed

½ teaspoon salt

¼ teaspoon freshly ground black pepper

1. In a small bowl, combine the prunes with the port and let stand at room temperature for 1 hour. Drain the prunes, reserving the port, and set both aside.

2. In a small skillet, heat 1 tablespoon of the goose fat over medium heat. Add the liver and cook, turning occasionally, until the liver is just cooked through, 8 to 10 minutes. Cool, then cut the liver into ½-inch cubes. Set aside.

3. In a large skillet, heat the remaining 4 tablespoons goose fat over medium heat. Add the onion and celery and cover. Cook, stirring occasionally, until the onion is golden, about 10 minutes. Add the port and cook, uncovered, until the port evaporates to a glaze, about 1 minute. Stir in the reserved liver and prunes, the chestnuts, parsley, and sage. Transfer to a large bowl. Add the bread cubes and stir in the melted butter. Stir in enough stock to moisten the stuffing. Season with the salt and pepper. Use immediately as a stuffing—do not pack the stuffing in the bird. (To bake the stuffing separately, transfer it to a lightly buttered 10 × 15-inch baking dish. Drizzle the stuffing with an additional ¼ cup stock or broth. Cover with aluminum foil. Bake in a preheated 350°F oven until heated through, about 30 minutes.)

Note: To roast chestnuts, preheat the oven to 400°F. Using a small, sharp knife, cut a deep X into the flatter side of each chestnut. Place in a single layer on a baking sheet and bake until the outer skin is split and crisp, about 30 minutes. Chestnuts never seem to be done at the same time, so work with the ones that are ready and continue roasting the others. Place the roasted chestnuts in a kitchen towel to keep them warm. Using a small, sharp knife, peel off both the tough outer and thin inner skins. To loosen the peels on stubborn, hard-to-peel chestnuts, return to the oven for an additional 5 to 10 minutes, or microwave on High for 1 minute.

Cranberry-Kumquat Chutney

Winter is the time for kumquats. They look like tiny, elongated oranges, with a pungent citrusy flavor. Kumquats can be eaten uncooked, but they really shine when they are simmered into a jam or chutney like this one. Buy extra kumquats to use as a garnish—they are gorgeous, and usually come attached to a spray of shiny dark green leaves.

Makes about 3 cups

Make Ahead: The chutney can be made up to 2 weeks ahead.

12 ounces fresh cranberries
8 ounces kumquats, cut into ¼-inch-thick rounds
1½ cups packed brown sugar
⅓ cup finely chopped onion
2 tablespoons shredded fresh ginger
1 teaspoon minced garlic
1 teaspoon yellow mustard seeds
1 cinnamon stick
¼ teaspoon salt
¼ teaspoon crushed hot red pepper

Combine all the ingredients in a medium, heavy-bottomed, nonreactive saucepan. Bring to a boil over medium heat, stirring often. Reduce the heat to medium-low and simmer, uncovered, stirring often, until the chutney is thick and the kumquats are translucent, about 20 minutes. Cool completely. Remove the cinnamon stick. (The chutney can be made up to 2 weeks ahead, cooled, covered, and refrigerated.)

Cranberry Maple Sauce

I always make my own cranberry sauce, even if I'm serving canned sauce for the traditionalists in the group. One of the best things about homemade cranberry sauce is that it can be made well ahead of serving, giving you one thing to scratch off your menu list. This sauce has become an oft-requested condiment—cranberries and maple are made for each other. The maple flavor will be subtle, so if you want to give it a boost, use the maple extract.

Makes about 2½ cups

Make Ahead: The sauce can be made up to 2 weeks ahead.

One 12-ounce package fresh cranberries
¾ cup pure maple syrup, preferably Grade B
½ cup water
½ cup packed light brown sugar
½ teaspoon maple extract (optional)

Combine all the ingredients in a medium, heavy-bottomed saucepan over high heat and bring to a boil, stirring often. Reduce the heat to medium and simmer until the cranberries have popped and the juices have thickened to a light syrup consistency, about 10 minutes. Cool completely. (The sauce can be made up to 2 weeks ahead, covered and refrigerated.) Serve chilled or at room temperature.

Festive Breads

While baking bread, and the enticing aromas that go with it, is not restricted to the holidays, this is the time for making extra-special breads, many of which have been handed down from generation to generation. No matter how good my great-aunt's gugelhopf was, Christmas was the only time of year she would make it. My friends say the same of their families' breads. Some of them are sweet, like stollen and panettone, and others are savory and stuffed with salami or prosciutto.

Baking bread is one of the most satisfying of all kitchen techniques. It connects the baker to the food in so many ways. If you like to roll up your sleeves and knead the bread by hand, great. But if you feel more confident with a machine to help you do the work, that's fine, too.

Here are some basics to help you carry on the tradition of Christmas bread baking.

Equipment

For mixing most doughs, all you need is a big bowl and a sturdy wooden spoon. Choose a thick pottery, glass, or ceramic bowl over a metal one—the former retains warmth better. If you plan to knead by hand, have a large work surface cleared and ready.

Heavy-duty electric mixers with large mixing bowls, such as KitchenAid, make short work of the dough-making process. Most handheld electric mixers aren't strong enough to mix yeast doughs. Using the paddle blade, mix the ingredients until a dough comes together and clears the bowl, then switch to the dough hook. Do not try to start the mixing process with the dough hook, which is specifically for kneading in the work bowl.

I don't recommend using a food processor for these recipes, because most food processors will only handle doughs containing about 3 cups of flour, and many of the recipes here call for larger amounts.

Check your oven temperature with an oven thermometer. Some bakers use baking stones to give their breads a flat, even baking surface. Baking stones are nice for making hard, crusty breads, but they're not that necessary for sweet, thin-crusted loaves. If you have one in your oven, place it on the oven rack, positioned as recommended in the recipe, and preheat the oven. Place the baking sheet with the bread directly on the stone.

Ingredients

The three most important ingredients in bread making are flour, yeast, and salt. Use *unbleached or bread flour* to make the breads in this book. Their high gluten content results in well-risen, firm-crumbed breads. Organic unbleached flour makes incredible bread, and is worth an extra trip to a natural foods store to get it.

Yeast, of course, causes the bread to rise. The live yeast grows in the dough, feeding on the sugars in the dough, and as it multiplies it gives off carbon dioxide. The gas is trapped in the dough, making it rise. If the yeast is too old or is killed by water that's too hot, the dough won't rise. *Active dry yeast* in ¼-ounce packages (about 2 teaspoons per envelope) is the most convenient yeast available. Be sure to note the expiration date, as the yeast quickly loses potency after that. Store yeast in the refrigerator to keep it fresh.

Instant or fast-acting yeast, which has a different formulation than active dry, sometimes is the only yeast you'll find at the supermarket. If you follow the instructions on the package, substituting it in exact amounts for active dry and using hot liquids to mix the dough, you will get a shorter rising time. However, along with many other bakers, I believe that a fast rise isn't necessarily a good thing, so I use slightly less (about a quarter less) instant yeast when substituting for active dry.

The yeast must be dissolved in warm water, about 105°F to 110°F. If the water is too hot, the yeast will be killed. If too cold, the yeast won't dissolve properly. (If you have to err, err on the cold side.) If you wish, check the temperature with an instant-read thermometer. After a few tries, you will be able to test the water with your fingers—it will be just warmer than body temperature. If another liquid, such as milk, is added to the dough, it should be warm, too. Instant yeast can be dissolved in warm water, just like active dry. While you can add instant yeast directly to the flour without dissolving in some bread dough recipes, sweet doughs, like many of those in this book, are heavier with their additional eggs, butter, and sugar. The yeast should be dissolved to distribute better throughout the sturdy dough.

Salt adds flavor to the bread and helps retard the rising action of the yeast. Without adding a little salt, the yeast could grow too rapidly. I prefer iodized salt because it dissolves easily with liquids. If you substitute fine sea salt or kosher salt, remember that these salts are about half as salty as iodized, so use about twice as much.

Mixing the Dough

As with any recipe, it helps to have all the ingredients measured out before proceeding. But with bread making, keep one important thing in mind. The exact amount of flour needed to make the dough will vary with the amount of humidity stored in the flour and in the air. Be flexible, and try not to add too much flour. Take special care with sweet breads that contain butter, eggs, and sugar that make the dough feel sticky.

Sprinkle the yeast over the warm water and let it stand for 5 to 10 minutes to soften. It will usually look creamy—not all yeast gets foamy when moistened. Stir well to dissolve the yeast. In some cases, the yeast and water are mixed with some of the flour to make a thick batter called a sponge, which is allowed to rise before proceeding. This lengthens the rising period by an hour or so and adds extra flavor to the bread.

In a large bowl or the bowl of a heavy-duty electric mixer fitted with the paddle blade set at low speed, mix the dissolved yeast with the remaining liquid ingredients (and butter, if using). Gradually mix in enough of the flour to get a stiff dough that clears the sides of the bowl. The dough is now ready for kneading.

Kneading

Manipulating the dough by hand or by machine activates the gluten in the flour, strengthening the dough so it won't collapse when the yeast multiplies and gives off its carbon dioxide.

To knead by hand, lightly flour the work surface. Turn the dough onto the work surface. Fold about a quarter of the dough over onto the top of the dough and press it down. Turn the dough a quarter turn, and repeat. Keep repeating the folding and turning, adding more flour as needed to keep the dough from sticking to the work surface (but not so much that the dough becomes dry). Do this rhythmically and enjoy the sensual pleasure of handling the dough. After 8 to 10 minutes, the dough will be smooth, somewhat firm, and elastic (if you pull opposite ends of the dough apart slightly, the dough will snap back into shape).

To knead in a heavy-duty electric mixer, change to the dough hook. Knead the dough, adding more flour as needed, until smooth and elastic. Sweet, soft doughs will have a tendency to climb up on the hook—just stop the machine, form the dough into a rough ball, and resume kneading. Knead for the minimum amount of time, as the motor is strong and it is easy to overknead. To check the consistency, transfer the dough to an unfloured work surface and knead by hand. If the dough doesn't stick to the surface, it has enough flour.

To add fruit or nuts to the dough, press the dough into a thick disk. Sprinkle with some of the fruit, roll up, and knead a couple of times. Continue the procedure until all of the fruit is incorporated. If you're using a mixer, gradually mix in the fruit—don't add it all at once.

Rising

Lightly oil or butter a clean, large bowl. Form the dough into a ball. Place your hands on the opposite sides of the dough, and tuck them under the dough to stretch the top surface of the dough. Rotate the dough and repeat the tucking movement. After a few tucks, the dough will shape itself into a ball. Place the ball, smooth side down, in the bowl and coat the underside with oil. Turn the dough, oiled side up, and cover tightly with plastic wrap. Let the dough stand in a warm place (near a turned-on stove or water heater is ideal, as is the top of a running clothes dryer) until it doubles in volume. To check the volume, push your finger $1/2$ inch into the dough. If the indentation remains, the dough has risen enough.

Shaping

Follow the individual instructions for shaping the loaves. If any seams are formed, pinch them shut. Place the loaves on nonstick baking sheets (or in their molds or pans), cover loosely with plastic wrap, and let rise until they look doubled in volume (use the finger test again if you wish).

Baking

Preheat the oven thoroughly before baking the bread. Sweet breads with sugar and butter have a tendency to brown quickly, and should be baked at moderate temperatures, around 375°F. If the bread browns too fast, tent it with aluminum foil. The bread is done when it is golden brown and sounds hollow when tapped on the bottom with your knuckles. An absolutely failproof method of checking is to insert an instant-read thermometer in the center of the loaf—it will read 195°F or above.

Cooling

Bread baked in a pan or mold should be cooled in the pan for a few minutes, then removed from the pan, or trapped steam will make the bread soggy. Cool the bread on a wire rack for at least 30 minutes before slicing. If sliced too soon, the steam will escape and you'll have bread that dries out before its time.

Gugelhopf

Another one of my Auntie Gisela's specialties, this beautiful sweet bread (sometimes called *kugelhopf*) can be found year-round at bakeries in northern Europe, but Auntie Gisela served her homemade version as a holiday treat. It has a light, dry texture that is perfect for dipping into hot tea or coffee. The sticky batterlike dough requires a heavy-duty standing mixer or a hand mixer with a strong motor and kneading beaters. It is usually made in the traditional turban-shaped gugelhopf pan, but any 10- to 12-cup decorative tube cake pan will do.

Makes 1 large loaf, 12 to 16 servings

Make Ahead: The cake is best served the day baked, but can be baked up to 2 days ahead.

1 cup raisins
3 tablespoons dark rum

SPONGE
One ¼-ounce package active dry yeast or
    1¾ teaspoons instant yeast
¼ cup warm (105°F to 110°F) water
¾ cup milk
1 cup unbleached all-purpose flour

GUGELHOPF
1 cup (2 sticks) unsalted butter, at room
    temperature
¾ cup granulated sugar
5 large eggs, at room temperature
½ teaspoon salt
½ teaspoon pure lemon oil or 1 teaspoon lemon
    extract
Grated zest of 1 lemon
3 cups unbleached all-purpose flour

GLAZE
1 cup confectioners' sugar, sifted
3 tablespoons dark rum
2 tablespoons sliced almonds

1. Place the raisins in a small bowl and stir in the rum. Let stand for at least 1 hour or up to overnight.

2. To make the sponge, in a medium bowl, sprinkle the yeast over the water. Let stand 5 minutes, then stir to dissolve the yeast.

3. In a small saucepan or a microwave, heat the milk to 105°F to 110°F. Stir the warmed milk into the yeast mixture. Add 1 cup of the flour and stir with a wooden spoon for 100 strokes. (This helps develop gluten and improves the cake's texture.) Scrape down the bowl and cover tightly with plastic wrap. Let stand in a warm place until the sponge doubles in volume, about 1½ hours.

4. Butter a 10-inch gugelhopf mold (or use a plain or fluted tube pan) well. Drain the raisins well (if you like you can save any drained rum to use in the glaze) and set aside.

5. To make the gugelhopf, using a heavy-duty standing mixer fitted with the paddle blade, set on high speed, beat together the butter and granulated sugar until light in color and texture, about 3 minutes. One at a time, beat in the eggs, then the salt, lemon oil, and lemon zest. The mixture will be soupy. Reduce the speed to low. Scrape the sponge into the butter mixture. Gradually beat in the remaining 3 cups flour, ½ cup at a time, to make a thick batter. Beat for about 10 minutes. The batter will feel sticky, look elastic, and cling to the sides of the bowl. Beat in the raisins just until incorporated.

6. Spread the batter evenly into the prepared pan. Cover tightly with plastic wrap and let stand in a warm place until the batter rises to the top of the pan, about 1¼ hours.

7. Position a rack in the center of the oven heated to 350°F. Bake until the top is golden brown and a long wooden skewer inserted in the center of the bread comes out clean, about 1 hour. Cool in the pan on a wire rack for 10 minutes. Run a sharp knife around the inside of the mold and the tube to release the bread. Unmold onto the rack and cool completely.

8. To make the glaze, in a small bowl, using a rubber spatula, mix the confectioners' sugar with the rum until very smooth. Place the cooled bread on the wire rack placed over a piece of waxed paper. Pour the glaze over the top and around the sides of the bread, then thinly spread the glaze all over the bread with a pastry brush. Immediately sprinkle the almonds over the wet glaze, patting them if necessary to adhere. Allow the glaze to set, about 30 minutes. Serve immediately, or wrap tightly in plastic and store at room temperature for up to 2 days.

Moravian Sugar Cakes

The culinary traditions of the Moravian sect run strong near Winston-Salem, North Carolina, where every Christmas bakeries struggle to keep up with the demand for these flat coffee cakes with a sugary topping. This home-baked recipe was supplied by my friend Cary Kirk's sister, Grigg K. Murdoch (although she leaves out the cinnamon). The cakes can be baked in four 9-inch round cake pans (aluminum foil pans are fine) or in two jelly-roll pans and cut in half vertically to make four cakes.

Makes 4 cakes

Make Ahead: The cakes can be prepared up to 2 days ahead.

2 medium baking potatoes, peeled and cut into 1-inch chunks
Two ¼-ounce packages active dry yeast or 3½ teaspoons instant yeast

12 tablespoons (1½ sticks) unsalted butter, at room temperature

½ cup granulated sugar

1 teaspoon salt

2 large eggs, at room temperature

About 6½ cups unbleached all-purpose flour

TOPPING

¾ cup plus 2 tablespoons packed light brown sugar

6 tablespoons (¾ stick) unsalted butter

½ teaspoon ground cinnamon

1. Place the potatoes in a medium saucepan and add enough cold water to cover by 2 inches. Do not add salt. Bring to a boil over high heat. Reduce the heat to medium-low and cook until the potatoes are very tender, about 20 minutes. Drain the potatoes, reserving the potato cooking liquid. Rub the potatoes through a wire sieve. Measure 1 packed cup of the potatoes, and set aside at room temperature; discard any remaining potatoes. Measure 1½ cups of the potato cooking liquid, and cool to 105°F to 115°F; discard the remaining potato liquid.

2. In a medium bowl, sprinkle the yeast over the warm potato water and let stand until the yeast is creamy, about 5 minutes. Stir to dissolve the yeast.

3. In a large mixing bowl using a handheld electric mixer or the bowl of a heavy-duty standing mixer fitted with the paddle blade, beat together the butter and granulated sugar on medium speed until light in texture, about 2 minutes. On low speed, beat in the cooled potatoes and salt, then the eggs. On low speed, beat in the yeast mixture (the mixture may look curdled, but don't worry). Gradually beat enough of the flour to form a soft, shaggy dough that just clears the sides of the bowl. If using a handheld mixer, switch to a wooden spoon when necessary.

4. Turn out the dough onto a lightly floured work surface and knead, adding more flour as needed, until the dough is smooth and elastic but still somewhat soft and slightly sticky, about 10 minutes.

If kneading by machine, switch from the paddle blade to the dough hook and knead on medium-low speed, adding more flour as needed, about 8 minutes. If you like you can transfer the dough to a floured surface and knead briefly by hand to check the consistency; it should be slightly sticky but smooth.

5. Shape the dough into a ball. Place in a buttered large bowl and turn to lightly coat the underside with butter. Cover tightly with plastic wrap and let stand in a warm place until doubled, about 1 hour.

6. Lightly butter four 9-inch round cake pans or two 15½ × 10½ × 1-inch jelly-roll pans. Stretch and pat the dough into the prepared pans. Cover loosely with plastic wrap and let stand in a warm place until puffy, about 30 minutes.

7. To make the topping, in a medium saucepan, bring ¾ cup of the brown sugar, 4 tablespoons of the butter, and 2 tablespoons water to a boil over medium heat, stirring often. Pour into a glass measuring cup and let stand until cooled but pourable, about 30 minutes.

8. In a small saucepan, melt the remaining 2 tablespoons of butter over medium heat. Brush the tops of the cakes lightly with the melted butter. Using a finger, punch 12 evenly spaced indentations into each round pan of dough (if you're using jelly-roll pans, punch 24 indentations into each). Pour the syrup into the indentations. In a small bowl, combine the remaining 2 tablespoons brown sugar and the cinnamon using your fingers, and sprinkle over the cakes.

9. Position racks in the top third and center of the oven heated to 375°F. Bake, switching the position of the pans from top to bottom and front to back halfway through baking, until the cakes are golden brown, about 35 minutes. Cool in the pans on wire racks for 10 minutes. If baking in jelly-roll pans, cut each cake in half vertically to make 4 cakes. Slide the cakes out of the pans onto wire racks and cool right side up. (The cakes can be baked up to 2 days ahead, stored in self-sealing plastic bags at room temperature. To refresh, wrap in aluminum foil and bake in a preheated 350°F oven for 15 to 20 minutes, until heated through.)

Panettone

In Italian-American neighborhoods, the holiday season is announced by the arrival of panettone, the dome-shaped Christmas bread of Italy. The factory-baked varieties are good (and seem to stay fresh forever thanks to a special commercial yeast), but like so many other things, homemade is better. Make it to have on hand to serve to friends with a cup of dark-roast coffee. Slightly stale slices are revived by a light toasting, or can be turned into excellent French toast. There is a fairy tale–like story on how panettone got its name. A poor baker named Antonio (nicknamed Tone) created a special bread to convince the stubborn king that he should be allowed to marry his beautiful daughter. Tone's bread (or the *pane di Tone*) did the trick, and the couple lived happily ever after.

Makes 1 large loaf

Make Ahead: The panettone can be baked up to 5 days ahead.

½ cup dark raisins
½ cup golden raisins
½ cup chopped candied orange peel or glacé orange slices
3 tablespoons brandy, grappa, or dark rum

SPONGE

1 cup warm (105°F to 110°F) milk
One ¼-ounce package active dry yeast or 1¾ teaspoons instant yeast
1 cup unbleached all-purpose flour

DOUGH

8 tablespoons (1 stick) unsalted butter, at room temperature
½ cup sugar
3 large eggs plus 1 large egg yolk
1 teaspoon vanilla extract
Grated zest of 1 orange
½ teaspoon salt
About 3 cups unbleached all-purpose flour

1 large egg white, beaten, for the glaze
2 tablespoons sliced almonds, for garnish

1. In a medium bowl, mix the dark and golden raisins and candied orange peel with the brandy. Cover and let stand for 1 hour.

2. To make the sponge, in another medium bowl, mix the milk and yeast to combine (no need to dissolve the yeast). Add the flour and stir for 100 strokes to make a thick batter. Cover tightly with plastic wrap and let stand in a warm place until the sponge is bubbly, about 1 hour.

3. To make the dough, drain the fruit, reserving the brandy. Pat the fruit dry with paper towels and set aside. In a large bowl using a handheld electric mixer or in the bowl of a heavy-duty standing mixer fitted with the paddle blade, beat the butter on high speed until creamy, about 1 minute. Add the sugar

and beat until light in color and texture, about 2 minutes. Beat in the eggs and yolk, one at a time. Beat in the reserved brandy, vanilla, orange zest, and salt. On low speed, beat in the sponge. Gradually beat enough of the flour to form a soft, shaggy dough that just clears the sides of the bowl. If using a handheld mixer, switch to a wooden spoon when necessary.

4. Turn out the dough onto a lightly floured work surface and knead until supple but still slightly sticky, about 5 minutes. If the dough holds its shape when formed into a ball, it has been kneaded enough. Do not add too much flour. Gradually knead in the fruit.

If kneading by machine, switch from the paddle blade to the dough hook and knead on medium-low speed until the dough is supple but still slightly sticky, about 5 minutes. Gradually add the fruit and knead until incorporated. If you like you can transfer the dough to a floured surface and knead briefly by hand to check the consistency.

5. Shape the dough into a ball. Place into a buttered large bowl and turn to lightly coat the underside with butter. Cover tightly with plastic wrap and let stand in a warm place until doubled in volume, about 2 hours.

6. Position a rack in the center of the oven and preheat to 350°F. Lightly butter an 8½-inch springform pan with 3-inch sides.

7. Turn out the dough onto the work surface and knead briefly. Shape into a flat disk and transfer to the prepared pan, stretching the dough to fill the pan. Cover loosely with plastic wrap and let stand in a warm place until the dough barely reaches the top of the pan, about 45 minutes.

8. Brush the top of the bread lightly with egg white and sprinkle with the almonds. Bake for 40 minutes. Loosely cover the top of the bread with aluminum foil, and continue baking until the top is golden brown and a thin knife inserted in the center comes out clean, about 35 minutes. Do not overbake. Cool in the pan on a wire rack for 15 minutes. Remove the sides and bottom of the pan and cool completely on the rack. (The panettone can be stored, wrapped well in plastic, for up to 5 days. Stale panettone is excellent toasted.)

Prosciutto, Rosemary, and Pepper Bread

With the additions of prosciutto, fresh rosemary, and cracked pepper, a basic bread becomes a festive loaf. The extra rising period gives the bread a more compact crumb and deeper flavor. If your main course is a simple roast, the bread can be served with dinner, or slice and serve as an appetizer with a glass of wine.

Makes 1 large loaf, about 12 servings

Make Ahead: The bread can be baked up to 8 hours before serving.

One ¼-ounce package active dry yeast or 1¾ teaspoons instant yeast
1¼ cups warm (105°F to 110°F) water
2 tablespoons extra virgin olive oil
1½ teaspoons salt
¾ teaspoon coarsely cracked black pepper
About 3½ cups bread flour or unbleached all-purpose flour
4 ounces (¼-inch-thick) sliced prosciutto, chopped into ¼-inch dice
1½ tablespoons chopped fresh rosemary or 2 teaspoons dried rosemary

1. In a large bowl or in the bowl of a heavy-duty electric mixer, sprinkle the yeast over the water. Let stand until the yeast softens, about 10 minutes. Stir to dissolve the yeast.

2. Using a wooden spoon or the paddle blade on low speed, mix in the oil, salt, and pepper. Beat in enough of the flour to make a shaggy dough that clears the sides of the bowl.

3. If kneading by hand, turn out the dough onto a lightly floured work surface. Knead the dough, adding more flour as needed, until the dough is smooth and elastic, about 10 minutes.

If kneading by machine, change to the dough hook and knead on medium-low speed until the dough is smooth and elastic, about 8 minutes. If you like you can knead on the work surface to check the consistency.

4. Shape the dough into a ball. Transfer the dough to a lightly oiled large bowl. Turn to coat the dough with oil. Cover tightly with plastic wrap. Let stand in a warm place until doubled in volume, about 1 hour.

5. Punch down the dough and shape into a ball. Return the dough to the bowl, turn to coat with oil, cover, and let rise until doubled again, about 45 minutes.

6. Position a rack in the center of the oven and preheat to 400°F. Lightly oil a large baking sheet.

7. Turn out the dough onto the work surface. Knead, gradually working in the prosciutto and rosemary. Flatten the dough into a 12-inch disk, then roll up jelly roll–style. Pinch the seams shut. Place on the baking sheet, seam side down. Cover loosely with plastic wrap. Let rise until doubled in volume, about 30 minutes.

8. Using a very sharp knife, cut 3 shallow diagonal slashes in the top of the bread. Bake until the bread is golden brown and sounds hollow when tapped on the bottom, 35 to 40 minutes. Cool completely on a wire rack. (The bread can be baked up to 8 hours before serving, cooled, wrapped in aluminum foil, and stored at room temperature.)

Salami and Cheese Stuffed Bread

Put slices of this bread out on a buffet, and watch it disappear. It looks great, and tastes even better. My friend Shirley Corriher, author of the indispensable *Cookwise,* taught me to bake the roll immediately after stuffing (without a second proofing) to make the bread rise in a thinner layer that will adhere the filling to the bread without any gaps.

Makes 1 long loaf, about 16 servings

Make Ahead: The bread can be baked up to 8 hours before serving.

One ¼-ounce package active dry yeast or
   1¾ teaspoons instant yeast
1¼ cups warm (105°F to 110°F) water
2 tablespoons extra virgin olive oil
1½ teaspoons salt
About 3½ cups unbleached all-purpose flour
2 tablespoons Dijon mustard
1 cup (4 ounces) shredded mozzarella
4 ounces thinly sliced Genoa salami
1 cup (4 ounces) shredded provolone cheese
2 tablespoons finely chopped fresh basil or
   1½ teaspoons dried basil
1 teaspoon dried oregano
¼ teaspoon crushed hot red pepper
2 tablespoons milk
1 large egg yolk
2 teaspoons sesame seeds

1. In a large bowl or in the bowl of a heavy-duty standing mixer, sprinkle the yeast over the water. Let stand until the yeast softens, about 10 minutes. Stir until the yeast dissolves.

2. Using a wooden spoon or the paddle blade on low speed, stir in the oil and salt. Beat in enough of the flour to make a shaggy dough that clears the sides of the bowl.

3. Turn out the dough and knead, adding more flour as needed, until smooth and elastic, about 10 minutes.

If kneading by machine, switch to the dough hook and knead on medium-low speed until the dough is smooth and elastic, about 8 minutes. If you like you can transfer the dough to a work surface and knead briefly by hand to check the consistency.

4. Shape the dough into a ball. Transfer the dough to a lightly oiled large bowl. Turn to coat the ball with oil. Cover tightly with plastic wrap. Let stand in a warm place until doubled in volume, about 1 hour.

5. Position a rack in the center of the oven and preheat to 375°F. Lightly oil a 17½ × 11½ × 1-inch jelly-roll pan (preferably nonstick).

6. Punch down the dough to deflate, and knead briefly on the work surface. Place the dough in the pan and pat it out to fit the pan. (If the dough seems too elastic and snaps back instead of staying in place, cover the dough in the jelly-roll pan with plastic wrap and let stand for 5 to 10 minutes to relax, and try stretching again.) Spread the mustard over the dough. Sprinkle with the mozzarella, leaving a ½-inch-wide border. Layer the salami over the mozzarella, then sprinkle with the provolone. Sprinkle with the basil, oregano, and crushed red pepper. Starting at a long end, roll up the dough as tightly as possible, and pinch the seams shut. Arrange the dough so the long seam faces down.

7. In a small bowl, mix together the milk and yolk well. Lightly brush the top of the roll with some of the mixture, then sprinkle the dough with the sesame seeds. Using a very sharp knife, cut 3 shallow diagonal slashes in the top of the bread. Bake until the bread is golden brown, about 35 minutes. (An instant-read thermometer inserted in the center of the bread will register above 195°F.) Cool

completely on a wire rack. (The bread can be baked up to 8 hours before serving, cooled, wrapped in aluminum foil, and stored at room temperature.)

Overnight Sticky Maple-Pecan Buns

What's better than waking up to freshly baked sweet rolls? With this recipe, even the baker doesn't have to get up at the crack of dawn to enjoy the aroma of sugar and spice wafting through the kitchen. Make a pan of sticky buns the night before and refrigerate them until ready to bake the next morning—the dough will rise slowly and develop flavor.

- **The buttermilk gives the dough a light flakiness. I always use liquid dairy buttermilk because it is thicker and has more flavor than dried buttermilk powder. Reconstituted buttermilk powder is too thin, and the dough may require too much flour. Gently heat the dairy buttermilk in a small saucepan over low heat or in the microwave. It should be just above body temperature.**

- **Maple syrup is one of Mother Nature's great culinary gifts, but it has a mild flavor that is best savored over pancakes or waffles. Pancake syrup (really just flavored corn syrup) works best here. Not only does it give the buns more maple flavor, it also remains gooey when the buns cool, while true maple syrup hardens.**

Makes 16 buns

Make Ahead: The sticky bun dough can be prepared the night before serving.

One ¼-ounce package active dry yeast or
    1¾ teaspoons instant yeast
¼ cup warm (105°F to 110°F) water
¾ cup warm (105°F to 110°F) buttermilk
¼ cup granulated sugar
4 tablespoons (½ stick) unsalted butter, melted
1 large egg plus 1 large egg yolk
½ teaspoon salt
¼ teaspoon baking soda
About 2¾ cups unbleached all-purpose flour
5 tablespoons unsalted butter, melted
⅓ cup packed light brown sugar
½ cup chopped pecans
¾ cup maple-flavored pancake syrup

1. In a small bowl, sprinkle the yeast over the warm water. Let stand until the yeast is creamy, about 10 minutes. Stir to dissolve the yeast.

2. In a large bowl or the bowl of a heavy-duty standing mixer, mix the yeast mixture with the warm buttermilk, the granulated sugar, melted butter, egg, egg yolk, salt, and baking soda. Using a wooden spoon or the paddle blade on low speed, add enough of the flour to make a soft dough.

3. If kneading by hand, turn out the dough onto a lightly floured work surface. Knead the dough, adding more flour as needed, until the dough is smooth and elastic, about 10 minutes.

If kneading by machine, change to the dough hook and knead on medium-low speed until the dough is smooth and elastic, about 8 minutes. If you like you can knead on the work surface to check the consistency.

4. Shape the dough into a ball. Place in a lightly buttered large bowl and turn to coat the dough with butter. Cover tightly with plastic wrap and let stand in a warm place until the dough doubles in volume, about 1¼ hours.

5. Turn out the dough onto a lightly floured work surface. Roll, pat, and stretch the dough into a 14 × 10-inch rectangle. If the dough

retracts, cover it loosely with plastic wrap, let stand 5 minutes or so, then try again. Brush the dough with 1 tablespoon of the melted butter. Leaving a 1-inch border at the long ends, sprinkle with the brown sugar, then the pecans. Starting at a long end, roll up the dough into a long cylinder. Pinch the long seam shut.

6. Using a sharp knife, cut the dough into 16 slices. Pour the remaining 4 tablespoons melted butter into a 13 × 9-inch metal baking dish. Brush the butter evenly onto the bottom and sides of the pan. Pour the pancake syrup into the pan, tilting to coat the bottom of the pan. Place the dough slices, flat side down, side by side in the pan. Cover tightly with plastic wrap and refrigerate for at least 8 hours and up to 12 hours.

7. Position a rack in the center of the oven and preheat to 375°F. Remove the pan of prepared buns from the refrigerator and let stand in a warm spot near the stove while the oven preheats.

8. Uncover the pan. Bake until the rolls are golden brown, about 30 minutes. Immediately invert the hot rolls onto a large platter, scraping any syrup in the pan over the rolls. Let cool for 5 minutes, then cut or break apart into individual rolls. Serve warm or cooled to room temperature.

Savory Walnut Rolls

To the average American, these rolls are out of the ordinary, but in France they are a familiar sight, especially on cheese platters. Not only are they studded with walnuts but the dough is made with ground walnuts and walnut oil to give them a deeper nutty flavor. Serve them with your holiday meal, and they will be a hit.

Makes 12 rolls

Make Ahead: The dough can be made up to 18 hours ahead of baking; the rolls can be baked up to 12 hours ahead.

STARTER

2 teaspoons active dry yeast or 1¾ teaspoons instant yeast
½ cup warm (105°F to 110°F) water
½ cup bread flour or unbleached all-purpose flour

DOUGH

1 cup coarsely chopped walnuts
About 2½ cups unbleached all-purpose flour
3 tablespoons walnut oil or vegetable oil
1½ teaspoons fine sea salt or table salt

1. To make the starter, sprinkle the yeast over the water in a large bowl or the bowl of a heavy-duty standing mixer. Let stand 5 minutes, then stir until the yeast dissolves. Add the flour and stir for 100 strokes (this activates the gluten in the flour). Cover with plastic wrap and let stand in a warm place until very bubbly, about 40 minutes.

2. Meanwhile, to make the dough, process ½ cup of the walnuts and the flour in a food processor fitted with the metal blade until the walnuts are ground into a powder. Set aside.

3. Add 1 cup water, the walnut oil, and salt to the starter and stir well. Using a wooden

spoon or the paddle blade on low speed, add enough of the walnut flour to make a soft, pliable dough that barely clears the sides of the bowl.

4. If kneading by hand, turn out the dough onto a lightly floured work surface. Knead the dough, adding more flour as needed, until the dough is smooth and elastic, about 10 minutes. Gradually knead in the remaining ½ cup walnuts.

If kneading by machine, change to the dough hook and knead on medium-low speed until the dough is smooth and elastic, about 8 minutes. Gradually add the remaining ½ cup walnuts. If desired, knead on the work surface to check the consistency.

5. Gather up the dough into a ball. Lightly oil a medium bowl. Add the ball of dough and turn to coat the dough with oil. Cover tightly with plastic wrap and let stand until the dough doubles in volume, about 1½ hours. (The dough can also be covered and refrigerated for up to 18 hours. Remove the bowl from the refrigerator and let stand for about 2 hours to come to room temperature before proceeding.)

6. Position a rack in the center of the oven and preheat to 350°F. Turn out the dough onto an unfloured work surface, and knead lightly to expel the air. Cut the dough into 12 equal pieces. Shape each piece into tight balls. Arrange the balls a few inches apart, smooth side up, on an ungreased baking sheet. Cover loosely with plastic wrap and let stand until almost doubled, about 30 minutes.

7. Discard the plastic wrap. Bake the rolls until crusty, about 20 minutes. To double-check for doneness, insert an instant-read thermometer into the center of a roll—it should read about 200°F. Cool slightly or to room temperature. (The rolls can be baked up to 12 hours ahead, loosely covered with plastic wrap and stored at room temperature.)

Stollen

Stollen is the festive Christmas bread of Germany. Its unusual folded shape is said to represent the baby Jesus in swaddling clothes. It is an authentic dessert to follow a German-style dinner of roast goose.

Makes 2 large stollen, about 10 servings each

Make Ahead: The stollen can be baked up to 1 day ahead.

½ cup dried cranberries or chopped candied red cherries
½ cup chopped candied orange peel or glacé orange slices
½ cup dark raisins
½ cup golden raisins
½ cup dark rum

SPONGE

1 cup warm (105°F to 110°F) milk
Two ¼-ounce packages active dry yeast or 3½ teaspoons instant yeast
1 cup unbleached all-purpose flour

DOUGH

12 tablespoons (1½ sticks) unsalted butter, at room temperature
½ cup granulated sugar
2 large eggs
Grated zest of 1 lemon
½ teaspoon salt
About 3½ to 4 cups unbleached all-purpose flour
1 cup slivered almonds
⅔ cup diced (½-inch) almond paste

4 tablespoons (½ stick) unsalted butter, melted, for assembly
4 tablespoons granulated sugar, for assembly
Confectioners' sugar, for serving

1. In a medium bowl, mix the cranberries, orange peel, dark raisins, and golden raisins with the rum. Cover and let stand for 1 hour.

2. To make the sponge, in another medium bowl, stir together the milk and yeast to combine (no need to dissolve the yeast). Add 1 cup of flour and stir for 100 strokes to make a thick batter. Cover tightly with plastic wrap and let stand in a warm place until the sponge is bubbly, about 1 hour.

3. To make the dough, drain the fruit, reserving the rum. Pat the fruit dry with paper towels and set aside. In a large bowl using a handheld electric mixer or in the work bowl of a heavy-duty standing mixer fitted with the paddle blade, beat the butter at high speed until creamy, about 1 minute. Add the granulated sugar and beat until light in color and texture, about 2 minutes. Beat in the eggs, one at a time. (The mixture may curdle, but don't worry.) Beat in the reserved rum, lemon zest, and salt. Reduce the speed to low. Beat in the sponge. Gradually beat in enough of the flour to form a soft, shaggy dough that just clears the sides of the bowl. Switch to a wooden spoon when necessary if making with the handheld mixer.

4. Turn out the dough onto a lightly floured work surface and knead until supple but still slightly sticky, about 5 minutes. If the dough holds its shape when formed into a ball, it has been kneaded enough. Do not add too much flour. Gradually knead in the fruit and almonds.

If kneading by machine, switch from the paddle blade to the dough hook and knead on medium-low speed until the dough is supple but still slightly sticky, about 5 minutes. Gradually add the fruit and almonds and knead just until incorporated. Do not overmix, or the fruit will color the dough. If you like you can transfer the dough to a floured surface and knead briefly by hand to check the consistency.

5. Shape the dough into a ball. Place into a buttered large bowl and turn to coat the dough with butter. Cover tightly with plastic wrap and let stand in a warm place until doubled, about 1 hour.

6. Position racks in the center and top third of the oven (see Note) and preheat to 350°F. Lightly butter two large baking sheets.

7. Turn out the dough onto the work surface and knead briefly. Cut the dough in half. On a prepared baking sheet, stretch and pat out the dough to form a 12 × 8-inch oval. (If the dough resists shaping, cover loosely with plastic wrap and let rest for 5 minutes, then try again.) Sprinkle ⅓ cup of the almond paste down the center of the oval. Fold one long side of the dough over, about 1 inch past the center. Fold the other side of the dough over, about 1 inch past the center. Pinch the seams closed. Brush the dough generously with 2 tablespoons of the melted butter and sprinkle with 2 tablespoons of the granulated sugar. Repeat with the remaining dough, butter, and sugar. Loosely cover the dough with plastic wrap and let stand in a warm place until almost doubled, about 30 minutes.

8. Bake until the tops are golden brown and a thin knife inserted in the thickest part of the dough comes out clean, about 45 minutes. Transfer the stollen to a wire rack and sift generously with confectioners' sugar. Cool completely on wire racks. Sift again with confectioners' sugar just before serving.

Note: If your oven isn't big enough to accommodate both stollen at the same time, position the rack in the center of the oven. Bake one stollen, refrigerating the other one while the first bakes.

Candies

For most of the year, making candy at home isn't a top priority. Then, at Christmas, cooks bring out their favorite recipes for gift giving and filling up the holiday candy dish, and rediscover how much fun candy making can be. My dad always makes a few pounds of rocky road to hand out, a tradition he carries on from Grandma Rodgers.

Candies don't have to be complicated or difficult to make. The candies offered in this chapter are among the simplest around, and you will get lots of sweets for your efforts. Only a few of them require a candy thermometer. It's helpful to have an understanding of the basic techniques, though. You could just leave all the responsibility to a candy thermometer, but if you take a minute to read these tips, then the mysteries of candy making won't seem daunting at all.

Cooked Syrup Temperatures

Many candies are based on a cooked sugar syrup. As the sugar boils, the water evaporates and the syrup becomes denser. The higher the temperature, the denser the syrup. The different syrup stages are identified by how the syrup will behave when a spoonful is dropped into a glass of cold water, which imitates how the candy will set when cooled. For example, when cooked to 300°F to 310°F, the syrup is at the hard-crack stage, and the cooled candy will be brittle. On the other hand, if the syrup is cooked to only 270°F, the soft-crack stage, the candy will harden, but with a softer texture. Because I do not use the entire range of cooked syrup temperatures in this book, I will not go into more detail, but that's the general idea.

Syrups usually are cooked without stirring. If a foreign object like a spoon is introduced into the syrup, the sugar crystals attach themselves to the intruder and the syrup could crystallize, resulting in a grainy candy—if you get it to turn into candy at all. Butter, and some other foods, like corn syrup, will hinder the crystallization process, so syrups with a high proportion of these ingredients can be stirred to ensure that the mixture doesn't scorch.

A good candy thermometer is an important tool. Plaque-attached, alcohol-filled glass candy thermometers are best because the tip of the thermometer is lifted from the bottom of the pot (if it touches the bottom, it will give an inaccurate reading). If you have a dial, clip-type thermometer, adjust it so it doesn't touch the bottom of the pot.

One very important piece of advice: Do not make sugar syrup–based candy in humid or rainy weather. The moisture in the air wreaks havoc with the syrup. The only two recipes in the book that have this caveat are Macadamia Milk Chocolate Toffee (page 102) and Homemade Peppermint Taffy (page 103).

Types of Chocolate

When choosing chocolate, buy the best you can afford. For most of my chocolate making, I prefer a high-quality bittersweet chocolate. You can't go wrong with European brands like Lindt, Callebaut, or Valrhona. These chocolates have a high cocoa butter content, which gives them a high gloss and that unmistakable, melt-in-your-mouth quality. *Couverture chocolate* has a very high cocoa butter content, and is preferred by professionals for hand dipping, but is not necessary in any of these recipes.

Unsweetened chocolate is pure chocolate liquor, the dark brown mass obtained from grinding cacao beans. It is most often used in baking, as in The Best Chocolate-Pecan Brownies (page 134).

Bittersweet chocolate is chocolate liquor that has been mildly sweetened. Many chocolate manufacturers are now selling chocolates with varying amounts of chocolate liquor. The amount is usually stated in a percentage on the label. A 70% cacao so-called bittersweet chocolate will be quite a bit more bitter than one with a 64% cacao content. Most European chocolates are bittersweet. I like chocolates with a cacao content of about 60%. *Semisweet* chocolate is slightly sweeter, and in most cases interchangeable with bittersweet. *Milk chocolate* is sweetened not only with sugar but with milk. *White chocolate* (not used in this book) is not chocolate at all, but sweetened cocoa butter. Milk and white chocolates scorch easily, so watch out when melting. *Chocolate chips* include lecithin, which helps them hold their shape when baked.

Chocolate is delicious but temperamental. Take care when melting chocolate, as it hates water and high heat. A single drop of water in melted chocolate will make it clump up and "seize" into a thick mass. When chocolate is overheated, it gets grainy.

The best way to melt chocolate is in a double boiler. Chop the chocolate finely with a large knife—finely chopped chocolate melts more evenly and quickly. Don't try to save time by chopping it in a food processor—the friction in the bowl will heat up the chocolate and melt it. Place the chopped chocolate in the double boiler insert or a heatproof bowl. Bring the water to a boil, then turn it off. If the water isn't simmering, it won't build up steam that could collect and drip into the bowl of chocolate. Set the insert over the hot water (it should not touch the water) and let stand, stirring occasionally, until the chocolate is smoothly melted.

Chocolate can also be melted in a microwave at Medium (50 percent) power. Microwave the chocolate in 1-minute intervals, stirring after each interval (the chocolate may look shiny and unmelted but will smooth out when stirred), until melted. I prefer the double-boiler method because it is easy to scorch chocolate in a microwave unless you are very attentive.

Finishing Touches

Until recently you didn't have much choice when it came to giving your homemade candies to friends. You put them in a jar or a box of some kind, and added a ribbon. Now kitchenware and crafts stores, catalogues, and online sources abound with candy boxes, cellophane bags, and candy papers to present your handiwork. For an especially nice gift, put the candies in a candy dish and wrap in colored cellophane or plastic wrap.

Chocolate, Cranberry, and Walnut Fudge

There are a lot of fudge recipes out there, but most of them are for experienced candymakers. This one is carefree, as it "fudges" with the help of marshmallows.

Makes about 2¼ pounds

Make Ahead: The fudge must stand at least 8 hours or overnight before serving. It can be made up to 1 week ahead.

8 tablespoons (1 stick) unsalted butter, cut into pieces
6 ounces semisweet chocolate, coarsely chopped
1¾ cups (3 ounces) miniature marshmallows
¾ cup (3 ounces) coarsely chopped walnuts
½ cup (2 ounces) dried cranberries
1 ounce unsweetened chocolate, finely chopped
1 teaspoon vanilla extract
2¼ cups sugar
One 5-ounce can evaporated milk

1. Line an 8- or 9-inch baking pan with a double thickness of aluminum foil with the foil extending 2 inches over opposite ends of the pan. Fold the overhang to form handles. Butter the inside of the foil-lined pan.

2. In a large bowl, combine the butter, semisweet chocolate, marshmallows, walnuts, cranberries, unsweetened chocolate, and vanilla.

3. In a large, heavy-bottomed saucepan, combine the sugar and evaporated milk. Lightly butter the exposed sides of the saucepan above the surface of the sugar mixture. Bring to a boil over medium heat, stirring constantly with a flat wooden spatula to prevent scorching. Attach a candy thermometer to the pan. Boil, stirring constantly, until the mixture

reaches 238°F degrees (soft-ball stage) on the thermometer.

4. Pour the hot mixture over the ingredients in the bowl. Let stand for 30 seconds. Stir with a wooden spoon until the chocolate and marshmallows are melted and the thickened mixture begins to have a sheen, about 1 minute. Spread evenly in the prepared pan. Let stand at room temperature to cool and mellow the flavors for at least 8 hours or overnight.

5. Lift up on the foil handles to remove the fudge from the pan. Using a sharp knife, cut the fudge into squares and lift them up from the foil. (The fudge can be made up to 1 week ahead, stored in an airtight container at room temperature.)

Chocolate Peanut Butter Meltaways

Once when our friend Marion Hampton was staying with us, a holiday care package that included a box of these chocolate morsels arrived from her mother, Caroline Cox. It wasn't long before I was on the phone getting the recipe. Bringing the temperature of the chocolate up to about 115°F and then cooling it to about 90°F helps it to set better.

Makes about 4 dozen candies

Make Ahead: The candies can be made up to 2 weeks ahead.

One 12-ounce jar crunchy peanut butter
5 tablespoons (½ stick plus 1 tablespoon) unsalted butter, at room temperature, plus more if needed
2 cups confectioners' sugar, sifted
1½ cups crispy rice cereal

11 ounces bittersweet or semisweet chocolate, finely chopped
1 tablespoon vegetable shortening

1. Line a baking sheet with aluminum foil. In a medium bowl, using a wooden spoon, cream the peanut butter with the butter until combined. Gradually stir in the confectioners' sugar. Stir in the cereal, which will crumble. (The moisture in the peanut butter varies from brand to brand—if the peanut butter mixture seems too crumbly, mix in more softened butter until it is malleable.) Using about 1 tablespoon for each, roll the mixture into balls, placing them on the prepared baking sheet. Refrigerate the balls while melting the chocolate.

2. In the top part of a double boiler placed over hot, not simmering, water, melt the chocolate with the shortening, stirring occasionally until smooth and an instant-read thermometer inserted in the chocolate reads 115°F to 120°F. Remove from the heat. Transfer the chocolate mixture to a small bowl and let cool to 88°F to 90°F, stirring occasionally.

3. Place a dab of the chocolate in the palm of one hand. Pick up a peanut-butter ball and roll it between your palms to coat lightly with the chocolate. Return the chocolate-coated ball to the foil-lined baking sheet. Repeat with the remaining balls. Refrigerate until the chocolate is set and the balls release easily from the foil, about 30 minutes. (The candies can be made up to 2 weeks ahead, stored in airtight containers and refrigerated.)

S'mores Rocky Road

My dad is the family candy maker, and his holiday specialty is rocky road. I stir graham crackers into my rocky road to make it a delicious variation on the s'mores theme. Do not substitute miniature marshmallows for the hand-snipped large ones, as the former tend to melt completely into the chocolate.

Makes about 2¼ pounds

Make Ahead: The candy can be made up to 2 weeks ahead.

1½ pounds milk chocolate, finely chopped
6 ounces marshmallows, snipped into quarters
    with lightly oiled scissors
1 cup coarsely chopped walnuts
1 cup mini-graham crackers (or break large
    crackers into bite-size pieces)

1. Line a baking sheet with aluminum foil and lightly butter the foil. In a large stainless steel bowl set over a large saucepan of *barely* simmering water, melt the chocolate, stirring occasionally, until almost but not completely melted. (The water must be at the barest simmer to efficiently melt this amount of chocolate.) Remove from the water and let stand, stirring occasionally, until the chocolate is completely melted and slightly thickened.

2. Stir in the marshmallows, walnuts, and graham crackers. Scrape the mixture out onto the prepared baking sheet and spread into a 1-inch-thick layer. Refrigerate until the chocolate is firm. Using a sharp knife, cut into 1- to 2-inch pieces. (The rocky road can be made up to 2 weeks ahead, stored in an airtight container at room temperature.)

Macadamia Milk Chocolate Toffee

Make a batch of this buttery, crunchy toffee for gift giving, and you may end up keeping a good bit of it for yourself. Use other nuts if you like—cashews, almonds, or even peanuts. Settle in to stir the syrup over medium heat for about 15 minutes. Don't rush it, or the butter may separate.

Makes about 35 pieces

Make Ahead: The toffee can be made up to 2 weeks ahead.

2 cups sugar
1½ cups (3 sticks) unsalted butter, cut into pieces
1 cup (4 ounces) macadamia nuts, rinsed of any
    salt if salted and patted dry, coarsely chopped
1 cup (6 ounces) milk chocolate chips

1. Lightly butter a 15½ × 10½ × 1-inch jelly-roll pan. In a large, heavy-bottomed saucepan cook the sugar and butter over medium heat, stirring constantly, until the mixture comes to a boil.

2. Attach a candy thermometer to the pan. Cook, stirring constantly at a steady but not rapid pace until the syrup reaches 310°F, about 15 minutes. Remove the pan from the heat and stir in ½ cup of the macadamia nuts. Pour the mixture into the prepared pan, letting it spread naturally. Let stand for 5 to 10 minutes to cool slightly. The chocolate must be warm enough to melt the chocolate topping, so don't let it cool too much.

3. Using a lint-free kitchen towel, blot any butter that has separated out of the toffee (a small amount is to be expected, but if a lot separates, it means you cooked the toffee too quickly). Sprinkle the chocolate chips in a single layer over the surface of the hot toffee.

Let stand until the chocolate softens, about 5 minutes. Using a metal spatula, spread the chocolate evenly over the surface of the toffee. Sprinkle with the remaining ½ cup macadamia nuts. Using a large, sharp knife, score the toffee into 2-inch pieces. As the toffee cools, retrace the score lines occasionally with the knife to reach the bottom of the pan so the toffee will break apart easily.

4. When the toffee is cooled and the chocolate is firm, use a metal spatula to remove the toffee from the pan. Following the score lines, break into pieces and serve. (The toffee can be made up to 2 weeks ahead, stored in an airtight container at room temperature.)

Homemade Peppermint Taffy

If you have a hankering to make homemade candy canes, make these instead. Candy canes are very difficult (if not impossible) to master at home. These are good old-fashioned pulled taffy hard candies, and not difficult at all to make. Supply yourself with a pair of rubber gloves to protect your hands from the heat of the candy during the pulling process, and you can have a batch ready in no time. Peppermint candies make a wonderful gift packaged in a beribboned glass jar.

- **This basic recipe can be flavored with any kind of food-quality oil or extract and tinted with food coloring to identify the flavor. Oil-based flavorings are preferred, because the flavor won't evaporate when it hits the hot syrup. You will find them at well-stocked kitchenware and crafts stores. Alcohol-based extracts, which are more common, will evaporate a bit, so the amount should be increased slightly.**

Makes about 14 ounces

Make Ahead: The candy can be made up to 1 month ahead.

Nonstick cooking spray
1½ cups sugar
½ cup corn syrup
2 tablespoons unsalted butter
⅛ teaspoon salt
½ teaspoon peppermint oil or ¾ teaspoon clear peppermint extract
Red liquid food coloring

1. Lightly butter a nonstick baking sheet. Spray a pair of kitchen scissors, a pair of rubber gloves, and an offset metal spatula with nonstick cooking spray.

2. In a medium saucepan fitted with a candy thermometer, bring the sugar, corn syrup, ¼ cup water, the butter, and salt to a boil over high heat, stirring constantly to help dissolve the sugar. Boil without stirring until the syrup reaches 270°F.

3. Remove the saucepan from the heat. Add the peppermint oil to the syrup. Color the syrup with 2 or 3 drops of red food coloring. Swirl the syrup by the handle of the saucepan to incorporate the oil and coloring. Pour onto the prepared baking sheet.

4. Let the syrup cool until a skin begins to form on top, about 3 minutes. Put on the rubber gloves. Using the oiled spatula, continuously fold the syrup back on itself until it is cool enough to handle. Pick up the mass of syrup and pull the candy, stretching it between your hands and folding it back on itself, until it is opaque but still warm, about 3 minutes, depending on the heat of the kitchen.

5. Twist and pull the candy into a long rope about ¾ inch thick, letting the rope fall onto the baking sheet as it is pulled. Work quickly, as the candy hardens as it cools. Using the oiled scissors, snip the candy rope into ¾-inch-long candies. (If the candy cools until hard, crack the candy into pieces.) Cool completely. (The candy can be made up to 1 month ahead, stored in an airtight container at room temperature.)

Striped Peppermint Candy: Lightly butter two baking sheets. Make the candy syrup through step 2. Add the peppermint oil and swirl to incorporate. Pour two-thirds of the syrup onto a baking sheet. Add 2 or 3 drops of red food coloring to the remaining syrup in the pan and swirl to incorporate. Pour the red syrup onto the other baking sheet and cover with an inverted bowl to keep warm. Pull the plain syrup until white and opaque. Flatten into a 6-inch square, place on the baking sheet, and cover with an inverted bowl to keep warm. Pull the red syrup just until it turns deep pink, and form into a thick 6-inch-long cylinder. Place the red candy in the center of the white candy square and roll up the square to enclose the red candy. Twist and pull the candy into a rope and cut into pieces.

Chocolate-Orange Truffles

There's a very nice story connected with these truffles. When I was working as a Manhattan restaurant manager, I became friendly with many customers, but Susan Ginsburg was a favorite. She always gave me a bottle of Grand Marnier for Christmas, and I used it to make these truffles to give to her. Years went by, and we lost track of one other until we accidentally crossed paths again. She is now my literary agent. When I became a caterer, I took out the recipe again and

turned these out by the thousands. Now I make them in more modest batches, but I always try to have some tucked away in the freezer to finish holiday meals with a flourish.

- **Dutch-process cocoa has been treated with alkali. Because it has a milder flavor than natural, nonalkalized cocoa, it is preferred for rolling the truffles, but regular cocoa will do. If you want to cut the bitterness of either cocoa, sift ¼ cup cocoa with ¼ cup confectioners' sugar, and use the mixture for rolling the truffles.**

- **It's simple to vary the flavors with different preserves and liqueurs. Instead of orange marmalade and Grand Marnier, substitute strawberry preserves and brandy, strained raspberry preserves (not seedless preserves, which are too thin) and Chambord or framboise, apricot preserves and dark rum, or cherry preserves and Kirschwasser.**

Makes about 3 dozen truffles

Make Ahead: The truffles can be made up to 1 week ahead.

12 tablespoons (1½ sticks) unsalted butter, cut into pieces
1 pound bittersweet chocolate, finely chopped
½ cup orange marmalade, preferably bitter orange
¼ cup Grand Marnier or other orange-flavored liqueur
½ cup Dutch-process cocoa powder, such as Droste, for rolling

1. In a medium heatproof bowl set over a large saucepan of hot, not simmering, water, melt the butter. Add the chocolate and melt, stirring often, until smooth. Remove from the heat. Whisk in the marmalade and liqueur. Cover loosely with plastic wrap and refrigerate until firm and chilled, at least 4 hours or overnight.

2. Place the cocoa powder in a shallow medium bowl. Line a baking sheet with aluminum foil. Using a melon baller, scoop the chilled chocolate mixture and roll between your palms to form a round truffle. (If the chocolate is too firm, let stand at room temperature to soften slightly.) Roll the truffle in the cocoa and place on the prepared baking sheet. Repeat with the remaining chocolate. (The truffles can be made up to 1 week ahead, stored in airtight containers and refrigerated, or frozen for up to 2 months. Remove the truffles from the refrigerator 10 minutes before serving, or about 30 minutes if frozen.)

Chocolate-Dipped Truffles: Do not roll the truffles in cocoa powder. Refrigerate the truffles on the foil-lined baking sheet until firm, at least 10 minutes. In the top part of a double boiler over hot, not simmering, water, melt 12 ounces finely chopped bittersweet chocolate, stirring often, until smooth and an instant-read thermometer inserted in the chocolate reads 115°F to 120°F. Remove from the heat and cool, stirring occasionally, until the chocolate is about 90°F. Place a dab of chocolate in the center of your palm. Pick up a truffle and roll in between your palms to coat with chocolate. Place on the foil-lined baking sheet. Repeat with the remaining truffles and chocolate. Refrigerate until the chocolate is set and the truffles release easily from the foil, about 30 minutes. You can roll the coated truffles in cocoa powder to give them their traditional look (which is supposed to resemble a fresh truffle coated with earth). Transfer the truffles to airtight containers to store.

Sweet and Spicy Candied Walnuts

It's a toss-up. Should I make candied walnuts with the familiar cinnamon-and-spice flavors? Or do I give them a savory twist with orange zest, rosemary, and cracked pepper? They're so easy to make, why not try both?

Makes ¾ pound

Make Ahead: The walnuts can be made up to 1 week ahead.

1 large egg white
¼ cup sugar
½ teaspoon salt
½ teaspoon ground cinnamon
¼ teaspoon ground ginger
¼ teaspoon freshly grated nutmeg
¼ teaspoon ground cloves
1½ cups (12 ounces) walnuts, preferably walnut halves

1. Position a rack in the center of the oven and preheat to 300°F.

2. In a medium bowl, whisk together the egg whites and sugar until very foamy. Whisk in the salt, cinnamon, ginger, nutmeg, and cloves. Add the walnuts and stir to coat.

3. Spread the nuts on an ungreased baking sheet. Bake for 10 minutes. Stir and separate any walnuts that are sticking together, then bake for another 10 minutes. Stir and continue baking until the coating is dry and the walnuts are crisp, 5 to 10 minutes. Cool completely.

Savory Orange-Rosemary Walnuts: Substitute the grated zest of 1 orange, 1 teaspoon crumbled dried rosemary, and 1 teaspoon coarsely cracked black pepper for the cinnamon, ginger, nutmeg, and cloves. If you like you can substitute pecans for the walnuts.

It Wouldn't Be the Holidays Without . . . Candy Canes

The hooked shape of the candy cane represents the crook of the shepherds who were present at the Nativity. Surprisingly, cellophane-wrapped striped candy canes are a fairly recent addition to the list of edible Christmas traditions.

The first candy canes were created in 1670, when the choirmaster at Cologne Cathedral handed out candy sticks to the children in his choir to keep them quiet during the long Living Nativity ceremony. To keep the children in a religious state of mind, he bent the sticks into shepherds' crooks to remind them that they were no longer just eating candy but commemorating the Nativity itself. Eventually, hooked candy canes became a German holiday tradition.

Like many other Yuletide traditions (notably the Christmas tree), the candy cane came to America with the first wave of German immigrants in the early 1800s. Its first documented stateside appearance was in 1847, on the Christmas tree of Wooster, Ohio, citizen August Imgard, a German-Swedish immigrant.

But how did the American candy cane become the red-and-white, peppermint-flavored Christmas icon we know today? The technical advances of the Industrial Revolution made sugar inexpensive and mechanized candy making. One of the most popular sweets of the nineteenth century was the peppermint stick. Its shape was perfect for bending into a crooked candy cane, but this still had to be done by hand, one cane at a time. The cooling menthol flavor of peppermint was distinctly wintry, and to some, the red-and-white coloring was a metaphor for Christ's blood and the purity of the Christ child.

In the 1920s, a candy manufacturer in Albany, Georgia, Bob McCormack of Bobs Candies, began making handmade candy canes. Because the canes were so difficult to make and transport, they were reserved for his family and local customers. And so they remained until the 1950s, when Bob's brother-in-law, Gregory Keller, a Catholic priest, invented a machine to automate candy cane production. Packaging innovations such as the individual cellophane wrap (pioneered by Bobs Candies in the 1920s when they became the first candy manufacturer to use the transparent paper) and special boxes to nestle the canes soon made Bobs the largest producer of candy canes in the world. The McCormack family sold Bobs in 1995 to Farley's and Sathers Candy Company, Inc.

If you want to mail-order the granddaddy of all contemporary candy canes (which now come in such flavors as piña colada and bubble gum), you can find them at such sellers as Blair's Candy (www.blaircandy.com or call 1-800-698-3536, ext. 202).

Cookies

Of all the Christmas edibles, cookies are most beloved. Every year, I bake sheet after sheet of my favorites, then pack them up for delivery to my friends (keeping plenty for myself). I love everything about the process: poring over cookbooks to decide which new recipes to try, mixing the dough (and trying not to eat too much of the unbaked dough), the rhythm of rolling the dough, searching kitchenware stores and catalogues for new cookie cutters, inhaling the aromas of sugar and spice from the oven as they fill the kitchen, packing up the trays and boxes of cookies, and most of all, the look and sounds of pleasure as my friends bite into their cookies. But none of this happens without advance planning.

Balance your cookie menu just like you balance a dinner menu. Choose cookies to give a variety of visual looks and flavors. You don't want them all to be homey (but delicious) drop cookies, nor do you want them all to be heavily spiced with ginger and cinnamon. Also, try to bake cookies that are specific to Christmas. If pressed for time and you want a familiar recipe to flesh out a cookie platter, then bake the chocolate chip cookie you make the rest of the year.

By nature, many traditional Christmas cookies are time-consuming. I am a very experienced baker, and I can tell you that there aren't too many shortcuts to baking and decorating gorgeous cut-out cookies. But you can balance the more time-intensive, hands-on cookies with some that are quickly made. In this chapter, I share plenty of easy cookie recipes that my friends, many of whom are food professionals, and I have baked for years. We all agree that our favorites are often the ones that give the cook the most cookies with the least effort.

In the spirit of a basic cookie cooking class (this is *Christmas 101*, not *202*), I stayed away from recipes that required special equipment (including German *springerle* and Dutch *spekulatius*, which call for special molds for stamping them with intricate designs). I do include a recipe for Spritz Butter Cookies (page 130), requiring a cookie press, because even though it isn't an absolutely necessary kitchen utensil, it can be used throughout the year. But don't look for a gingerbread house—it takes too much time. And as no one has the nerve to bite into such an ornate creation, I think they're a waste of time and ingredients. I did make one with my niece and nephew, and we all agreed that gluing candies on a cookie roof gets old fast.

Set up your cookie-baking kitchen like a factory. In other words, get organized, and finish one job before you move on to the next. Don't let those bowls and spoons pile up in the sink. Owning more than one or two cookie sheets will definitely move things along. Have the entire batch of cookies baked and cooled before you begin any icing or decorating. Have plenty of small custard cups or paper cups with separate spoons ready to hold different colored icings.

Whenever possible, enlist another pair of hands. Cookie making is so much easier, quicker, and more fun when you are sharing with a friend. Every year, my friends Diane and I get together to bake her Ultimate Thumbprint Cookies (page 132). In a couple of hours, we have literally hundreds of them.

Types of Cookies

The most basic categories of cookies are rolled cookies, formed cookies, drop cookies, and bar cookies.

Rolled Cookies

Rolled cookies are created from chilled, rolled-out dough, and usually cut into shapes and decorated with icing. Sugar cookies and gingerbread cookies, two Christmas traditions, are examples of rolled cookies. The dough must be chilled to give it a firm texture that can be rolled out. Let the chilled dough stand at room temperature for a few minutes to warm and soften slightly, or it may crack during rolling. The work surface should be floured somewhat generously to cut down on the sticking problem. Don't forget to dust the top of the dough with flour, too, so the rolling pin doesn't stick to it. While you're rolling, occasionally run a long, thin metal spatula or knife under the dough to make sure it isn't sticking.

Formed Cookies

Formed cookies are made into shapes without the help of cookie cutters, although other utensils or your hands may be used. The dough can be chilled or at room temperature. When forming balls of dough, use measured amounts (I usually use one level tablespoon) so the cookies are uniform. Measure out all of the dough balls at once, placing them on an extra cookie sheet or jelly-roll pan (or even in a shallow baking dish). When cutting out squares or strips, use a ruler as a guide. Thin doughs are best cut with a pizza wheel. To give the cookies attractive wavy edges, use a fluted ravioli wheel.

Drop Cookies

Drop cookies are made from dough dropped in measured amounts onto baking sheets. They spread quite a bit, so always allow 2 inches between the cookies so they don't run into each other when baked. They aren't the prettiest cookies, but they are among the most popular.

Bar Cookies

Bar cookies are baked in a baking pan, cooled, and cut into bars. They are very sturdy, and are great cookies for mailing. I used to be frustrated trying to dig the first bar out of the pan and ruining it in the process (well, I did get to eat it . . .), so I developed a method to solve the problem. To remove bar cookies easily from the baking pan, line the bottom and short sides of the pan with a long piece of aluminum foil (preferably nonstick foil), folding the excess foil to form "handles." When the cookies are baked and cooled, lift up on the handles to remove them from the pan in one piece. They can now be cut into uniform bars without any waste.

Ingredients

As I always say in my cooking classes, baking is nothing but chemistry that tastes good. It is important to understand the ingredients that go into the recipes. Too often cooks are tempted to substitute ingredients and then have problems. During the holiday season, when I know I will be doing a lot of baking, I buy many of my staple ingredients in quantity at a wholesale club to get the best prices.

Butter and Other Fats

Fats add tenderness and moisture to baked goods. There are many cooking fats available, and they all have unique qualities that make them behave differently in recipes.

Butter is the fat backbone for most cookies. Butter gives cookies a crisp texture and an irreplaceable flavor. Buy a high-quality butter for the best results. Some inexpensive brands have off flavors or a high water content that will affect the taste and texture of the dough. Most bakers prefer *unsalted butter* for many reasons. First, unsalted butter allows the baker to be in control of how much salt is needed to bring out the flavors in the dough. Also, because the addition of salt to butter hides off flavors and rancidity, unsalted butter is likely to be fresher than salted. If you must use salted butter, omit the salt in the recipe. There are

reduced-fat butters on the market, but I have not tested these recipes with them, and do not guarantee the results.

In most recipes, to start the dough, butter is creamed with sugar. Properly softened butter is the key, because you want to use the electric mixer to beat in little bubbles of air that will expand in the oven (thanks to the chemical reaction of the baking soda or baking powder). If the butter is too warm or too cold, the bubbles won't form properly, and you'll have hard, flat cookies.

To soften butter, cut the chilled butter into 1-inch pieces and place in the mixing bowl. Let stand until soft but still slightly pliable, about 30 minutes in an average-temperature kitchen. The butter shouldn't look shiny or oily. To save time, using the large holes on a box grater, grate the cold butter into the bowl. It will be softened by the time you gather the rest of the ingredients. Butter can also be softened in a microwave oven, if you keep an eye on it. The exact length of time depends on the wattage power of the oven. Use Low (20 percent) power, as higher settings tend to melt holes in the butter before it is completely softened.

Margarine is softer and more oily than butter. Some bakers indiscriminately substitute it for butter, but the cookies will have a softer texture. I rarely bake with margarine because I like the flavor and texture of butter-baked cookies, but some recipes (none in this book) require it to give the cookies a tender crumb. If you use margarine, choose a reliable stick brand. Never use tub or whipped margarine (or butters, for that matters), as their added water gives them unreliable cooking qualities.

Vegetable shortening is used in some recipes to lend extra tenderness to the cookie. Measure shortening in level amounts in a metal measuring cup. Shortening now comes in easy-to-measure sticks, which are especially convenient to use during the busy holiday baking season.

Eggs

I use large, Grade A eggs in my baking. If you substitute another egg size, you could throw off the liquid content of the recipe. Store eggs in their carton in the refrigerator, not in the egg holders in the refrigerator door (it really isn't cold enough in the door and reduces the time they stay fresh). When a recipe calls for room-temperature eggs, remove them from the refrigerator about 1 hour before using. Never let eggs stand at room temperature for longer than 2 hours. To speed the warming-up process, place the whole uncracked eggs in a bowl and cover them with hot tap water. Let the eggs stand for 3 to 5 minutes and the hot water will remove their chill. Drain and use the eggs.

Royal icing, a common decorating icing, usually is made with raw egg whites. Knowing that some cooks prefer to avoid uncooked eggs, I use dehydrated egg white powder (which is salmonella-safe) in my royal icing. It is available in most supermarkets, craft and baking supply stores, and from online sources.

Flour

All-purpose flour is preferred for cookie baking. It has a moderate amount of gluten, the protein combination that gives strength to dough. *Unbleached flour* (even if it is called "all-purpose") has a high gluten content, and is really best for yeast dough. However, as most cookie recipes contain enough butter to tenderize the gluten, if you only have unbleached flour, you can use it. *Cake flour* has a very low gluten content, and should only be used in recipes that call for it. *Use the flour indicated in the recipe.*

White rice flour, available in natural foods stores, or *cornstarch* (both gluten-free ingredients) is sometimes added to cookie dough to further reduce the gluten content and give the cookies a meltingly tender crumb.

These recipes were tested with the dip-and-sweep method of measuring. Dip the metal measuring cup or measuring spoon into the bag of flour (or any dry ingredient) and fill the cup without packing the ingredient. Using the flat side of a knife, sweep the excess from the top of the cup to get a level measurement. When following a recipe in other cookbooks, read the introductory remarks to see what dry measuring method the cook prefers. Some bakers insist that you spoon the flour into a cup and level it off, but that makes a mess. Others insist that you weigh the flour on a scale.

Sugar Products

Most cookie doughs use *granulated sugar*. I have come to experience a difference in quality among sugars (cane sugar has finer crystals than beet sugar), so buy a well-known brand and read the label to be sure you are getting cane sugar.

Confectioners' sugar, sometimes called powdered sugar, is used primarily for icings and decorating. Confectioners' sugar is usually sifted over baked cookies as a garnish. If you plan to garnish a lot of cookies, purchase a confectioners' sugar shaker with a mesh wire top so you don't have wash a sieve every time you need a little sprinkle.

Light brown sugar is granulated sugar with molasses added. *Dark brown sugar* simply has more molasses. They are interchangeable, but I find light brown sugar milder and more versatile. Always store brown sugar at room temperature in an airtight container or tightly closed in its plastic bag secured with a sturdy rubber band, or it will dry out and harden. There are a number of remedies to soften hard brown sugar (place a wedge of apple in the bag for a couple of days, for example), but nothing is faster or easier than running out and buying a new, inexpensive box of fresh brown sugar. I do not use "granulated" brown sugar or liquid brown sugar. Brown sugar should be measured in packed, level amounts.

Molasses is a by-product of the sugar-refining process. *Unsulfured molasses* (often called light molasses) is extracted from the sugar cane without sulfur dioxide. *Sulfured molasses* (sometimes labeled "robust") is strongly flavored. *Blackstrap molasses* is very bitter. I only use unsulfured molasses. When measuring molasses, lightly spray the inside of the liquid measuring cup with nonstick vegetable oil spray so it doesn't stick as much.

Honey is often categorized by the type of flower nectar that the bees collect in the vicinity of their hive—thyme, lavender, and so on. I use a full-flavored, high-quality, blended supermarket honey like Golden Blossom because I can be sure of the flavor from jar to jar.

Nuts

Many holiday cookies are loaded with nuts. For the best price (and usually the best, freshest flavor, because of fast turnover) buy nuts in bulk at natural foods stores. The high oil content of nuts encourages rancidity, so store them, tightly wrapped, in the refrigerator or freezer, not at room temperature.

Baking Perfect Cookies

Get Organized

Before you start baking, read the entire recipe to be sure you have all the ingredients and utensils. Measure all of the ingredients accurately, and have them ready in the order used. Prepare all of the baking sheets according to the recipe (although most of these recipes use nonstick baking sheets). Adjust the oven racks in the recommended positions before preheating the oven.

Baking Basics

Do you want great cookies? Then get good cookie sheets. Over the years, I think I have tried every cookie sheet on the market. I had a love affair with nonstick insulated cookie sheets, but I had to admit that the insulation kept some cookies from getting sufficiently crisp. At first the nonstick surface seemed handy, until it scratched and chipped. And there have been a number of innovations lately that make the nonstick sheets obsolete in my view.

Practically every baker I know recommends the same baking sheet—the sturdy aluminum *half-sheet pan*. The 18×13-inch pan holds a lot of cookies, and its heavy-gauge construction absorbs heat evenly in the oven, discouraging the hot spots that are the bane of cheap, thin sheets. It does have shallow rimmed sides. Some cooks argue that the sides inhibit air flow, affecting the browning of the cookies, but I have never experienced this problem. However, if it concerns you, turn the cookie sheet upside down and bake on its underside, where the rims will be hidden out of the way.

Back when I started baking at my mom's side, there was only one way to give a baking sheet a nonstick surface—with fat, flour, and elbow grease. Then parchment paper made its appearance, and it is still a reliable way to keep cookies (and other baked goods) from sticking. But the real discovery is *nonstick baking pads*, made from thin sheets of silicone. Unlike parchment paper, which is disposable after only one or two uses at the most, these pads can be used up to one thousand times. That is a lot of cookies. They used to be pricey, but now every large housewares shop on the planet carries them. They are an indispensable investment.

During the holidays, you will appreciate having more than one baking sheet with a single nonstick pad. Three or four sheets, each with its own pad, are ideal. This way you won't have to wash and dry the sheets between batches, a chore that can really slow the process down.

In a gas oven, the heat rises from the bottom, so the cookies in the top third of the oven will bake more quickly than those in the center. Therefore, the position of the baking sheets should be switched from top to bottom and from front to back halfway through baking to ensure even baking. For the best results, *bake the cookies one sheet at a time on the center rack*. This may be absolutely necessary in electric ovens with top-heating elements. If you have a convection oven, you can bake on two or even three racks, but reduce the oven temperature by 25°F, lower the estimated baking time by about one-third, and keep an eye on the cookies.

Check the cookies for doneness at the beginning of the recommended baking time. Not all cookies turn golden brown when done—I have given specific visual tests as well as timings. It is a good idea to make a test run of the first tray so you can judge whether you like the cookies more or less baked according to your taste. I mention this because I prefer soft, just-baked cookies myself, but you may like them well-done and crisp.

Let the cookies stand on the baking sheet to cool and firm slightly before removing them from the sheet. Transfer them to wire racks to cool completely. I love my stackable cake racks, which are especially helpful in a cramped kitchen. Cool cookies completely before decorating, stacking, or storing.

Allow the cookie sheets to cool completely before baking another batch. If you put the dough on warm cookie sheets, the cookies will melt and spread before they have a chance to bake. There is a trick to save the cooling time: Arrange the cookies on a baking pad, and slide the cookie-covered pad on the cookie sheet. The pad will protect the dough from the hot sheet. However, it is still better to have plenty of cookie sheets and pads on hand.

Making Masterpieces

Some cookies come out of the oven already beautiful. Others want to be decorated. Those blond-gold sugar cookies really aren't Christmas cookies until they are embellished with icing and dusted with colored sugar or sprinkles.

The dough for rolled cookies is prepared for cutting out with a rolling pin. If you are a dedicated baker, invest in a *silicone rolling pin*. Cookie doughs have a high proportion of butter and sugar, and they love to stick to wooden rolling pins. With a nonstick silicone pin, however, all but the most temperamental doughs behave. You will still have to use some flour on the work surface and top of the dough, but not nearly as much as with regular wooden pins.

With little more than some good food coloring to create nicely colored icing, and a selection of attractive sugars, jimmies, and sprinkles, I can accomplish a lot. And a collection of well-shaped cookie cutters also helps. Some people are driven to create cookies that are so intricately painted that I don't see how anyone could bear to bite into them! Just use your imagination and your color sense, and you'll be fine. When I decorate my sugar cookies, I stick to green Christmas trees decorated with round sprinkles to represent ornaments, yellow bells garnished with a single silver dragée for a clapper, and white snowflakes sparkling with colored sugar crystals.

If you don't consider yourself an artist and are afraid of making garnished cookies with mismatched colors, there is help. Just go to an art supply store and purchase an inexpensive color wheel. This is a tool that artists use to match up colors. The colors opposite each other on the wheel are considered compatible. Purple and yellow, for example, are opposites but compatible. Other color theories and suggested combinations are often explained on the wheel. Now you don't have to let your own (possibly misguided) sense of color lead you astray. Of course, if you stick to the basics, you'll have the least trouble.

Most cookies can be decorated with just two icings. For a shiny icing to spread over cookies, use the Decorating Icing on page 138. If you want to pipe line decorations from a pastry bag, use the Royal Icing on page 136. If you wish, frost the cookies with an undercoat of decorating icing, let dry, then detail with the royal icing. Or the royal icing can be thinned with water to a spreadable consistency that will dry on the cookie into a shiny surface. When not using the icing, cover with plastic wrap or moist paper towels pressed onto the surface so they don't crust over. A metal icing spatula, preferably offset, will make icing the cookies a breeze. I have two sizes, one large and one small, to use on different sizes of cookies.

Both icings can be colored. For the truest, brightest tones, use high-quality food coloring, found at kitchenware and crafts stores. Supermarket-quality liquid food colorings are only OK. Their colors aren't very exciting, and the icing often ends up pastel no matter how much coloring is added. Use these colorings in very judicious amounts, stirring well before you judge the color—it is easy to go overboard. Food coloring drops or gels are the easiest to use because they mix well with the icing. Food coloring pastes give very intensely colored results but need to be scooped out of the jar with the tip of a toothpick or wooden skewer and require a good amount of stirring to dissolve.

When mixing different colors of icing, disposable cups and spoons work well because they can be thrown away. When washing bowls and utensils used to color icing, be careful not to splash colored water all over the sink and kitchen.

Cookies can also be painted before baking with an egg yolk–based glaze. For each color, stir 1 large egg yolk with ¼ teaspoon water in a small bowl, custard cup, or disposable cup. Using a small whisk or spoon (the whisk works best), mix in the desired amount of high-quality food coloring drops. You must use good food coloring to override the bright yellow of the yolk. Use small paintbrushes to paint unbaked cookies. It's up to you how intricate you want to get.

Storing Cookies

Store cookies in airtight containers. Throughout the year, I look for covered metal boxes or containers (such as those that hold gift bottles of liquor and coffee cans with snap-shut plastic lids) that I can press into service. During the holidays, decorated gift boxes show up in crafts stores, but they can disappear fast—buy them when you find them.

When layering cookies, separate the layers with double sheets of waxed paper. Some sturdy cookies can be stored in self-sealing plastic bags. Wrap bar cookies individually in plastic. Especially during the holidays, supermarkets carry colored plastic wrap, which will give the cookies a holiday look.

For long-term storage, do not store different cookies in the same container, as they may pick up flavors from each other. Also, when combined, moist cookies will soften the crisp ones. You can't help mixing cookies if you are giving out a selection, but in general it's never mix, never worry.

Mailing Cookies

Use a gift box just large enough to hold the amount of cookies you want to send. Choose sturdy cookies and wrap individually with plastic. Bar and drop cookies are good choices.

If baking and sending rolled cookies, roll them on the thick side so they hold up better during shipping. Place double layers of waxed paper between the layers of cookies. Crumple waxed paper to fill any spaces in the gift box. Place the gift box in a larger mailing box, surround the gift box with plastic pellets, and seal.

Sugar Cookies 101

My perfect sugar cookie must have buttery flavor and melt-in-your-mouth texture yet be firm enough to stand up to a fair amount of decorating. (After all, undecorated sugar cookies may taste good, but they are a bit plain until you roll up your sleeves and ice them.) Typical sugar cookie recipes call for creaming the butter and sugar together, but I cut the butter into the dry ingredients like you would for a pie dough to increase the flakiness of the cookies. For added tenderness, I combine shortening with the butter and cornstarch with the flour.

● If you want to freeze these, freeze *undecorated* baked cookies, as the icing won't hold up well in the freezer. They can be frozen for up to 1 month. About a week before you plan on serving the cookies, defrost them, decorate, and store in airtight containers at room temperature.

Makes about 3½ dozen cookies

Make Ahead: The dough must chill for at least 1½ hours or up to 1 day. The cookies can be baked up to 1 week ahead.

2¾ cups all-purpose flour
¼ cup cornstarch
1 cup sugar
1½ teaspoons baking powder
½ teaspoon salt
8 tablespoons (1 stick) unsalted butter, at room temperature
½ cup vegetable shortening, at room temperature
⅓ cup heavy cream
1 large egg plus 1 large egg yolk
1½ teaspoons vanilla extract
Decorating Icing (page 138)

1. Position racks in the top and bottom thirds of the oven and preheat to 350°F.

2. In a large bowl, whisk the flour, cornstarch, sugar, baking powder, and salt to combine. Add the butter and shortening. Using a handheld electric mixer at low speed, move the beaters through the mixture until the butter and shortening are uniformly cut into tiny crumbs and the mixture resembles coarse cornmeal, 2 to 3 minutes. In a small bowl, whisk together the heavy cream, whole egg, egg yolk, and vanilla. Using a wooden spoon, stir the heavy cream mixture into the dry ingredients and mix well to form a soft dough. Gather the dough together and divide into two thick disks. Wrap each disk in plastic. Refrigerate until chilled, about 1½ hours. (The dough can be prepared up to 1 day ahead.)

3. To roll out the cookies, work with one disk at a time, keeping the other disk refrigerated. Remove the dough from the refrigerator and let stand at room temperature until malleable enough to roll out without cracking, 5 to 10 minutes. (If the dough has been chilled for longer than 1½ hours, it may take a few more minutes.) Unwrap the dough and place on a floured work surface. Lightly sprinkle the top of the dough with flour. Roll out the dough ⅛ inch thick, or slightly thicker for softer cookies. (A silicone rolling pin works best for this somewhat sticky dough.) As you roll out the dough, it will become easier to work with, and tiny cracks on the surface will smooth out and disappear. Occasionally run a long knife under the dough to make sure it isn't sticking, and dust more flour under the dough if needed.

4. Using cookie cutters, cut out the cookies and transfer to cookie sheets lined with nonstick baking pads or parchment paper, placing the cookies 1 inch apart. Gently knead the scraps together and form into another disk.

Wrap and chill for 5 minutes before rolling out again to cut out more cookies.

5. Bake, switching the position of the cookie sheets from top to bottom and front to back halfway through baking, just until the edges of the cookies are barely beginning to turn golden, about 10 minutes. Do not overbake. Let stand on the cookie sheets for 2 minutes, then transfer to wire racks to cool completely. Decorate as desired with Decorating Icing. (The cookies can be baked up to 1 week ahead, stored in airtight containers at room temperature.)

Gingerbread Cookies 101

It took me many batches to finally master the perfect gingerbread cookie. When the dough is rolled thin, it will bake crisp and almost crackerlike. Yet when rolled thick (my preference), the cookies turn out plump and moist. In either case, the flavor will be complex and slightly hot-spicy. I use large gingerbread cookies as place cards for my holiday dinner table, with the guests' names written onto them, and everyone gets to take theirs home (if they don't nibble them with their coffee after dinner).

Makes about 3 dozen cookies

Make Ahead: The dough must be chilled for at least 3 hours or up to 2 days. The cookies can be baked up to 1 week ahead.

3 cups all-purpose flour
1 teaspoon baking soda
¾ teaspoon ground cinnamon
¾ teaspoon ground ginger
½ teaspoon ground allspice
½ teaspoon ground cloves
½ teaspoon salt
¼ teaspoon freshly ground black pepper
8 tablespoons (1 stick) unsalted butter, at room temperature
¼ cup vegetable shortening
½ cup packed light brown sugar
⅔ cup unsulfured molasses
1 large egg
Royal Icing (page 136)

1. Position racks in the top and bottom thirds of the oven and preheat to 350°F.

2. Sift the flour, baking soda, cinnamon, ginger, allspice, cloves, salt, and pepper through a wire sieve into a medium bowl. Set aside.

3. In a large bowl, using a handheld electric mixer set at high speed, beat the butter and vegetable shortening until well combined, about 1 minute. Add the brown sugar and beat until the mixture is light in texture and color, about 2 minutes. Beat in the molasses and egg. Using a wooden spoon, gradually mix in the flour mixture to make a stiff dough. Divide the dough into two thick disks and wrap each disk in plastic wrap. Refrigerate until chilled, about 3 hours. (The dough can be prepared up to 2 days ahead.)

4. To roll out the cookies, work with one disk at a time, keeping the other disk refrigerated. Remove the dough from the refrigerator and let stand at room temperature until just malleable enough to roll out without cracking, about 10 minutes. (If the dough has been chilled for longer than 3 hours, it may need a few more minutes.) Place the dough on a lightly floured work surface and sprinkle the top of the dough with flour. Roll out the dough ⅛ inch thick, making sure that the dough isn't sticking to the work surface (run a long metal spatula under the dough occasionally just to make sure, and dust the surface with more flour if needed). For softer cookies, roll out slightly thicker. Using cookie cutters, cut out the cookies and transfer to cookie sheets lined with nonstick baking pads, placing the cookies 1 inch apart. Gently knead the scraps together and form into another disk. Wrap and chill for 5 minutes before rolling out again to cut out more cookies.

5. Bake, switching the position of the cookie sheets from top to bottom and back to front halfway through baking, until the edges of the cookies are set and crisp, 10 to 12 minutes. Cool on the sheets for 2 minutes, then transfer to wire racks to cool completely. Decorate with Royal Icing. (The cookies can be made up to 1 week ahead, stored in airtight containers at room temperature.)

Chocolate-Hazelnut Biscotti

Biscotti are great for gift giving because they get better as they age a bit. Dip these into hot coffee or tea. They are also wonderful dipped into sweet wine, so a bottle of port makes a nice auxiliary gift to these cookies. While chocolate chips hold their shape better during baking, chopped bittersweet chocolate has the best flavor, so the choice is yours.

Makes about 28 biscotti

Make Ahead: The biscotti can be baked up to 2 weeks ahead.

½ cup (2 ounces) hazelnuts
2 cups plus 2 tablespoons all-purpose flour
1 teaspoon baking powder
¼ teaspoon salt
8 tablespoons (1 stick) unsalted butter, at room
    temperature
1 cup sugar
Grated zest of 1 large orange
2 large eggs
1 teaspoon vanilla extract
3 ounces (½ cup) mini-chocolate chips or
    coarsely chopped bittersweet chocolate

1. Position the racks in the top third and center racks of the oven and preheat to 350°F. Spread the hazelnuts on a baking sheet. Bake until the skins are cracked, about 10 minutes. Place the hazelnuts in a clean kitchen towel and rub together to remove as much skin as possible. (Some skin will remain on the nuts, but that's fine.) Cool, then coarsely chop. Place the chopped hazelnuts in the freezer to cool quickly. Keep the oven on.

2. In a large bowl, whisk the flour, baking powder, and salt together to combine. In another large bowl, using a handheld electric mixer set at high speed, beat together the butter, sugar, and orange zest until very light in color and texture, about 2 minutes. One at a time, beat in the eggs, then the vanilla.

3. Using a wooden spoon, gradually beat in the flour mixture just until a smooth dough forms. Using a wooden spoon, stir in the chocolate chips and chopped hazelnuts.

4. Divide the dough in half. Using lightly floured hands on a floured work surface, form the dough into two 10 × 2-inch rectangular logs. Place the logs on an ungreased baking sheet at least 2 inches apart. Bake until the logs are set and golden brown, about 30 minutes. Remove from the oven and let cool on the baking sheet for 20 minutes.

5. Using a serrated knife and a sawing motion, carefully cut the logs into diagonal slices about ½ inch wide. Place the slices on ungreased baking sheets. Bake until the undersides of the biscotti are lightly browned, about 8 minutes. Turn the biscotti over. Switch the positions of the baking sheets from top to bottom and front to back. Continue baking until lightly browned on the other side, about 8 minutes longer. Cool completely on the baking sheets. (The biscotti can be baked up to 2 weeks ahead, cooled and tightly covered in an airtight container at room temperature.)

Cinnamon Stars

This recipe was brought from the old country by my great-grandmother Kindle, where they are called *Zimt Sternen*, literally "Cinnamon Stars." Favoring ground almonds over flour gives these cookies an intense flavor and crisp texture. Almond flour used to be difficult to find, but it is now easily available at natural foods stores, many supermarkets, and by mail order. Allow about an hour for the ground almonds in the dough to soak up the moisture from the egg whites before rolling out. These cookies can be stored for weeks, but do not try to make them during rainy or humid weather, as the meringue in the dough will keep it from firming up.

- If you cannot find almond flour, you can grind the nuts at home. There are many ways to grind the nuts. I use a tabletop Zylis-brand rotary grinder that I not only use for nuts, but hard cheese as well. Use the attachment with the finest holes. The almonds can also be ground in a handheld rotary grater. If using a hand grater, use whole blanched almonds.

- As a last resort, you can grind the nuts in a food processor, although you will get the best results from the store-bought almond flour or almonds ground in a rotary grinder. Combine blanched, sliced almonds with 2 tablespoons of the confectioners' sugar from the recipe. (The confectioners' sugar acts as a buffer to keep the almonds from turning into almond butter. In step 2, beat the egg whites, lemon zest, and cinnamon with the remaining confectioners' sugar.) Pulse until the almonds are very finely ground but not oily, about 25 pulses. Use as directed.

- It is best to bake these cookies one sheet at a time in the center of the oven. If you only have one cookie sheet, be sure to let it cool completely before placing the next batch of dough onto the sheet.

Makes about 3 dozen cookies

Make Ahead: The dough must stand at room temperature for about 1 hour before rolling out. The cookies can be baked up to 2 weeks ahead.

2 cups confectioners' sugar
3 large egg whites
Grated zest of 1 lemon
½ teaspoon ground cinnamon
2 cups almond flour (also called almond meal)

1. Position a rack in the center of the oven and preheat to 350°F.

2. Sift the sugar into a medium bowl. Add the egg whites, lemon zest, and cinnamon. Using a handheld electric mixer set at high speed, beat until the mixture is thick and shiny, about 5 minutes. Transfer ¾ cup of the meringue mixture to a small bowl, cover tightly with plastic wrap, and set aside. Add the almond flour to the remaining meringue and stir to make a soft dough. Cover with plastic wrap and set aside until the mixture is stiff enough to roll out, about 1 hour. (The exact amount of time depends on the humidity when the dough is made.)

3. On a lightly floured work surface, roll out the dough to ⅛-inch thickness. Using a 2½-inch star-shaped cookie cutter, cut out the cookies and place about 1 inch apart on a nonstick baking sheet. Spoon about ½ teaspoon of the meringue onto the center of each cookie, and use the back of a spoon to spread to the edges of the cookie.

4. Bake until the glaze is set and the tips of the cookies are barely beginning to brown, about 12 minutes. Cool on the sheets for 1 minute, then transfer to a wire rack to cool completely. Knead the dough scraps and repeat the procedure to bake more cookies. You will

have leftover meringue. (The cookies can be baked up to 2 months ahead, stored in airtight containers at room temperature.)

Lebkuchen

In my family, these cookies epitomized Christmas baking. Great Auntie Gisela would bake her lebkuchen into large oblong cookies and decorate them with paper stamps of St. Nicholas, using the glaze as glue. The stamps were imported and beautifully designed in an Old World attention to detail. Nonetheless, my cousin Lisa and I would complain that our friends didn't have to scrape paper off *their* cookies. Now, as adults, we have great nostalgia for our great aunt's famous lebkuchen, and we got all choked up when we found the same paper stickers.

Full of honey and spices, these bake into aromatic, hard bars that keep forever. My cousin Suzie still has some of Gisela's old St. Nick lebkuchen stashed away with her ornaments and brings them out every year to admire—if not eat. (There are tales of lebkuchen getting better with years of aging, but you have to draw the line somewhere.) If you like softer cookies, place a sliced apple on waxed paper in the closed cookie container for a day or two.

- If you want to make St. Nicholas cookies (which are often made from gingerbead as well), you can find the appropriate cookie cutters and papers in the online shop www.stnicholascenter.org or at European delicatessens during the holiday season.

Makes about 40 cookies

Make Ahead: The dough must be chilled for at least 4 hours or overnight. The cookies can be baked up to 2 months ahead. Age the cookies for at least 3 days before serving.

3 cups all-purpose flour

1 teaspoon baking soda

1 teaspoon ground cinnamon

½ teaspoon freshly grated nutmeg

½ teaspoon ground cloves

½ teaspoon salt

1 cup honey

¾ cup packed light brown sugar

1 large egg

Grated zest of 1 lemon

1 tablespoon fresh lemon juice

1 cup (4 ounces) very finely chopped walnuts

½ cup very finely chopped candied peel

ICING

1 cup confectioners' sugar

1 teaspoon fresh lemon juice

½ teaspoon almond extract

1. Sift the flour, baking soda, cinnamon, nutmeg, cloves, and salt into a medium bowl and set aside. In a large bowl, whisk together the honey, brown sugar, egg, lemon zest and juice, and 2 tablespoons water. Gradually stir in the flour mixture, then the walnuts and candied orange peel. If the dough seems too dry, sprinkle with water, 1 tablespoon at a time, and mix with your hands until moistened. Gather up the dough. Divide the dough into 2 flat disks and wrap in plastic. Refrigerate until firm and chilled, at least 4 hours or overnight. (If chilled overnight, allow the dough to stand at room temperature for 30 minutes before rolling out. The dough will crack if it is too cold.)

2. Position racks in the center and top third of the oven and preheat to 375°F.

3. On a lightly floured work surface, roll out one disk of dough into a ½-inch rectangle, about 12 × 8 inches. Using a sharp knife, trim the dough to a 7½ × 10-inch rectangle, discarding the trimmings. Cut the dough into 20 bars. Place the bars on cookie sheets lined

with nonstick baking pads, about 1 inch apart. Repeat the procedure with the remaining dough. (If you want to make St. Nicholas cookies, roll out the dough, skip trimming the edges, and cut the dough with a St. Nicholas–shaped cookie cutter.)

4. Bake, switching the positions of the cookie sheets from top to bottom and back to front halfway through baking, until the edges of the cookies are beginning to brown, about 15 minutes. Transfer to wire racks and cool completely.

5. To make the icing, sift the confectioners' sugar into a small bowl. Add the lemon juice and almond extract. Stir in 2 tablespoons water to make a thin, spreadable icing. Using a small metal spatula, spread the icing over the tops of the cookies, and let stand until the icing is dry. If making St. Nicholas cookies, attach the paper stamps to the icing and let dry. (The cookies can be baked up to 2 months ahead, stored in airtight containers at room temperature. If possible, age the cookies for at least 3 days before serving.)

Moravian Spice Wafers

The Moravians were a Protestant sect that settled in Pennsylvania and North Carolina. They were well-known for their belief in the spiritual rejuvenation that comes from breaking bread with loved ones. (Their religious services were called "love feasts," and lasted so long that refreshments of coffee and buns had to be served.) These plain-looking but delicately crisp wafers have been baked for generations by families in the Winston-Salem area, and they are one of my absolute favorite cookies for gift giving.

- **Bakers who enjoy the zen of rolling dough should try these cookies, because the dough is rolled quite thin. Even if you don't consider yourself a master "roller-outer," the dough is very easy to work with. And don't let the large yield scare you off. When you get into a rhythm, you'll knock out the entire batch in no time, and you'll have a mountain of cookies that store very well.**

Makes about 10 dozen cookies

Make Ahead: The dough must be chilled for at least 4 hours or overnight. The cookies can be baked up to 2 months ahead.

2¾ cups all-purpose flour
1 teaspoon baking soda
1 teaspoon ground cinnamon
½ teaspoon ground ginger
½ teaspoon ground cloves
½ teaspoon ground allspice
½ teaspoon freshly grated nutmeg
½ teaspoon salt
½ cup vegetable shortening
½ cup packed light brown sugar
1 cup unsulfured molasses
1 tablespoon brandy

1. Sift the flour, baking soda, cinnamon, ginger, cloves, allspice, nutmeg, and salt together into a large bowl. In another large bowl, using a handheld electric mixer set at high speed, beat the shortening and brown sugar together until light in color and texture, about 2 minutes. Beat in the molasses and brandy. Using a wooden spoon, gradually stir in the flour to make a stiff dough. (If the dough seems too dry, sprinkle with additional brandy and mix with your hands until moistened.) Gather up the dough and divide into 4 thick disks. Wrap each disk in plastic. Refrigerate until well chilled, at least 4 hours or overnight.

2. Position a rack in the center of the oven and preheat to 350°F. (These cookies are best

 Old-fashioned Eggnog (page 20)

 Above: Greek Snowballs (page 126), Cinnamon Stars (page 118), Diane's Ultimate Thumbprint Cookies (page 132). *Opposite:* Red and Green Lasagna (page 64)

 Opposite: Pannettone (page 90). *Above:* S'mores Rocky Road (page 102), Macadamia Milk Chocolate Toffee (page 102), Chocolate, Cranberry, and Walnut Fudge (page 100)

Following pages: Crown Roast of Pork with Apple Stuffing and Hard Cider Sauce (page 52), Baby Carrots and Green Beans in Tarragon Butter (page 74)

 Chocolate Bûche de Noël (page 140) with Chocolate-Orange Truffles (page 104)

when baked one sheet at a time in the center of the oven.)

3. Work with one disk of chilled dough at a time. (Unlike many other refrigerated doughs, this dough is easy to roll, even when chilled.) Unwrap the dough, place on a lightly floured work surface, and sprinkle the top of the dough with flour. Roll out the dough $1/16$ inch thick, making sure that the dough isn't sticking to the work surface (run a long metal spatula or knife under the dough occasionally just to make sure, and dust the surface with more flour if needed). Brush any excess flour from the top of the dough with a soft pastry brush. Using a 2-inch round cookie cutter (preferable with a fluted edge), cut out the cookies. Place the cookies $1/2$ inch apart on cookie sheets lined with nonstick baking pads. Place the scraps in a plastic bag.

4. Bake the cookies, one sheet at a time, turning the sheet from front to back halfway during cooking, until the edges are very lightly browned, about 8 minutes. Do not overbake the cookies or they will taste bitter. Transfer to wire racks to cool completely. Repeat the procedure with the remaining dough, placing any scraps in the plastic bag.

5. To bake more cookies, knead all of the scraps from the 4 disks together. (If the dough seems dry, sprinkle with 2 teaspoons of brandy and knead until moistened.) Working with half of the dough at a time, roll out more cookies and bake. Do not roll out the scraps a third time, as they will have picked up too much flour and will be tough. (The cookies can be baked up to 2 months ahead, stored in airtight containers at room temperature.)

Tannenbaum Cookies

Christmas cookies don't come prettier than this. With the help of a pastry tube, round holes are cut out from Christmas tree–shaped butter cookies. The holes are filled with crushed sour ball candies that melt during baking into colorful transparent sheets that resemble glass ornaments. They are a little fussy but worth the effort.

- Don't bother to crush an entire 10-ounce bag of sour balls. Crush only the colors you like (the white ones don't look like much when they are melted). You'll only need about $1/2$ cup crushed candies for the entire batch, so 2 tablespoons each of 4 colors will be plenty.

Makes about 4 dozen cookies

Make Ahead: The dough must chill for 3 hours. The cookies can be baked up to 5 days ahead.

2½ cups all-purpose flour
1 teaspoon baking powder
½ teaspoon salt
8 tablespoons (1 stick) unsalted butter, at room temperature
1 cup sugar
2 large eggs, at room temperature
1 teaspoon vanilla extract
About 5 ounces (half of a 10-ounce bag) sour ball candies
Nonstick cooking oil spray

1. In a large bowl, whisk the flour, baking powder, and salt together. In a medium bowl, using a handheld electric mixer set on high speed, beat the butter until creamy, about 1 minute. Add the sugar and beat until light in color and texture, about 2 minutes. Beat in the eggs, one at a time, then the vanilla. Using a wooden spoon, gradually stir in the flour

mixture. Gather up the dough and divide into two flat disks. Wrap in waxed paper and refrigerate until well chilled, about 3 hours.

2. Unwrap the candies and separate them by color. Place each color in a small plastic bag and crush with a rolling pin or flat meat pounder. Set aside.

3. Position racks in the center and top third of the oven and preheat to 350°F. Line cookie sheets with foil.

4. Working with one disk at a time, on a lightly floured work surface, dust the top of the dough with flour, and roll out to ⅛-inch thickness. Using a 3-inch tree-shaped cookie cutter, cut out the cookies. Place the cookies 1 inch apart on the foil. Using a plain pastry tip with a ½-inch opening, cut out 3 or 4 holes from each cookie. Using a small spoon (an espresso spoon works well), fill the holes with the crushed candies. You will have leftover candies.

5. Bake, switching the position of the cookie sheets from top to bottom and back to front halfway through baking, until the cookies are lightly browned and the candies have melted, 10 to 12 minutes. Cool completely on the cookie sheets. If you wish, let stand 5 minutes, then slide the foil with the cookies off the sheets to cool. (The cookies can be baked up to 5 days ahead, stored in an airtight container at room temperature.)

Linzer Cookies

The Austrian city of Linz is famous for its special lattice-topped tart created from a cinnamon-scented nut dough filled with raspberry jam. This recipe makes beautiful sandwich cookies from the same formula. You will need two round cookie cutters, one 2 inches in diameter, and the other ¾ inch in diameter.

Makes about 3½ dozen

Make Ahead: The cookies can be baked up to 5 days ahead.

1½ cups (6 ounces) walnuts
¾ cup granulated sugar
2 cups all-purpose flour
½ teaspoon baking powder
½ teaspoon ground cinnamon
½ teaspoon salt
¼ teaspoon ground cloves
1 cup (2 sticks) unsalted butter, chilled, cut into small cubes
2 large eggs
About ¾ cup raspberry preserves (not jelly or jam)
Confectioners' sugar, for serving

1. Position racks in the center and top third of the oven and preheat to 350°F.

2. In a food processor fitted with the metal blade, pulse the walnuts with ¼ cup of the granulated sugar until finely ground, about 20 pulses. Transfer to a large bowl. Add the flour, the remaining ½ cup granulated sugar, the baking powder, cinnamon, salt, and cloves and mix well. Add the butter. Using a pastry blender, cut the butter into the flour mixture until it looks like cornmeal. In a small bowl, beat one of the eggs and stir into the flour

mixture to make a dough. Gather up the dough into a ball.

3. Work with half of the dough at a time, keeping the remaining dough covered with plastic wrap. On a lightly floured work surface, roll out the dough ⅛ inch thick. Using a 2-inch round cookie cutter (preferably with a fluted edge), cut out cookies. Transfer to cookie sheets lined with nonstick baking pads, placing the cookies about 1 inch apart. Gather up the scraps and knead together briefly. Roll and cut out more cookies until the first half of the dough is used up. Place 1 teaspoon of the raspberry preserves in the center of each cookie round.

4. On a lightly floured work surface, roll out the reserved dough ⅛ inch thick and cut out 2-inch round cookies. Using a ¾-inch round cookie cutter, cut holes in the center of each round. Place over the preserve-topped cookies with the holes centered over the preserves to make sandwiches, lightly pressing the edges of the two layers together. Gathering up the scraps, roll and cut out more cookies until the dough is used up. In a small bowl, beat the remaining egg. Using a pastry brush, lightly brush the tops of the cookies with the egg.

5. Bake, switching the position of the baking sheets from top to bottom and back to front halfway through baking, until the cookies are golden and the preserves are bubbling in the center, about 15 minutes. Transfer the cookies to wire racks to cool completely. (The cookies can be baked up to 5 days ahead, stored in an airtight container at room temperature.) Just before serving, sift confectioners' sugar over the cookies.

Polish Bowknot Cookies

Every European culture has a fried Christmas cookie, but this recipe for Polish *chrusciki* has become my favorite. The smooth silky dough, rich with sour cream and fragrant with a bit of rum, is a pleasure to roll out, and it fries into flaky, delicate bow knot cookies. To ensure a safe, easy, deep-frying procedure and the best results, take a few minutes to set yourself up properly for deep-frying with a deep pot and a deep-frying thermometer. And, above all, use fresh vegetable oil.

- Deep-frying is an easy cooking technique to master if you have the right tools. Use a large (5-quart) heavy pot that will hold at least 2 to 3 inches of oil. Deep-fried food should swim in the oil so it can cook properly. The cookies will be greasy and heavy if you skimp on the oil and use less than is required.

- The type of oil isn't especially important, as long as it is tasteless. I usually deep-fry with generic vegetable oil or vegetable shortening. Canola oil sometimes leaves a thick, sticky coating on utensils, so I don't recommend it for deep-frying.

- Even if you are frugal, do not save the deep-frying oil for another use. Reheated oil never tastes the same, and subsequent food fried in it won't be as tasty. Just factor the cost of the oil into the recipe and discard it after you have finished.

- Use a deep-frying thermometer to check the temperature of the oil. Let the oil return to 360°F between batches. Do not crowd the cookies in the pot, or they will bring down the temperature of the oil too much.

- Use a very large mesh wire strainer, like the kind that comes with wok sets, to remove the cookies from the hot oil. A slotted spoon collects too much oil.

- **Drain the fried cookies on wire racks set over a jelly-roll pan. This drains the cookies much more effectively than placing them on paper towels. When fried food is placed on paper towels, steam is created and trapped where the food touches the paper. This steam makes the food soggy. The cooled cookies can be placed on crumpled paper towels to remove any excess oil. (Crumpled paper towels get into the nooks and crannies of the cookies better than flat paper.)**

Makes about 7 dozen

Make Ahead: The cookies can be fried up to 3 days ahead.

3 large egg yolks
3 tablespoons granulated sugar
¼ teaspoon salt
1 tablespoon dark rum or brandy
1⅔ cups all-purpose flour
½ cup sour cream, at room temperature
 Vegetable oil, for deep-frying
Confectioners' sugar, for serving

1. In a medium bowl, using a handheld electric mixer set at high speed, beat the egg yolks, granulated sugar, and salt until the yolks are thick and pale yellow, about 2 minutes. Beat in the rum. Using a wooden spoon, a third at a time, alternately beat in the flour and sour cream, beating well after each addition.

2. Transfer the dough to a floured surface and knead until smooth, about 3 minutes. Wrap in plastic and let stand at room temperature for 20 minutes.

3. Work with half of the dough at a time, leaving the other half covered. On a lightly floured work surface, dust the dough with flour, and roll out to ¹⁄₁₆-inch thickness. Using a fluted ravioli cutter or pizza wheel, cut 1-inch-wide strips of dough. Cut the dough crosswise into 3-inch lengths. In the center of each strip, cut a slit about 1½ inches long. Pull one end of the dough through the slit to make a bow-tie shape. Place the cookies on cookie sheets. Repeat with the remaining dough.

4. Pour enough vegetable oil into a 5-quart pot to come halfway up the sides. Heat over high heat to 360°F. In batches, without crowding, fry the cookies until golden brown, turning halfway through frying, about 3 minutes. Using a large wire-mesh skimmer, transfer the cookies to wire racks set over jelly-roll pans to drain and cool. Place the cooled cookies on crumpled paper towels to remove any excess oil. (The cookies can be fried up to 3 days ahead, stored in airtight containers at room temperature.) Just before serving, sift confectioners' sugar over the cookies.

Florentines

My cooking teacher/friend Vicki Caparulo says that these are among her favorite Christmas cookies, and she often makes them for gifts because they look so great but don't take much effort. Crisp and crunchy with a luscious caramel flavor, and drizzled with chocolate, these are sometimes called lace cookies because of the tiny holes that form during baking.

- Be sure to leave plenty of room between the balls of dough so they can spread out without running into one another.

- Remove the cookies from the baking sheet when they are set but still warm. If they cool and can't be removed easily from the baking sheet, return to the oven for a minute or two to warm up.

Makes about 7½ dozen cookies

Make Ahead: The cookies can be baked up to 1 week ahead.

8 tablespoons (1 stick) unsalted butter, cut into pieces
½ cup light corn syrup
½ cup packed light brown sugar
1 cup all-purpose flour
1 cup (5 ounces) finely chopped walnuts
1 teaspoon vanilla extract
3 ounces bittersweet chocolate, finely chopped

1. Position racks in the center and top third of the oven and preheat to 350°F.

2. In a medium saucepan, bring the butter, corn syrup, and brown sugar to a full boil over medium heat, stirring constantly. Remove from the heat and wait until the mixture stops bubbling, then stir in the flour, walnuts, and vanilla and mix well. Transfer the dough to a bowl and cool for 20 minutes.

3. Using ½ teaspoon for each, form the dough into ¾-inch balls and place 2 inches apart on cookie sheets lined with nonstick baking pads. Bake, switching the position of the cookie sheets from top to bottom and front to back halfway through the baking time, until the cookies are golden brown, bubbling, and covered with tiny holes, 8 to 10 minutes.

4. Let the cookies cool on the sheets until firm enough to remove but still warm, 1 to 2 minutes. Using a spatula, transfer the cookies to wire racks to cool completely. When cooled, arrange the cookies in a single layer on paper towels to absorb the excess butter from the cookies.

5. In the top part of a double boiler over hot, not simmering, water, melt the chocolate, stirring occasionally. Transfer to a small plastic bag. Force the chocolate into the corner of the bag. Using scissors, snip a tiny hole from the corner. Drizzle the melted chocolate over the tops of the cookies. Let stand until the chocolate is firm. If the kitchen is warm, transfer the cookies to baking sheets and chill in the refrigerator until the chocolate sets. (The cookies can be baked up to 1 week ahead, stored in airtight containers at room temperature.)

Florentine Sandwich Cookies: These cookies are doubly rich and very impressive. Increase the chocolate to 6 ounces. Using a small icing spatula or a dinner knife, spread the flat back of a cookie with a thin layer of melted chocolate, then sandwich with a second cookie. Makes about 4 dozen cookies.

Greek Snowballs
Kourabiedes

Every Greek family has a recipe for these melt-in-your-mouth cookies. Glancing at the ingredients, you can see that *kourabiedes* are closely related to Nutty Angel Fingers (page 129), but the Greek cookies are rolled into balls, not logs, and scented with brandy. As an alternative, substitute anise-flavored ouzo or sambuca for the brandy. Many bakers stud each cookie with a whole clove, but I prefer them plain.

Makes about 30 cookies

Make Ahead: The cookies can be baked up to 1 week ahead.

1½ cups all-purpose flour
1 teaspoon baking powder
⅛ teaspoon salt
1 cup (2 sticks) unsalted butter, at room temperature
⅓ cup confectioners' sugar, plus an additional ½ cup for rolling the cookies, and more for rolling just before serving
1 large egg yolk
1 tablespoon brandy or anise liqueur
1 cup (5 ounces) finely chopped walnuts or almonds
About 30 whole cloves (optional)

1. Position racks in the center and top third of the oven and preheat to 350°F.

2. In a large bowl, whisk the flour, baking powder, and salt together. In another large bowl, using a handheld electric mixer set at high speed, beat the butter until light in color and texture, about 2 minutes. Beat in the ⅓ cup confectioners' sugar, then the egg yolk and brandy, just until combined. Using a wooden spoon, stir in the flour mixture, then the walnuts, mixing just until smooth.

3. Using a level tablespoon for each, roll the dough into 1-inch balls. Place the balls 1 inch apart on a nonstick cookie sheet. Stud each cookie in the center with a whole clove, if using.

4. Bake, switching the position of the cookie sheets from top to bottom and front to back halfway through baking, until the cookies are firm to the touch and lightly browned around the edges, about 20 minutes. Let the cookies cool on the sheets for 5 minutes. Roll the cookies in the remaining ½ cup confectioners' sugar, then transfer to wire racks to cool completely. Before serving, roll the cookies again in more confectioners' sugar to freshen their coating. (The cookies can be baked up to 1 week ahead, stored in an airtight container at room temperature.)

Mocha Nut Crinkles

Deeply flavored with chocolate and espresso, these drop cookies are a mocha lover's dream. Kids love to make them because even though they're easy to make, there's a lot of fun hands-on work involved. Instant espresso coffee powder, found at Italian delicatessens and many supermarkets, gives the strongest coffee flavor, although you can substitute ½ teaspoon coffee extract or regular instant coffee if you wish.

Makes 4 dozen cookies

Make Ahead: The dough must be chilled for at least 2 hours. The cookies can be baked up to 1 week ahead.

2 ounces unsweetened chocolate, finely chopped
5 tablespoons milk
1½ teaspoons instant espresso powder
2 cups all-purpose flour
2 teaspoons baking powder

½ teaspoon salt

1⅔ cups granulated sugar

½ cup vegetable shortening

2 large eggs, at room temperature

2 teaspoons vanilla extract

½ cup (2 ounces) coarsely chopped walnuts

¾ cup confectioners' sugar, for rolling

1. In the top part of a double boiler set over barely simmering water, melt the chocolate, stirring occasionally. Remove from the water and cool the chocolate until tepid.

2. In a glass measuring cup, heat 1 tablespoon of the milk in a microwave on High until boiling. Add the espresso powder and stir to dissolve. Stir in the remaining ¼ cup milk.

3. In a large bowl, whisk the flour, baking powder, and salt together. In another large bowl, using a handheld electric mixer set at high speed, beat together the granulated sugar and shortening until well combined. Beat in the eggs, one at a time, then the vanilla. Reduce the mixer speed to low. Mix in the melted chocolate. A third at a time, alternately beat in the flour and milk mixtures. Stir in the walnuts. Cover with plastic wrap and refrigerate until chilled and firm, at least 2 hours.

4. Position racks in the center and top third of the oven and preheat to 350°F. Place the confectioners' sugar in a small bowl. Using 1 tablespoon for each, roll the dough into 1-inch balls. Roll the balls in the confectioners' sugar to coat, then place 2 inches apart on baking sheets lined with nonstick baking pads.

5. Bake, switching the position of the baking sheets from top to bottom and back to front halfway through baking, until the cookies are set with crisp edges, about 15 minutes. Cool on the baking sheets for 5 minutes, then transfer to wire racks to cool completely. (The cookies can be baked up to 1 week ahead, stored in airtight containers at room temperature.)

Chewy Molasses Drops

Mary-Lynn Mondich has been my friend for years, and her exceptional skills as a cookie baker led her to establish American Vintage, a bakery that specializes in her family's secret-recipe wine biscotti. So when Mary-Lynn shared this recipe with me many Christmases ago, I paid attention. Now a holiday baking season doesn't pass that I don't make these chewy, moist, spicy, I-could-eat-the-whole-batch cookies.

Makes about 3 dozen

Make Ahead: The dough must be chilled for at least 1 hour. The cookies can be baked up to 1 week ahead.

6 tablespoons (¾ stick) unsalted butter

6 tablespoons vegetable shortening

1⅓ cups sugar

¼ cup unsulfured molasses

1 large egg, at room temperature

2 cups all-purpose flour

2 teaspoons baking soda

1 teaspoon ground cinnamon

½ teaspoon ground ginger

½ teaspoon salt

¼ teaspoon ground cloves

1. In a medium saucepan, melt the butter and shortening together over medium heat. Transfer to a large bowl and let cool until tepid. (Place the saucepan in a large bowl of ice water to speed up the process if you wish.)

2. Whisk in 1 cup of the sugar, the molasses, and egg. In another large bowl, sift the flour, baking soda, cinnamon, ginger, salt, and cloves together. Using a wooden spoon, gradually stir the flour mixture into the wet ingredients. Cover tightly with plastic wrap and refrigerate until well chilled, at least 1 hour.

3. Position racks in the center and top third of the oven and preheat to 350°F. Place the remaining ⅓ cup sugar in a small bowl. Using 1 tablespoon of dough for each, roll into 1-inch balls. Roll in the sugar to coat, then place 2 inches apart on baking sheets lined with nonstick baking pads.

4. Bake, switching the position of the baking sheets from top to bottom and back to front halfway through baking, until the cookies are evenly browned and the edges are set, about 12 minutes. Cool briefly on the sheets, then transfer to wire racks to cool completely. (The cookies can be baked up to 1 week ahead, stored in an airtight container at room temperature.)

Peppernuts

Just about every country in northern Europe has some version of these spicy drops in its Christmas cookie culture. The cookies are often allowed to dry out until they are rock hard. In my recipe, they aren't exactly soft, but they aren't dangerous to your teeth either. They are properly spicy with pepper, cinnamon, cloves, and anise.

Makes about 4 dozen cookies

Make Ahead: The cookies can be baked up to 2 months ahead. Age the cookies for 2 days before serving.

1 cup honey
4 tablespoons (½ stick) unsalted butter, cut into
    pieces
3 large eggs
4 cups all-purpose flour
½ cup granulated sugar
1½ teaspoons ground cinnamon
1 teaspoon anise seed, crushed in a mortar or
    under a heavy pot
1 teaspoon freshly grated nutmeg
1 teaspoon freshly ground black pepper
1 teaspoon baking powder
½ teaspoon baking soda
½ teaspoon ground cloves
½ teaspoon salt
½ cup finely chopped candied citron or candied
    lemon or orange peel
¼ cup dark rum or brandy

GLAZE
1½ cups confectioners' sugar, sifted
About 4 tablespoons water

1. Position racks in the center and top third of the oven and preheat to 350°F.

2. In a medium saucepan, bring the honey and butter to a boil over medium heat, stirring to melt the butter. Transfer to a large bowl and cool to room temperature. (Place the saucepan in a large bowl of ice water to speed up the process if you wish.) Add the eggs and mix well.

3. In a large bowl, sift the flour, granulated sugar, cinnamon, anise, nutmeg, pepper, baking powder, baking soda, cloves, and salt together. In three additions, stir the dry ingredients into the honey mixture, adding the candied citron with the last addition of flour. Stir in the rum to make a stiff dough.

4. Using a level tablespoon for each, roll the dough into 1-inch balls. Place the balls about 1 inch apart on cookie sheets lined with nonstick baking pads.

5. Bake, switching the position of the cookie sheets from top to bottom and back to front halfway through baking, until the cookies are lightly browned and feel firm when pressed with a finger, about 20 minutes. Cool for 5 minutes on the cookie sheets.

6. To make the icing, mix together the confectioners' sugar with enough water in a small bowl until the glaze is the thickness of heavy cream. One at a time, holding the cookies upside down, dip the tops of the cookies into the glaze. Let the excess glaze drip off, then place the cookies right side up on wire racks to cool completely. (The cookies can be stored for up to 2 weeks in airtight containers at room temperature.) If possible, age the cookies for 2 days before serving.

Pine Nut Amaretti

Amaretti are crisp Italian almond macaroons that can be bought at many specialty food shops. In this homemade version from Vicki Caparulo, the lily has been gilded by pressing pine nuts into the cookies before baking. These cookies are almost ridiculously easy to make, and they are different from the others in this chapter. First they are slowly baked in a low oven to create their special texture. Then the cookies must dry at room temperature on their baking sheet for at least 4 hours before baking. When you have a whole day of cookie baking ahead of you, you might not have an extra cookie sheet handy, so let them stand on a sheet of parchment paper or aluminum foil and slip the paper onto the sheet when ready to bake.

Makes about 2 dozen cookies

Make Ahead: The cookies must stand at room temperature for 4 hours before baking. The cookies can be baked up to 3 weeks ahead.

One 7-ounce tube almond paste (see Note)
2 large egg whites
½ cup sugar
½ cup (2 ounces) pine nuts, coarsely chopped

1. Grate the almond paste on the large holes of a box grater (or crumble as finely as possible with your fingertips) into a medium bowl. Add the egg whites. Using a handheld electric mixer at low speed, beat until the mixture is well combined. Add the sugar, increase the speed to medium-high, and beat until smooth.

2. Using a rounded teaspoon for each, roll the dough into ¾-inch balls. Place the pine nuts in a small bowl. One at a time, press one side of the ball into the nuts, then place the balls 1 inch apart on a cookie sheet lined with a nonstick baking pad. Set aside, uncovered, at room temperature for 4 hours.

3. Position a rack in the center of the oven and preheat to 300°F. Bake until the cookies are deep golden brown and the pine nuts are lightly toasted, about 40 minutes. Cool on the cookie sheet for 2 minutes, then transfer to wire racks to cool completely. (The cookies can be baked up to 3 weeks ahead, stored in an airtight container at room temperature.)

Note: Almond paste, made from ground almonds and sugar, is available at specialty food shops and many supermarkets. Do not confuse it with marzipan, which is prepared with ground almonds and syrup, and has a softer consistency and sweeter flavor.

Nutty Angel Fingers

My family has always called these "angel fingers," although I've seen similar recipes called "Mexican Wedding Cakes" and "Russian Tea Cakes." The latter are rolled into balls, but the Rodgerses have always rolled them into finger-shaped logs. These cookies are perfect to make with kids—they couldn't be easier and everyone loves them. My brother Doug, who isn't much of a baker at other times of the year, bakes these by the bushel every Christmas, to an appreciative audience of coworkers and family members.

Make Ahead: The cookies can be baked up to
1 week ahead.

1 cup (2 sticks) unsalted butter, at room
    temperature
6 tablespoons confectioners' sugar, plus about
    1 cup for coating the cookies
2 teaspoons vanilla extract
2 cups all-purpose flour
2 cups (8 ounces) finely chopped pecans or
    walnuts

1. Position racks in the top and bottom
thirds of the oven and preheat to 350°F.

2. In a large bowl, using a handheld electric
mixer set on medium-high speed, beat the
butter with 6 tablespoons confectioners' sugar
until light in texture and color, about 2
minutes. Mix in the vanilla. Using a wooden
spoon, work in the flour, then the chopped
nuts, to make a crumbly dough. Gather up the
dough and press it together.

3. Using 1 tablespoon of dough for each
cookie, squeeze the dough in your fist to make
a rough 2½-inch log. Roll the log between your
palms to smooth it. Place the logs 1 inch apart
on cookie sheets lined with nonstick baking
pads. (These cookies don't spread during
baking, but don't put them too close together
or they won't brown as nicely.)

4. Bake, switching the position of the cookie
sheets from top to bottom and back to front
halfway through baking, until lightly browned,
about 20 minutes. Don't underbake the cookies
or they will crumble. Place ½ cup of the
remaining confectioners' sugar into a small
bowl. Let the cookies stand on the cookie sheets
for 5 minutes, then roll the warm cookies in
the sugar. Transfer to wire racks to cool
completely. Before serving, roll the cookies
again in the remaining ½ cup confectioners'

sugar to freshen their coating. (The cookies can
be baked up to 1 week ahead, stored in an
airtight container at room temperature.)

Spritz Butter Cookies

**In the introduction to this chapter, I said that I
wouldn't include cookies that called for special
equipment. These beautiful and buttery shaped
cookies are the exception. Because you get a
variety of shapes for your money and the press
can be used throughout the year to decorate
appetizers and make shapes out of softened
butter, I consider a cookie press a good
investment and not an esoteric piece of kitchen
equipment. To decorate these cookies, use high-
quality dried or candied fruit.**

Makes about 5 dozen cookies

Make Ahead: The cookies can be baked up to
1 week ahead.

1 cup (2 sticks) unsalted butter, at room
    temperature
¾ cup sugar
1 large egg
1 teaspoon vanilla extract
½ teaspoon almond extract (optional)
2 cups all-purpose flour
½ teaspoon baking powder
¼ teaspoon salt
About 60 pieces candied cherry halves or glacé
    apricots, cut into ½-inch cubes, for decoration

1. Position racks in the center and top third
of the oven and preheat to 400°F.

2. In a large bowl, using a handheld electric
mixer set at high speed, beat the butter and
sugar together until light in color and texture,
about 2 minutes. Beat in the egg, vanilla, and
almond extract, if using. Sift the flour, baking

powder, and salt. Using a wooden spoon, add the flour mixture and mix to make a soft dough.

3. In batches, transfer the dough to the baking press and fit with the desired plate. Holding the press about ½ inch above a nonstick baking sheet, press out cookies, placing them about 1 inch apart. Place a cherry half in the center of each cookie.

4. Bake, switching the position of the cookie sheets from top to bottom and front to back halfway through baking, until the edges of the cookies are lightly browned, 8 to 10 minutes. Transfer to wire racks to cool completely. (The cookies can be baked up to 1 week ahead, stored in airtight containers at room temperature.)

Gingered Shortbread

Shortbread is the ultimate sugar cookie, crisp yet tender, and bursting with buttery flavor. It's a good cookie to make when the cookie monster in you growls but you don't have any eggs in the house. Gluten-free rice flour (cornstarch can be substituted) is used with the all-purpose flour to give it a delicate crumb.

- The shortbread's ancestor is the bannock, a round oatmeal cake that symbolizes the sun and was a part of pagan Yule celebrations. While some bakers roll and cut out shortbread dough into shapes, I prefer to mark the round of dough into the traditional "petticoat tail" wedges with the tines of a fork. If you make shortbread around New Year's and you are superstitious, you should know that it is considered unlucky to cut shortbread with a knife—you should break it along the perforations.

Makes 12 large cookies

Make Ahead: The shortbread can be baked up to 5 days ahead.

1 cup (2 sticks) unsalted butter, at room temperature
½ cup sugar
1⅔ cups all-purpose flour
⅓ cup white rice flour (available at natural foods stores, Asian grocers, and many supermarkets) or cornstarch
1 teaspoon ground ginger
½ cup (about 2 ounces) finely chopped crystallized ginger

1. Position a rack in the center of the oven and preheat to 350°F. Lightly butter a 9½-inch springform pan.

2. In a large bowl, using a handheld electric mixer set at high speed, beat the butter until creamy, about 1 minute. Add the sugar and beat until the mixture is light in color and texture, about 2 minutes. Using a wooden spoon, stir in the all-purpose flour, rice flour, and ground ginger to make a soft dough. Stir in the crystallized ginger. Press the dough evenly into the prepared pan. Using the tines of a fork, press around the perimeter of the dough. Prick the dough, reaching down to the bottom of the pan, into 12 wedges.

3. Bake until lightly browned, about 30 minutes. Cool completely in the pan, then remove the sides of the pan. Break the shortbread into wedges following the perforations in the dough. (The shortbread can be baked up to 5 days ahead, stored in airtight containers at room temperature.)

Diane's Ultimate Thumbprint Cookies

Every holiday season my friend Diane Kniss and I make mountains of these delectable cookies— small mounds of walnut-coated cookies filled with glistening preserves. They are related to thumbprint cookies but are smaller and more delicate. Diane's original recipe card calls them "Sonja Henies," after the famous and elegant ice skating star of the thirties and forties. The first time you make them, you may think they are somewhat time-consuming, but I've included some tips to help you along. And when you taste them, you won't mind the extra effort.

Makes about 3½ dozen cookies

Make Ahead: The cookies can be baked up to 1 week ahead.

1 cup (2 sticks) unsalted butter, at room
    temperature
½ cup packed light or dark brown sugar
2 large eggs, separated
½ teaspoon vanilla extract
2 cups all-purpose flour
1½ cups (6 ounces) walnuts
¼ cup granulated sugar
Pinch of salt
⅔ cup fruit preserves, such as raspberry or
    apricot (see Note)

1. Position racks in the top and bottom thirds of the oven and preheat to 350°F.

2. In a large bowl, using a handheld electric mixer set on medium-high speed, beat the butter until creamy, about 30 seconds. Add the brown sugar and beat until light in color and texture, about 2 minutes. Beat in the egg yolks, then the vanilla. Using a wooden spoon, gradually mix in the flour to make a soft dough. Using a rounded teaspoon for each, roll the dough into 1-inch balls. Place the balls on baking sheets lined with nonstick baking pads. Let stand in a cool place (near an open window or in the refrigerator) until slightly chilled and firm, about 10 minutes. (Don't skip this step— the dough must be slightly chilled in order to make the holes in the dough that hold the filling.)

3. In a food processor fitted with the metal blade, pulse the walnuts and granulated sugar together until the walnuts are finely chopped. Set aside.

4. In a small bowl, beat the egg whites with the salt until foamy. Pour about a third of the chopped walnut mixture into a shallow bowl. Dip each ball of dough in the egg whites, then roll in the walnut mixture to coat, and place 1 inch apart on the baking sheets. Holding a ball of dough on the sheet with one hand, use the tip of your little finger of the other hand to press a ¼-inch-wide hole into the center, about ¼ inch deep. (If you have long fingernails, use the inverted tip of a ¼-inch-wide wooden spoon handle or a dowel.) If the ball cracks, just press the crack together to smooth. Repeat with the other balls of dough, gradually adding more of the walnut mixture to the shallow bowl as needed. (It is important use the walnut mixture in batches, as it will collect moisture from the egg whites, and if used all at once, it will get so wet that it won't adhere properly. Also, you probably will have leftover chopped walnuts— but that's better than running out of them.)

5. Bake, switching the position of the baking sheets from top to bottom and front to back halfway through baking, until the cookies feel set but not completely baked, about 10 minutes. Meanwhile, place the preserves in a small self-sealing plastic bag and squeeze the preserves into one corner of the bag. Using scissors, snip off the corner of the bag to make

an opening about ¼ inch wide. When the cookies are set, pipe the preserves from the bag into the hole in each cookie. Return the cookies to the oven, switching the position of the baking sheets from top to bottom and front to back. Bake until the cookies are lightly browned, 5 to 8 more minutes. Cool on the baking sheets for 2 minutes. Transfer to wire racks to cool completely. (The cookies can be baked up to 1 week ahead, stored in airtight containers at room temperature.)

Note: Be sure to use preserves—jellies and jams are too thin and will melt into the cookies. If your preserves are especially chunky, chop up the fruit pieces with a knife before using, otherwise the fruit can clog the hole in the bag as you fill the cookies.

Brandied Fruitcake Drops

These moist and chewy cookies have been gobbled up by many an unsuspecting professed fruitcake hater. The recipe is easily doubled.

Makes 3 dozen

Make Ahead: The cookies can be baked up to 1 week ahead.

8 tablespoons (1 stick) unsalted butter, at room temperature
1 cup packed light brown sugar
1 large egg
½ cup buttermilk
¼ cup brandy or bourbon
1 teaspoon vanilla extract
2 cups all-purpose flour
½ teaspoon baking soda

¼ teaspoon salt
1 cup chopped candied fruit for fruitcakes (a combination of candied orange and lemon peels, candied cherries, pineapple, and citron) or any dried or candied fruit you prefer
¾ cup coarsely chopped walnuts
36 walnut halves, for decoration

1. Position racks in the center and top third of the oven and preheat to 350°F.

2. In a large bowl, using a handheld electric mixer set at high speed, beat the butter and brown sugar together until light in color, about 2 minutes. Beat in the egg. Add the buttermilk, brandy, and vanilla, and beat until the mixture is fluffy, about 1 minute. Sift together the flour, baking soda, and salt. Using a wooden spoon, add the flour mixture and mix to make a soft dough. Stir in the chopped candied fruit and chopped walnuts.

3. Using about 1 tablespoon for each cookie, drop the dough about 1 inch apart onto nonstick cookie sheets. Press a walnut half into the center of each cookie. Bake, switching the position of the cookie sheets from top to bottom and front to back halfway through the baking time, until the edges of the cookies are lightly browned, about 20 minutes. Transfer the cookies to a wire rack and cool completely. (The cookies can be baked up to 1 week ahead, stored in airtight containers at room temperature.)

The Best Chocolate-Pecan Brownies

Brownies are just as appropriate for a Fourth of July celebration as a Christmas cookie platter. Yet I always find reasons to include them in the annual holiday selection. Everyone loves them, they are a great "bang for your buck" cookie (you get a lot of cookies with little work), and they are easy to pack up and send. And most important, this recipe is absolutely the best. Two kinds of chocolate give it a complex flavor, but one that kids won't turn their noses up at. A dose of light corn syrup ensures that they will come out moist and chewy—just be sure not to overbake them.

Makes 24 brownies

Make Ahead: The brownies can be baked up to 5 days ahead.

1 cup (2 sticks) unsalted butter, cut into pieces
6 ounces bittersweet chocolate, finely chopped
4 ounces unsweetened chocolate, finely chopped
2 cups packed light brown sugar
4 large eggs, at room temperature
¼ cup light corn syrup
2 teaspoons vanilla extract
2½ cups all-purpose flour
½ teaspoon baking soda
½ teaspoon salt
2 cups (8 ounces) coarsely chopped pecans

1. Position a rack in the center of the oven and preheat to 350°F. Fold a 20-inch-long piece of foil lengthwise to fit over the bottom of a 13 × 9-inch square baking pan, letting the ends of the foil hang over the sides as handles. Lightly butter the foil and sides of the pan, dust with flour, and tap out the excess.

2. In a large saucepan, melt the butter over medium heat. Remove the pan from the heat and add the bittersweet and unsweetened chocolates. Let stand until the chocolate softens, about 3 minutes. Whisk until smooth. Whisk in the brown sugar. One at a time, whisk in the eggs, then the corn syrup and vanilla.

3. In a large bowl, sift the flour, baking soda, and salt together. Now sift them over the chocolate mixture. Using a rubber spatula, fold together until combined. The batter will be thick. Stir in the pecans.

4. Spread the batter evenly into the prepared baking pan. Bake until a toothpick inserted in the center comes out with a moist crumb, 35 to 40 minutes. Do not overbake. Cool completely in the pan on a wire rack. Lift up on the handles to remove the brownies. Cut into bars. (The brownies can be baked up to 5 days ahead, wrapped individually in plastic, and stored at room temperature.)

Cranberry Oat Bars

Sturdy, hearty, and fruit filled, these bars are great for mailing. I cut them into fairly large bars that are good for a lunchbox or an afternoon pick-me-up, but they can be cut into daintier pieces for a Christmas cookie platter. The foil lining allows the baker to lift out the baked cookie in one big piece before cutting into bars—otherwise the first bar will get messed up as you try to dig it out.

Makes 16 bars

Make Ahead: The bars can be made up to 5 days ahead.

CRANBERRY FILLING

2 cups fresh or frozen cranberries
¾ cup granulated sugar
Grated zest of 1 orange

1½ cups all-purpose flour

1½ cups old-fashioned rolled oats (not quick-cooking or instant)

1 cup packed light brown sugar

1 teaspoon baking powder

½ teaspoon salt

12 tablespoons (1½ sticks) unsalted butter, cut into small cubes

1. Position a rack in the center of the oven and preheat to 350°F. Lightly butter an 8-inch square baking pan. Line the pan with a double thickness of aluminum foil so that the foil extends beyond the two opposite ends of the pan. Fold the overhang down to form handles. Lightly butter the foil.

2. To make the filling, bring the cranberries, granulated sugar, and orange zest to a boil in a medium saucepan, stirring to dissolve the sugar. Reduce the heat to medium and cook, stirring often, until thick and reduced to 1 cup, about 5 minutes. Transfer to a bowl and cool completely.

Auntie Gisela's Cookies

The culinary highlight of the Christmas season in my family was Auntie Gisela's enormous cookie platter, wrapped in colored cellophane and delivered to my grandmother's house. Auntie Gisela had brought many of the recipes over with her from Liechtenstein in the early 1920s. Some of the cookies were Old World favorites. Spicy lebkuchen were cut into shapes, then topped with icing and stuck with paper stamps of Saint Nicholas. Crisp cinnamon stars were shiny with meringue glaze. Linz sandwich cookies had glistening raspberry preserves peeking through a small hole in the center of the top cookie. As an added attraction, she tucked in slices of her deluxe fruitcake and yeasty gugelhopf coffee cake.

It was food like this that got me interested in becoming a food professional. When I asked Mom how Auntie Gisela made these wonderful desserts, she said, "Ask her. She'd love to show you." And she did. After I moved to New York from California, Auntie Gisela would occasionally send me a recipe or two in her Christmas card, hinting that one of these days I'd get the entire collection of her cookbooks and notebooks. And after she passed away, my cousin Suzie presented me with this treasure.

One day I found an example of why Auntie Gisela was such a special baker: She was always trying to improve her skills. On a page of her stationery with the heading "Christmas 1975," she meticulously listed the cookies she baked, the yield of the recipe, how to improve them the next time (use different cutters and frosting), and what cookies to bake *next* year so as not to serve too many of the same kinds two years in a row! And people ask me where I get my sense of organization at the holidays . . .

3. In a medium bowl, combine the flour, oats, brown sugar, baking powder, and salt. Add the butter. Using your fingertips, work the butter into the flour mixture until well combined and crumbly. Press half of the mixture firmly and evenly into the bottom of the prepared pan, and spread the cranberry filling on top. Sprinkle the remaining flour mixture over the filling, and gently press into an even layer.

4. Bake until the top is evenly browned, about 40 minutes. Cool completely on a wire rack.

5. Run a knife around the inside edges of the pan to release the bars from the sides. Lift up on the foil handles to remove the bars from the pan. Using a large, sharp knife, cut into 16 bars. (The bars can be baked up to 5 days ahead, individually wrapped in plastic, and stored at room temperature.)

Royal Icing

This icing hardens into shiny white lines, and is the one to use for piping decorations onto gingerbread people or other cookies. Traditional royal icing calls for raw egg whites, but as dried egg white powder is available at most supermarkets these days, I prefer it to avoid any consternation about uncooked whites.

- **Royal icing can also be used to decorate cookies to give them a smooth, shiny surface. Just thin the prepared icing with additional water until it is spreadable. Allow at least 1 hour for the icing to dry.**

- **When using a pastry bag, practice your decorating skills before you ice the cookies. Do a few trial runs to get the feel of the icing**

and the bag, piping the icing onto aluminum foil or waxed paper. If it hasn't crusted over, use a metal spatula to scrape the test icing back into the batch.

- **Dried egg white powder is available at baking supply and crafts stores and most supermarkets. Meringue powder, which is dehydrated egg whites with sugar already added, also makes excellent royal icing; just follow the directions on the package. The plain unsweetened dried egg whites are more versatile, though, as they can be used in savory dishes, too.**

Makes about 2 cups, enough for about 4 dozen cookies

Make Ahead: The icing can be made up to 2 days ahead.

1 pound (4½ cups) confectioners' sugar
2 tablespoons dried egg white powder

1. In a medium bowl, using a handheld electric mixer set at low speed, beat the confectioners' sugar, egg white powder, and 6 tablespoons water until combined. Increase the speed to high and beat, scraping down the sides of the bowl often, until very stiff, shiny, and thick enough to pipe, 3 to 5 minutes. (The icing can be made up to 2 days ahead, stored in an airtight container with a moist paper towel pressed directly on the icing surface, and refrigerated.)

2. To pipe line decorations, use a pastry bag fitted with a small writing tip about ⅛ inch wide, such as Ateco Number 7. It may be too difficult to squeeze the icing out of smaller tips. If necessary, thin the icing with a little warm water. To fill the pastry bag, first fit it with the tube. Fold the top of the bag back to form a cuff, and hold it in one hand. Using a rubber

spatula, scoop the icing into the bag. Unfold the cuff and twist the top of the bag closed. Squeeze the icing down to fill the tube. Always practice on a sheet of waxed paper or aluminum foil to check the flow and consistency of the icing.

Traditional Royal Icing: Substitute 3 large egg whites for the egg white powder and water.

It Wouldn't Be the Holidays Without . . . Cookies

The word *cookie* comes from the Dutch *koeptje*, which means "little cake." The Dutch brought their recipes to America when they settled in today's New York City, but the tradition of serving sweet little cakes at Christmas was already centuries old.

The first cookies were probably savory crackers. (To this day, sweet cookies are called "biscuits" in Britain.) Crisp baked cakes kept for a long time and were easy to transport on journeys, so they had a practical function. The Muslim invasion of Spain in the 700s, and later the Crusades, exposed Europe to Arabic foods. The Arabs loved sugar and spices, and European cooks soon incorporated both into their crackers, along with butter and other ingredients that lightened and tenderized the mix. However, the Arabs had a corner on the sugar market (they kept the refining process a secret for many centuries), so most cookies were sweetened with honey or dried fruits.

But it was in northern Europe, and Germany in particular, that the cookie reached its apotheosis. Nuremberg, a shipping center for the important spice trade, and with access to unlimited amounts of honey from the nearby forest, perfected gingerbread. Fairs were important social and economic events in medieval Nuremberg (a custom that lives on in Germany with the annual Oktoberfest and Christmas market festivals). Gingerbread cookies, cut into shapes of people, hearts, and other everyday images, and occasionally crafted into small houses, were a specialty of these fairs.

The practice of baking gingerbread into people-shaped cookies probably evolved from the pagan human sacrifice ceremonies that occurred around the winter solstice. Of course, human sacrifice was discouraged by the Church Fathers, so cookie-shaped people that could be dispatched with a bite replaced the real thing. The German fairy tale "Hansel and Gretel," with its gingerbread house, a witch that turns children into cookies, and an oven that turns out to be her sacrificial pyre, is a gold mine for sociologists, historians, and armchair psychiatrists alike.

Decorating Icing

When you want a thin, slick opaque surface on your cookies that can be sprinkled with colored sugar or other goodies, make this simple icing. For a thicker surface, use the minimum amount of milk. For a translucent look, use a bit more milk to make a thinner icing. The amount of milk needed to reach your desired thickness will vary depending on the humidity.

Makes about ¾ cup, enough for about 3 dozen cookies

2 cups confectioners' sugar
3 to 4 tablespoons milk, as needed
Food coloring, as needed (optional)

Sift the confectioners' sugar through a wire sieve into a medium bowl. Using a rubber spatula, blend enough milk into the sugar to reach the desired consistency. If desired, divide the icing into individual bowls or paper cups and tint with food coloring. When not using, cover each bowl tightly with plastic wrap or press a moist paper towel directly on the icing surface to prevent a crust from forming.

Desserts

So many Christmas desserts have entered the collective consciousness that it's not an easy task to choose which ones to make. Fruitcake, mincemeat pie, gingerbread, plum pudding . . . each one has its place of honor in the holiday dessert hall of fame. Every country with a substantial Christian population has its own special sweets, so the list is almost endless.

Yet there are common themes that run from dessert to dessert and country to country. Many of the desserts, like plum pudding and fruitcake, are doused with liquor and made well ahead of serving to age and mellow. Aromatic spices that warm the palate, such as ginger, cinnamon, cloves, nutmeg, and allspice, are used. Cakes and puddings are made in special shapes to show that they are extraordinary desserts, not just for everyday consumption.

Many Christmas desserts use *candied fruits*. Supermarket candied fruits are not very good—most of their natural flavor and color has been removed and artificially replaced. Specialty food stores and some candy stores, as well as online sources, will carry high-quality candied fruits. Instead of candied orange peels, I often chop glacé orange slices.

Dried fruits also play a big role in many of these desserts. Sulfur dioxide, an ingredient that some people choose to avoid, is often used to process the fruits. Sulfured dried fruits do have a brighter color, but that isn't always necessary. Unsulfured fruits can be found at natural foods stores. I prefer large, plump *Thompson raisins* for my holiday baking, but regular raisins will do. *Golden raisins* add color variety, but you can always substitute more dark raisins if you prefer. *Currants* are small raisins. *Dried apricots and pineapple* are common, but use apricots that aren't too sour and pineapple that isn't too sweet. (Glacé apricots are a great alternative to dried apricots.) When I see an old recipe that calls for candied cherries, I often substitute tasty *dried cherries*, and *dried cranberries* are a delicious addition to holiday baked goods.

Chocolate Bûche de Noël

Makes 8 to 12 servings

Make Ahead: The bûche de Noël can be baked up to 1 day ahead. The chocolate leaves can be made up to 3 days ahead.

CHOCOLATE ROLL

6 large eggs, separated, at room temperature

¼ teaspoon cream of tartar

¾ cup granulated sugar

⅓ cup Dutch-process cocoa powder, such as Droste, sifted, plus 2 tablespoons for finishing the cake

¼ teaspoon salt

FILLING

1 teaspoon unflavored gelatin

2 tablespoons boiling water

1½ cups heavy cream

2 tablespoons confectioners' sugar

Grated zest of ½ orange

½ teaspoon vanilla extract

GANACHE

½ cup heavy cream

6 ounces bittersweet chocolate, finely chopped

2 tablespoons light corn syrup

1 tablespoon Grand Marnier or other orange-flavored liqueur or frozen orange juice concentrate, thawed

Sprigs of fresh juniper or pine, for garnish

Chocolate Leaves (recipe follows, optional)

10 to 12 Chocolate-Orange Truffles (page 104) or store-bought truffles

2 tablespoons Dutch-process cocoa powder, such as Droste, for garnish

1. To make the chocolate roll, position a rack in the center of the oven and preheat to 350°F. Lightly butter a 15½ × 10½ × 1-inch jelly-roll pan. Lightly butter the pan and line with waxed paper.

2. In a greasefree large bowl, using a handheld mixer at low speed, beat the egg whites until foamy. Add the cream of tartar and increase the speed to high. Beat until soft peaks form. Gradually beat in ¼ cup of the granulated sugar and beat until stiff peaks form. Set aside.

3. In another large bowl, beat the egg yolks with the ⅓ cup cocoa powder, the remaining ½ cup granulated sugar, and the salt on high speed until the mixture forms a thick ribbon, about 2 minutes. Stir about a quarter of the whites into the yolk mixture, then fold in the remaining whites. Scrape into the prepared pan and spread evenly.

4. Bake until the cake springs back when pressed in the center, 12 to 15 minutes. Cool completely in the pan on a wire rack. Sift the remaining 2 tablespoons cocoa powder over the top of the roll. Place a large sheet of aluminum foil over the cake and place a baking sheet over the pan. Invert the cake onto the foil. Carefully peel off the waxed paper. Cool completely.

5. To make the filling, in a small bowl, sprinkle the gelatin over the boiling water. Let stand for 10 minutes to soften the gelatin. In a small saucepan over medium-low heat, heat ¼ cup of the heavy cream until just warm. Add to the gelatin mixture, stir to dissolve the gelatin, and cool for 10 minutes. In a chilled medium bowl, beat together the remaining 1¼ cups heavy cream, the confectioners' sugar, orange zest, and vanilla until just stiff. Beat in the gelatin mixture.

6. Spread the filling over the cake, leaving a 1-inch border. Using the foil as an aid, roll up the cake from a long end into a tight cylinder. Transfer the roll to a long platter, seam side down. Cover tightly and refrigerate until the filling sets, at least 1 hour or overnight.

7. To make the ganache, in a medium saucepan, bring the heavy cream to a simmer over medium-high heat. Remove from the heat and add the chocolate, corn syrup, and Grand Marnier. Let stand until the chocolate melts, about 5 minutes. Whisk until smooth and transfer to a medium bowl placed in a larger bowl of ice water. Let stand, stirring often, until chilled and thick, about 5 minutes. Whisk just until soft peaks form—do not overwhisk. Immediately spread the ganache over the roll. Using the tines of a fork, make wavy lines in the ganache to simulate bark. (The roll can be prepared up to 1 day ahead, tented with aluminum foil and refrigerated.)

8. To serve, tuck the juniper under the roll, decorate the cake with the chocolate leaves and truffles, and sift the cocoa powder over all. Serve chilled or at cool room temperature.

Chocolate Leaves: Line a baking sheet with waxed paper. Place 4 ounces finely chopped bittersweet chocolate in the top part of a double boiler over hot, not simmering, water. Stirring occasionally, heat the chocolate until almost completely but not quite melted. Remove from the heat and let stand, stirring occasionally, until completely melted and tepid, about 10 minutes. Holding a lemon leaf in the palm of your hand, and using the back of a teaspoon, coat the underside of the leaf evenly with the melted chocolate. Avoid getting the chocolate on the other side of the leaf. Place the coated leaves on the prepared baking sheet. Refrigerate until the chocolate is firm, at least 30 minutes. (The chocolate leaves can be prepared up to 3 days ahead and refrigerated.) Carefully pull the leaves away from the chocolate and discard. Store the chocolate leaves in the refrigerator until ready to serve. Makes about 12 chocolate leaves.

Gisela's Deluxe Fruitcake

Don't tell me that you don't like fruitcake until you've tried my Auntie Gisela's recipe. I never could understand all the jokes about fruitcake because when I was growing up, I only had Gisela's deluxe version, which wasn't made with the weird colored cherries and artificial booze flavor of commercial brands. The dried cranberries are my addition. Gisela stopped baking before dried cherries and cranberries came onto the market, so she used extra raisins. But, knowing her, she would have used the new dried fruits if she could have.

- The fruitcake must age at least 24 hours before slicing. This allows the flavors to mellow and the fruit and applesauce to give off some moisture into the cake.

- Some people like well-aged fruitcakes. (It also gives them the chance to make them weeks before serving or gift giving.) These fruitcakes are meant to be eaten within two weeks. If you like a cake with a spirited brandy and rum kick, unwrap the cakes after five days and brush them with a combination of brandy and rum, allowing about 2 tablespoons per cake. Rewrap the cakes and continue aging for up to 2 months.

- This recipe makes 5 loaves. It is a waste of time, money, and effort to make fewer. Because this cake is so delicious, you can easily give it as a gift. I assume that most people won't have five loaf pans, so I give baking instructions for the typical 8½ × 3¾ × 2½-inch disposable foil pans.

- You will need a very large bowl (8 to 10 quarts) to mix the batter. If you don't have one, make the cake batter in the largest bowl you have up to where the nuts and fruits are

added. Then scrape the batter into the largest kettle you own and stir in the nuts and fruits.

- Fruitcake bakes at a low temperature so the fruit on the outside of the cake doesn't scorch. Bake only until a wooden skewer inserted in the center comes out clean, or the cake will be dry.

Makes 5 fruitcakes

Make Ahead: The fruitcakes must be made at least 1 day before serving. They can be stored for up to 2 months (see headnote).

6 cups all-purpose flour
1½ teaspoons ground cinnamon
1½ teaspoons baking soda
1½ teaspoons baking powder
1½ teaspoons salt
¾ teaspoon ground cloves
¾ teaspoon freshly grated nutmeg
1½ cups (3 sticks) unsalted butter, at room temperature
2 cups packed light brown sugar
3 large eggs, at room temperature
1 cup store-bought applesauce
½ cup cognac or brandy
½ cup dark rum
3 cups coarsely chopped pecans or walnuts
1½ cups (14 ounces) coarsely chopped glacé oranges
2 cups (14 ounces) dark raisins
2 cups (14 ounces) golden raisins
1 cup (8 ounces) coarsely chopped pitted prunes
1 cup (6 ounces) coarsely chopped dried pineapple
1 cup (5 ounces) dried cranberries

1. Position racks in the center and top bottom third of the oven and preheat to 300°F. Lightly butter and flour five 8½ × 3¾ × 2½-inch

disposable aluminum foil loaf pans. Line the bottoms of the pans with waxed paper.

2. Sift the flour, cinnamon, baking soda, baking powder, salt, cloves, and nutmeg together into a large bowl. Set aside.

3. In a very large bowl, using a handheld electric mixer set at high speed, beat the butter until creamy, about 1 minute. Add the brown sugar and beat until light in texture and color, about 2 minutes. One at a time, beat in the eggs. Beat in the applesauce, ¼ cup of the cognac, and ¼ cup of the rum. Gradually beat in the flour mixture to make a stiff batter.

4. In a medium bowl, mix the pecans, glacé oranges, dark raisins, golden raisins, prunes, pineapple, and cranberries. (Combining the fruits first helps to distribute them more evenly in the batter.) Using a wooden spoon, stir into the batter until well distributed. Spread the batter evenly into the prepared pans, smoothing the tops. Place the pans on baking sheets (this makes it easier to get them in and out of the oven).

5. Bake for 1 hour, just until a wooden skewer inserted in the centers of the cakes comes out clean, 1 hour to 1¼ hours. Let cool in the pans on wire racks for 10 minutes.

6. Invert the cakes onto the racks and peel off the paper. In a small bowl, combine the remaining ¼ cup cognac and ¼ cup rum. Brush the mixture all over the cakes. Set the cakes right side up and cool completely.

7. Wrap each cake in plastic and then aluminum foil. Store in the refrigerator for up to 2 weeks. To store longer, see the recommendations on page 142. Let stand at room temperature for 24 hours before slicing.

Deep Dark Stout Gingerbread

A holiday season never goes by that I don't make this gingerbread at least once. The deep caramel notes of the stout complement the spices beautifully. It is a regular on my buffet tables, because its tight crumb makes it easy for guests to eat out of hand. Also, because it is firm and easy to transport, it is one of my favorite foods to make and give as a present. Serve it warm from the oven for a real treat.

- **Open the stout and pour it into a measuring cup about 1 hour before making the cake so the stout can go flat. Stir it occasionally to help expel the carbonation. Stout often comes in large bottles—if you have leftover stout, cover it tightly with plastic wrap and refrigerate for up to 1 week. You can use the flat stout in beef stew and, of course, plum pudding (see page 153).**

Makes 12 servings

Make Ahead: The gingerbread can be baked up to 2 days ahead.

2½ cups all-purpose flour
2 teaspoons ground ginger
2 teaspoons ground cinnamon
1½ teaspoons baking powder
½ teaspoon baking soda
½ teaspoon salt
1 cup (2 sticks) unsalted butter, at room temperature
1¼ cups packed light brown sugar
2 large eggs plus 1 large egg yolk
1 cup unsulfured molasses
¾ cup flat stout, at room temperature
Confectioners' sugar, for garnish

1. Position a rack in the center of the oven and preheat to 350°F. Lightly butter and flour the inside of a 12-cup fluted tube pan, tapping out the excess flour.

2. Sift the flour, ginger, cinnamon, baking powder, baking soda, and salt together into a medium bowl. In a large bowl, using a handheld electric mixer set at high speed, beat the butter until creamy, about 1 minute. Add the brown sugar and beat until the mixture is light in texture and color, about 2 minutes. One at a time, beat in the eggs, then the yolk. Beat in the molasses.

3. Reduce the mixer speed to low. In three additions, beat in the flour mixture, alternating with the stout, scraping down the sides of the bowl as needed, until the batter is smooth. Scrape into the prepared pan and smooth the top.

4. Bake until a toothpick inserted in the center of the cake comes out clean, 50 to 60 minutes. Cool in the pan on a wire rack for 10 minutes, then invert the cake onto the rack. Transfer to a serving platter, sift confectioners' sugar over the top, and serve warm. Or cool completely and serve at room temperature. (The gingerbread can be baked up to 2 days ahead, covered tightly with plastic wrap and stored at room temperature.)

Marie's Orange-Walnut Cake

My friend Marie Instaschi has been baking this cake as a Christmas gift for friends for years. At first I was just a lucky recipient, but as soon as I got her recipe, it became one of my holiday baking regulars, too. (In fact, I am copying this recipe from a page in my recipe book that is splattered with almost two decades' worth of batter.) Like Deep Dark Stout Gingerbread (page 143), it transports well (Marie's crosses the country to get to me, and it arrives in perfect condition). It also ages well—Marie always ages her cakes for a few days before giving them out, but I can never wait that long.

Makes 12 servings

Make Ahead: The cake can be baked up to 1 week ahead.

2 cups all-purpose flour
1 teaspoon baking powder
1 teaspoon baking soda
½ teaspoon salt
1 cup (2 sticks) unsalted butter, at room temperature
1 cup granulated sugar
3 large eggs, separated, at room temperature
Grated zest of 1 large orange
1 cup sour cream, at room temperature
¾ cup (3 ounces) chopped pecans or walnuts

GLAZE
½ cup Grand Marnier
½ cup confectioners' sugar
Juice of 1 large orange (about ¼ cup)

1. Position a rack in the center of the oven and preheat to 350°F. Lightly butter and flour the inside of a 12-cup fluted tube pan, tapping out the excess flour.

2. Sift the flour, baking powder, baking soda, and salt together into a medium bowl. In a large bowl, using a handheld electric mixer set at high speed, beat the butter until creamy, about 1 minute. Add the granulated sugar and beat until light in color and texture, about 2 minutes. One at a time, beat in the egg yolks, then the orange zest.

3. Reduce the mixer speed to low. In three additions, beat in the flour mixture, alternating with the sour cream, scraping down the sides of the bowl as needed, until the batter is smooth. Stir in the walnuts.

4. In a greasefree medium bowl, using the electric mixer with clean beaters, beat the egg whites just until stiff peaks form. Do not overbeat the whites or they will look lumpy and watery. Using a rubber spatula, stir about a quarter of the whites into the batter to lighten it. Pour the remaining whites on top, and fold them in until the whites are incorporated. Scrape the batter into the prepared pan and smooth the top.

5. Bake until a toothpick inserted in the center of the cake comes out clean, 50 to 60 minutes. Cool in the pan on a wire rack for 10 minutes.

6. To make the glaze, in a medium bowl, whisk together the Grand Marnier, confectioners' sugar, and orange juice to dissolve the sugar. Brush about half of the glaze over the cake, letting it soak in. Invert the cake onto the wire rack, and place the rack over a jelly-roll pan. Brush the remaining glaze over the cake. Cool completely. (The cake can be baked up to 1 week ahead, wrapped tightly in plastic and stored at room temperature.)

Chocolate-Cranberry Truffle Cake

Whenever chocolate is served for dessert, you are guaranteed an appreciative audience. This dense chocolate confection, with its shiny dark glaze, is almost like eating a cranberry-flavored truffle. The whipped cream actually helps balance the richness of the torte, so don't neglect it.

Makes 10 to 12 servings

The cake and sauce can be prepared up to 1 day ahead.

CAKE

¾ cup dried cranberries

⅓ cup red raspberry liqueur, Schnapps, or crème de cassis

1 cup (2 sticks) unsalted butter, cut into pieces

12 ounces bittersweet chocolate, finely chopped

1½ cups sugar

6 large eggs, at room temperature

⅔ cup all-purpose flour

½ teaspoon salt

GLAZE

½ cup plus 2 tablespoons heavy cream

5 ounces bittersweet chocolate, finely chopped

¼ cup dried cranberries, for garnish

SAUCE

1 cup fresh or frozen cranberries

⅓ cup sugar

3 tablespoons red raspberry liqueur, Schnapps, or crème de cassis

Sweetened whipped cream, for serving

1. To make the cake, position a rack in the center of the oven and preheat to 350°F. Lightly butter a 9-inch round springform pan. Line the bottom of the pan with a round of waxed paper or parchment paper. Dust the inside of the pan with flour and tap out the excess.

2. Combine the cranberries and liqueur in a small microwave-safe bowl. Microwave on High for 15 seconds, until the liqueur is hot. Cool. Drain the cranberries and reserve the liqueur.

3. Melt the butter in a medium heavy-bottomed saucepan. Remove from the heat and add the chocolate. Let stand for 1 minute, then whisk until smooth. Whisk in the sugar. One at a time, whisk in the eggs, then the reserved liqueur. Add the flour and salt and stir with a wooden spoon until smooth. Scrape the batter into the prepared pan.

4. Bake until a toothpick inserted 1 inch from the edge comes out with a moist crumb (the center will look barely set), about 45 minutes. Transfer to a wire rack and run a knife around the inside of the pan to release the cake. Cool completely in the pan.

5. Remove the sides of the pan. Place the wire rack over the cake, invert, and remove the pan bottom and waxed paper. Place the cake on the rack on a rimmed baking sheet.

6. To make the glaze, heat the heavy cream in a medium saucepan over medium heat until simmering. Remove from the heat and add the chocolate. Let stand for 1 minute, then stir until smooth. Let stand until slightly thickened but pourable, about 15 minutes.

7. Pour the glaze over the torte. Using a metal icing spatula and working quickly, smooth the glaze over the top and sides of the cake to cover it evenly. Refrigerate the cake until the glaze is beginning to set, about 20 minutes. Sprinkle the dried cranberries around the top edge of the cake to garnish. Refrigerate until the glaze is firm, about 15 minutes. (The cake can be made up to 1 day ahead, covered tightly with plastic wrap and refrigerated. Let

the cake stand at room temperature for 30 minutes before serving.)

8. To make the sauce, bring the cranberries, ¾ cup water, and the sugar to a boil in a small saucepan over high heat, stirring to dissolve the sugar. Reduce the heat to medium and cook until all of the cranberries have burst, about 5 minutes. Purée in a food processor. Rub through a wire sieve placed over a medium bowl; discard the solids in the sieve. Cool. Stir in the liqueur. Cover and refrigerate until chilled (the sauce will thicken), at least 2 hours. (The sauce can be made up to 1 day ahead, covered and refrigerated.)

9. Using a wide metal spatula, transfer the cake to a serving platter. Using a sharp knife dipped in hot water, slice the cake. For each serving, drizzle cranberry sauce onto a dessert plate, top with a slice of cake, and add a dollop of whipped cream.

Mincemeat Lattice Tart

Here's an encore of my favorite mincemeat recipe, first included in *Thanksgiving 101*. This time, instead of a pie, I serve it in a sweetened tart crust covered with a lattice topping. You will have about 3 cups of mincemeat left over. For a quick dessert, warm it over low heat, adding about ⅓ cup apple or orange juice to moisten, and spoon over ice cream.

Makes 8 servings

Make Ahead: The mincemeat can be prepared up to 1 month ahead; the tart can be baked up to 1 day ahead.

MINCEMEAT

2 Golden Delicious apples, peeled and grated (using the large holes of a box grater)

One 12-ounce container (1½ cups) frozen apple
   juice concentrate, thawed
3 ounces (1 packed cup) chopped dried apples
¾ cup (3 ounces) dark raisins
¾ cup (3 ounces) golden raisins
¾ cup (3 ounces) dried currants
¾ cup (3 ounces) dried cranberries
⅔ cup candied orange peel
⅓ cup chopped candied lemon peel
½ cup packed dark brown sugar
½ cup dark rum
½ cup cognac or brandy
4 tablespoons unsalted butter
½ teaspoon ground cinnamon
½ teaspoon ground allspice
½ teaspoon freshly grated nutmeg
½ teaspoon ground cloves

SWEET TART DOUGH
2 cups all-purpose flour
¼ cup granulated sugar

¼ teaspoon salt
9 tablespoons (1 stick plus 1 tablespoon)
   unsalted butter, chilled, cut into ½-inch pieces
2 large egg yolks
6 tablespoons ice water

2 tablespoons unsalted butter, cut into pieces, for
   topping

1. To make the mincemeat, in a large Dutch
oven, bring the fresh apples, apple juice
concentrate, dried apples, dark raisins, golden
raisins, currants, dried cranberries, candied
orange peel, candied lemon peel, brown sugar,
dark rum, cognac, butter, cinnamon, allspice,
nutmeg, and cloves to a boil over medium heat,
stirring often. Reduce the heat to medium-low
and cook, stirring often, until the fruits are
softened and the liquid almost completely
evaporates, about 25 minutes. Transfer to a
medium bowl and cool completely. Cover tightly

It Wouldn't Be the Holidays Without
. . . Mincemeat

The mincemeat we serve today is a
throwback to the days when meats were
preserved for long periods without
refrigeration. Tough pieces of meat, offal,
and suet were finely minced and cooked with
sugar and liquor (for preservation) and spices
and candied fruits (for flavor). The resulting
confection could be topped off with more
liquor for longer storage. Butchering usually

took place in the winter, so the minced meat
would age until the next year.

   It can be argued that without meat you
can't call it mincemeat, but modern tastes
have lightened the original recipe. Even in
England, where holiday mincemeat tarts are
piled high in bakery windows throughout the
season, you would be hard put to find any
that are made with real meat or suet.

with plastic wrap and refrigerate overnight or up to 1 week. (To store the mincemeat for up to 1 month, stir in an additional ¼ cup dark rum and ¼ cup cognac every week or so.)

2. To make the tart dough, in a medium bowl, whisk the flour, granulated sugar, and salt to combine. Using a pastry blender, cut in the butter until the mixture resembles coarse crumbs. In a small bowl, beat the egg yolks with the ice water. Stirring the dry ingredients with a fork, gradually mix into the flour mixture until completely moistened and clumping together. Gather the dough together. Divide the dough into 2 disks, one slightly bigger than the other. Wrap in waxed paper and refrigerate until chilled, about 1 hour.

3. Position a rack in the center of the oven, place a baking sheet on the rack, and preheat to 375°F. Lightly butter a 9-inch round tart pan with a removable bottom.

4. On a lightly floured work surface, dust the larger disk of dough with flour, and roll into a ⅛-inch-thick circle. Fit into the prepared pan, making sure that the crust fits snugly into the corners. Trim the dough overhang to ½ inch. Fill the tart shell with 3 cups of the mincemeat (reserving the rest) and dot with the butter.

5. On the floured work surface, dust the smaller disk of dough with flour and roll into a ⅛-inch-thick circle. Using a ruler and a pizza wheel (or a sharp knife), cut the dough into ¾-inch strips. Arrange the dough strips on top of the filling in a lattice pattern, trimming the edges of the strips where they touch the bottom crust. Fold over the edges of the bottom crust and press against the top edge of the pan.

6. Place the tart on the hot baking sheet. Bake until the crust is lightly browned, about 45 minutes. Cool on a wire rack for 30 minutes. Serve warm or at room temperature. The tart can be baked up to 1 day ahead; cover the tart loosely with aluminum foil and bake in a preheated 350°F oven for about 15 minutes.

Pear and Cranberry Crisp

Sometimes instead of the typical ornate Christmas sweet, I need a crowd-pleasing dessert. That's when I bake this homey, satisfying, and delicious crisp. If you wish, serve it with vanilla ice cream or sweetened whipped cream.

- **For best results, think ahead and buy the pears 3 or 4 days before you want to bake the crisp. Markets rarely carry ripe pears because they must be picked and transported while hard. Ripen them in a closed brown paper bag at room temperature. Do not try to ripen them in the refrigerator. Not only will they never ripen, but the cores will be brown and soft.**

Makes 8 to 12 servings

Make Ahead: The crisp can be baked up to 8 hours ahead.

FILLING

8 ripe medium Anjou or Bartlett pears, peeled, cored, and cut into ½-inch wedges
One 12-ounce bag fresh or frozen cranberries
1 cup granulated sugar
2 tablespoons all-purpose flour
2 tablespoons unsalted butter, cut into small pieces, chilled

TOPPING

½ cup all-purpose flour
½ cup packed light brown sugar
6 tablespoons unsalted butter, cut into small pieces, chilled
1 teaspoon ground cinnamon
1 cup chopped walnuts

1. Position a rack in the center of the oven and preheat to 350°F. Lightly butter a 13 × 9-inch glass baking dish.

2. To make the filling, in the prepared dish, toss together the pears, cranberries, granulated sugar, flour, and butter.

3. To make the topping, in a medium bowl, using your fingertips, work the flour, brown sugar, butter, and cinnamon until combined and crumbly. Work in the walnuts. Sprinkle the topping evenly over the filling. Place on a baking sheet.

4. Bake until the juices are bubbling and the pears are tender, about 45 minutes. Serve hot, warm, or at room temperature. (The crisp can be baked up to 8 hours ahead, cooled, covered, and stored at room temperature.)

Peppermint Profiteroles with Chocolate Sauce

The cooling flavor of peppermint is so refreshing after a big meal. I'm not saying that these ice cream–stuffed cream puffs with their warm chocolate sauce are light—just delicious. This is a restaurant-style dessert that really is easy to duplicate at home. The components can all be made well ahead of time and put together just before serving. (It helps to have someone help to fill the profiteroles.)

- **The profiteroles are most easily shaped with a pastry bag fitted with a ½-inch-wide plain tip. Or drop the dough by teaspoonfuls onto the baking sheet.**

Makes 8 servings

Make Ahead: The profiteroles can be baked up to 1 week ahead and frozen. The ice cream should be made at least 4 hours and up to 2 days ahead. The chocolate sauce can be prepared up to 2 days ahead.

CREAM PUFFS

6 tablespoons (¾ stick) unsalted butter, chilled, cut into ½-inch pieces

1½ teaspoons sugar

⅛ teaspoon salt

¾ cup unbleached all-purpose flour

4 large eggs, at room temperature

ICE CREAM

1½ pints high-quality vanilla ice cream, slightly softened

23 hard red-and-white-striped peppermint candies, crushed (about ⅓ cup)

1½ teaspoons clear peppermint extract

CHOCOLATE SAUCE

1 cup heavy cream

9 ounces bittersweet or semisweet chocolate, finely chopped

Additional red-and-white-striped peppermint candies, crushed, for garnish

Sprigs of fresh mint, for garnish

1. To make the cream puffs, position a rack in the center of the oven and preheat to 400°F. In a medium heavy-bottomed saucepan, bring ¾ cup water, the butter, sugar, and salt to a full boil over high heat, stirring occasionally to melt the butter. Reduce the heat to medium. Add the flour and stir until the dough forms a ball that clears the sides of the pan and lightly films the bottom of the pan, about 2 minutes. Remove from the heat and cool for 10 minutes.

2. Using a handheld electric mixer set at low speed, beat in 3 of the eggs, one at a time. Transfer to a pastry bag fitted with a plain ½-inch tip (such as Ateco No. 5). Pipe sixteen 1½-inch-wide mounds of dough onto an ungreased baking sheet. In a small bowl, beat the remaining egg. Lightly brush the tops of the mounds with the beaten egg, smoothing the pointed tops with a pastry brush. Do not drip egg onto the baking sheet.

3. Bake the cream puffs until golden, about 20 minutes. Reduce the oven temperature to 350°F and continue baking until the puffs are golden brown and crisp, about 10 minutes. Remove from the oven and pierce the side of each puff with a small, sharp knife tip. Return to the oven and bake for 5 more minutes. Transfer to wire racks and cool completely. (The profiteroles can be baked up to 1 week ahead, stored in self-sealing plastic bags and frozen. Thaw at room temperature, then recrisp in a preheated 400°F oven for 5 minutes. Cool before filling.)

4. At least 4 hours before serving, make the peppermint ice cream. Mix together the ice cream, crushed candy, and peppermint extract in a medium bowl. Transfer to an airtight container, cover, and freeze until solid, at least 4 hours or up to 2 days.

5. To make the sauce, heat the heavy cream in a medium saucepan over medium heat until simmering. Remove from the heat and add the chocolate. Let stand until the chocolate softens, about 5 minutes. (The sauce can be prepared up to 2 days ahead, cooled, covered, and refrigerated. Reheat in a double boiler.)

6. To serve, split the pastries in half crosswise. Place one scoop of ice cream into the bottom of each puff. Cover with the tops. Spoon equal amounts of sauce into 8 shallow bowls. Place 2 profiteroles in each bowl. Sprinkle with crushed candy and garnish with a mint sprig. Serve immediately.

Shortcakes with Pears in Brandied Cream Sauce

Strawberry shortcake has its place as a summertime masterpiece, but other seasonal fruits can be used to make shortcakes throughout the year. This version uses sautéed pears in a creamy, brandy-spiked sauce. If possible, use star-shaped cookie cutters for the biscuits—they will give a festive look to the dessert.

Makes 12 servings

Make Ahead: The shortcakes can be baked up to 8 hours before serving. The pears can be peeled and prepared up to 2 hours before serving.

BISCUITS

1¾ cups all-purpose flour

1 cup cake flour (not self-rising)

¼ cup plus 1 teaspoon granulated sugar

4 teaspoons baking powder

½ teaspoon baking soda

¾ teaspoon salt

10 tablespoons (1¼ sticks) chilled unsalted butter, cut into ½-inch pieces

About 1 cup buttermilk

1 large egg, beaten

PEARS

8 firm-ripe Bosc pears, peeled, cored, and cut into ½-inch-thick wedges

2 tablespoons fresh lemon juice

2 tablespoons unsalted butter

⅓ cup Poire Williams (clear pear-flavored brandy) or regular brandy

½ cup packed light brown sugar

2 cups heavy cream

Sprigs of fresh mint, for garnish

Fresh raspberries, for garnish

1. To make the biscuits, position racks in the center and top third of the oven and preheat to 400°F. Sift the all-purpose flour, cake flour, ¼ cup granulated sugar, the baking powder, baking soda, and salt into a large bowl. Add the butter and cut in with a pastry blender until the mixture resembles coarse crumbs with a few pea-size pieces. Stir in the buttermilk, adding a little more if needed to make a soft dough. Knead a few times in the bowl until the dough comes together.

2. On a lightly floured work surface, roll the dough out to a ½-inch thickness. Using a 3-inch diameter star-shaped biscuit cutter, cut out biscuits. Gather up the scraps, knead lightly, reroll, and cut out additional biscuits to make a total of 24. Place on two ungreased baking sheets, spacing 2 inches apart. Brush the tops of the biscuits lightly with the egg, then sprinkle with the remaining 1 teaspoon granulated sugar.

3. Bake until golden brown, switching the position of the baking sheets from top to bottom and front to back halfway through baking, 18 to 20 minutes. (The biscuits can be baked up to 8 hours before serving, cooled completely and wrapped in aluminum foil. Reheat the foil-wrapped biscuits in a preheated 350°F oven for 10 minutes before using.)

4. To make the filling, in a medium bowl, toss the pears with the lemon juice. (The pears can be prepared up to 2 hours ahead, covered and refrigerated.)

5. In a very large skillet, melt the butter over medium heat. Add the pears and cook, stirring occasionally, until just tender, about 6 minutes. Stir in the Poire Williams, then the brown sugar. Add the heavy cream, increase the heat to high, and bring to a boil. Cook until the cream reduces by about a third (it should coat a wooden spoon), about 5 minutes.

6. To serve, divide the hot pears among 12 shallow bowls. Top each serving with 2 biscuits, garnish with mint sprigs and raspberries, and serve warm.

Gingerbread Soufflés with Eggnog Sauce

It was my dear friend Kelly Polan who gave me the idea for this dessert—she had misplaced her original recipe and asked me to replicate it. Now they are one of my favorite holiday dinner finales. Soufflés are not hard to make, and, in fact, are practically all make ahead. However, you will need eight 6-ounce ramekins, and a quick step when it comes time to serve them.

Makes 8 soufflés

Make Ahead: The soufflé base can be prepared up to 4 hours ahead.

7 tablespoons unsalted butter, plus 1 tablespoon chilled unsalted butter, cut into pieces
⅓ cup plus 2 tablespoons all-purpose flour
1¾ cups half-and-half, warmed
1¾ cups packed dark brown sugar
2 tablespoons finely chopped crystallized ginger
2 teaspoons ground ginger
1 teaspoon ground cinnamon
½ teaspoon freshly grated nutmeg
¼ teaspoon ground cloves
6 large eggs, separated, plus 2 large egg whites (whites at room temperature)
1½ cups New Wave Eggnog (page 21) or store-bought eggnog, for serving

1. Lightly brush the insides of eight 6-ounce ramekins with butter, then coat the insides with granulated sugar, tapping out the excess sugar.

2. Melt the 7 tablespoons butter in a moderately large saucepan (it must be large

enough to fold in the egg whites later) over medium-low heat. Whisk in the flour. Let the roux bubble, without browning, for 1 minute. Gradually whisk in the warm half-and-half and brown sugar and increase the heat to medium. Cook, whisking constantly, until the mixture comes to a simmer and is very thick. Remove from the heat and stir in the crystallized ginger, ground ginger, cinnamon, nutmeg, and cloves. Dot the top with the butter pieces, and cover with a piece of plastic wrap, pressing the wrap directly on the surface of the soufflé base. (The soufflé base can be prepared up to 4 hours ahead, stored at room temperature. Stir over medium-low heat until warmed before proceeding.)

3. When ready to bake the soufflés, position a rack in the center of the oven and preheat to 400°F. Place the ramekins on a large rimmed baking sheet.

4. Whisk the 6 egg yolks into the warm soufflé base. Beat the 8 egg whites in a large bowl using an electric mixer set on high speed until soft peaks form. Stir a quarter of the whites into the soufflé base, then fold in the remaining whites.

5. Ladle the soufflé mixture into the ramekins, filling them about three-quarters full. Bake until the soufflés are fully puffed and the edges are lightly browned, about 15 minutes.

6. Serve the soufflés immediately (if not sooner!). Pass a pitcher of eggnog at the table, so each guest can poke a hole in their soufflé and add the eggnog as a sauce.

Figgy Pudding Noel

"Oh, bring me a figgy pudding . . ." The pudding made famous by the carol "We Wish You a Merry Christmas" is a delicious dessert that is much lighter than other steamed puddings from the British Christmas tradition. If you want to flambé the pudding with cognac or brandy, use apple juice to soak the figs, otherwise your pudding will be too spirited. Be sure to use a firm, high-quality sandwich bread to make the crumbs.

Makes 6 to 8 servings

2½ cups fine, dry, freshly ground bread crumbs (made from about 12 slices stale bread, crusts trimmed off)
½ cup milk
1 cup (about 8 ounces) finely chopped dried figs, preferably Calimyrna
3 tablespoons cognac, brandy, or apple juice
3 large eggs, at room temperature
1 cup granulated sugar
4 tablespoons unsalted butter, melted
1½ teaspoons baking powder
½ teaspoon salt
1 cup heavy cream
2 tablespoons confectioners' sugar
½ teaspoon vanilla extract

1. Generously butter the inside of a 1½- to 2-quart tubed steamed pudding mold. Dust with flour and tap out the excess.

2. In a medium bowl, moisten the bread crumbs with the milk. In a small bowl, combine the figs and cognac. Let both mixtures stand for 10 minutes.

3. In a large bowl, whisk together the eggs, granulated sugar, melted butter, baking powder, and salt until combined. Stir in the soaked bread crumbs and the figs with their cognac. Pour the batter into the prepared mold and cover with the lid.

4. Place a collapsible metal steamer in a large kettle. Add enough water to come just beneath the steamer and bring to a full boil over high heat. Place the mold on the steamer and cover tightly. Reduce the heat to low. Simmer, adding more boiling water as needed to keep a good head of steam, until a toothpick inserted in the center of the pudding comes out clean, about 2 hours. Let the pudding stand for 5 minutes.

5. Meanwhile, in a chilled medium bowl, using a handheld electric mixer set at high speed, beat the heavy cream, confectioners' sugar, and vanilla until stiff peaks form. Set aside.

6. Run a sharp knife around the inside of the mold to release the pudding. Unmold the pudding onto a platter. Slice and serve warm with a dollop of the whipped cream.

Yuletide Plum Pudding

Plum pudding is a Christmas classic that just doesn't get served at any other time of year. It is absolutely beloved by the British, but hasn't established itself as one of America's favorite Yuletide sweets. Nonetheless, I include it because the words "plum pudding" sing with holiday good cheer, and there is plenty of romance attached to it via Dickens's well-known Christmas stories. And the proliferation of steamed pudding molds in kitchenware shops in December shows that I am not alone in loving this kind of dessert!

It Wouldn't Be the Holidays Without . . . Plum Pudding

The "plum" in plum pudding refers to dried prunes. Over the years, some recipes evolved to omit the prunes in favor of raisins. Today it can be made with all manner of dried and candied fruits.

Plum pudding is another Christmas food with origins older than Christianity itself. Druids believed that Daga, the god of plenty, celebrated the winter solstice by mixing up a pudding of the earth's bounty, including meats, fruits, and spices. For centuries the pudding was somewhat unceremoniously boiled in a sack. The Victorians finally cosseted the pudding in a mold or basin to give it the more uniform shape we have today.

In England the fruits and liquors for the pudding are traditionally prepared on the last Sunday before Advent, called "Stir-Up" Day. One of the prayers for that day's service begins, "Stir up . . . ," which acts as a wake-up call for the task that awaits the parishioners when they return home. The mixture is stirred once a week or so by each family member for good luck, then steamed on Christmas morning.

Thanks to my British friends Howard Shepherdson and Rod Marten for invaluable research assistance. Not only did they both supply their mums' recipes, but they also hosted a taste test of packaged plum puddings in their London kitchen. What a feast for my fellow plum pudding lovers!

- In Britain and Australia, a homemade plum pudding is usually enormous and steamed in a big heatproof bowl for 8 hours or more. I use a typical 6-cup tubed steamed pudding mold to reduce the cooking time, though it still takes 5 hours. It can be aged for days, weeks, or even months, just like a fruitcake, doused every week with about ¼ cup of brandy, dark rum, or both. I find that for American tastes, a couple of days is enough. Steamed pudding molds are available by mail order through Sur La Table (1-800-243-0852) and other kitchenware shops.

- Old recipes for plum pudding call for beef suet, the hard, crisp fat around the kidneys. I prefer to use butter because it's easier to find, but you can substitute shredded beef suet, for a plum pudding that the Cratchits would admire.

- Some hard-line traditional cooks wouldn't dream of serving plum pudding without hard sauce (creamed butter and confectioners' sugar spiked with brandy). I prefer the coolness of vanilla ice cream or whipped cream with the warm pudding. It's up to you.

Makes 8 to 10 servings

Make Ahead: The plum pudding should be made at least 1 day or up to 3 days ahead. Allow 5 hours for the pudding to steam. The hard sauce can be prepared up to 1 day a head.

1 large Granny Smith apple, peeled, cored, and diced

½ cup chopped pitted prunes

½ cup dark raisins

½ cup golden raisins

½ cup dried currants or additional raisins

½ cup chopped candied lemon peel, candied orange peel, or a combination of both

½ cup finely chopped almonds

1½ cups fresh bread crumbs, prepared from firm white sandwich bread

¾ cup packed light brown sugar

⅔ cup all-purpose flour

½ cup stout

2 large eggs, beaten

4 tablespoons (½ stick) cold unsalted butter, shredded on the coarse holes of a box grater

2 tablespoons brandy or dark rum

1 teaspoon ground cinnamon

1 teaspoon ground ginger

½ teaspoon salt

½ teaspoon ground allspice

¼ teaspoon freshly grated nutmeg

¼ teaspoon ground cloves

Grated zest of 1 orange

¼ cup brandy, for flambéing

Hard Sauce (recipe follows), vanilla ice cream, or sweetened whipped cream, for serving

1. Butter well and flour the inside of a 1½-quart covered tubed steamed pudding mold.

2. In a large bowl, combine the apple, prunes, dark raisins, golden raisins, currants, citrus peel, and almonds. Add the bread crumbs, brown sugar, flour, stout, eggs, butter, 2 tablespoons brandy, cinnamon, ginger, salt, allspice, nutmeg, cloves, and orange zest. Mix very well. Spoon into the prepared pudding mold, smooth the top, and cover.

3. Place the pudding on a trivet or a collapsible steamer rack in a large kettle. Fill the pot with enough hot water to reach the bottom of the steamer rack. Cover the pot tightly and bring the water to a boil over high heat.

4. Reduce the heat to medium-low. Cook at a steady simmer, keeping a full head of steam going and adding boiling water to the pot as needed, for 5 hours. The pudding is done when it has lost its raw look, has a rich dark brown color, and is firm to the touch. You will have to remove the mold and open it to check the pudding's progress. Be careful of the steam and hot water!

5. Transfer the pudding mold to a wire rack and let cool for 10 minutes. Invert the pudding onto a plate. Cool completely. Wrap the pudding in aluminum foil and refrigerate at least overnight and up to 3 days.

6. To reheat, butter the steamed pudding mold well. Unwrap the pudding. To heat by steam, slip it back into the mold. Place the mold in the pot and steam again in simmering water until heated through, about 1 hour. To reheat in a microwave, place the pudding, upside down, in a large microwave-safe bowl. Cover the pudding with plastic wrap. Heat on Medium-High (70 percent power) until heated through, 10 to 15 minutes, depending on the wattage of your oven (the higher the wattage, the less time needed to reheat the pudding). The pudding is heated through when an instant-read thermometer inserted in the center reads 165°F. Be careful of the steam when you uncover the pudding. Invert the pudding onto a rimmed heatproof plate.

7. In a small saucepan, heat the brandy over low heat just until warm. Do not allow the brandy to come to a boil. (Brandy won't flame unless it is warm, but if overheated, it could unexpectedly ignite.) Pour the warm brandy over the pudding and light the brandy with a match. Present the flaming pudding, spooning the brandy over the top of the pudding until it extinguishes. Serve hot, with the Hard Sauce.

Hard Sauce: In a medium bowl, using a handheld electric mixer set at high speed, beat 1 cup (2 sticks) room temperature unsalted butter until creamy, about 1 minute. On low speed, gradually beat in 1 cup confectioners' sugar. Beat in 2 tablespoons brandy, 2 tablespoons dark rum, and ¼ teaspoon freshly grated nutmeg. Serve at room temperature. (The hard sauce can be prepared up to 1 day ahead, covered tightly and refrigerated. Return to room temperature.)

Classic Raspberry and Sherry Trifle

Lovers of gooey desserts will give this trifle high marks. Pound cake spread with raspberry jam, drizzled with sherry or apple juice, and layered in a glass trifle bowl with raspberries and custard sauce, the disparate ingredients marry into an impressively rich concoction that is perfect for feeding a crowd. But one word of advice: Trifle is only as good as its components. Buy a good pound cake from your favorite bakery, imported preserves, and a nice bottle of sherry, and you'll have a masterpiece.

- **A smooth custard sauce is one of the hallmarks of a good cook. It is stirred constantly to discourage the eggs from overcooking and scrambling. A wooden spatula works better than a wooden spoon because it scrapes the bottom of the pan more efficiently and can get into the corners more efficiently.**

- **Don't overcook the custard, or the eggs will scramble. The custard should cook to the point when it thickens enough to nicely coat a wooden spatula. Until you've done this frequently enough that you recognize the thickness by sight, use an instant-read thermometer to gauge when the custard is cooked to 185°F. If you cook the custard much** beyond this point, or anywhere near the boiling temperature of 212°F, it will become grainy. Some cooks rescue scrambled custard by whirling it in a blender until smooth again, but I find the fixed sauce tastes "eggy." If you do botch a batch, it's best to toss it out and start over again.

- Custards are strained before serving to remove any pieces of cooked egg white and to ensure a silky smooth texture. Egg whites set at a lower temperature than egg yolks, so there will always be a few strands of stray white or chalazae (the thin white cord attached to the yolks) in the sauce that should be removed.

- You can make the trifle in any 3-quart glass bowl, but a footed glass trifle bowl looks especially festive. (After the holidays, use the bowl to serve fruit or vegetable salads or tiramisù.) Trifle bowls are available at houseware stores during the holiday season.

Makes 10 to 12 servings

Make Ahead: The trifle should be prepared at least 8 hours ahead, and can be refrigerated for up to 1 day.

CUSTARD SAUCE

2½ cups milk

½ cup granulated sugar

7 large egg yolks, at room temperature

1 teaspoon vanilla extract

One 16-ounce store-bought pound cake, cut into ½-inch-thick slices

½ cup sweet sherry, such as cream or oloroso

1 cup high-quality raspberry preserves

2 pints fresh or frozen raspberries (see Note)

2 cups heavy cream

3 tablespoons confectioners' sugar

1½ teaspoons vanilla extract

⅓ cup sliced almonds, toasted

1. Start the trifle at least 8 hours before serving. To make the custard sauce, in a medium heavy-bottomed saucepan, heat the milk and granulated sugar over medium-low heat until very hot, stirring occasionally to dissolve the sugar.

2. In a medium bowl, whisk the egg yolks to combine. Gradually stir about 1 cup of the hot milk mixture into the yolks, then whisk them into the saucepan. Cook over medium-low heat, stirring constantly with a wooden spatula, until the custard is thick enough to coat the spoon, about 3 minutes. An instant-read thermometer inserted into the custard should read 185°F. Do not let the custard come to a boil. Strain the custard through a wire sieve into a medium bowl. Stir in the vanilla. Press a piece of plastic wrap directly onto the surface of the custard and pierce a few holes into the wrap with the tip of a sharp knife. Let stand on a wire rack until cooled to room temperature.

3. Stand cake slices around the inside of the bowl and more on the bottom, trimming the cake as needed. Drizzle about ¼ cup of the sherry over the cake. Using a rubber spatula, spread some of the preserves on the exposed sides of the cake slices (this doesn't have to look perfect). Fill the bowl with half the raspberries. Top with more cake slices, spread with preserves, and sprinkle with 2 tablespoons of the remaining sherry. Repeat with the remaining raspberries, cake slices, preserves, and sherry. (Don't be concerned if you have leftover cake or not quite enough.) Slowly pour the custard sauce over all. Cover tightly with plastic wrap and refrigerate for at least 8 hours, or preferably overnight.

4. Just before serving, in a chilled large bowl, using a handheld electric mixer set at high speed, beat together the heavy cream, confectioners' sugar, and vanilla until stiff peaks form. Spread over the top of the trifle and sprinkle with the almonds. Serve chilled, topping each portion with some of the whipped cream topping and almonds.

Note: Use individually frozen raspberries, not block-frozen. Place the frozen raspberries in a wire sieve and rinse under cold running water to remove any ice crystals. Do not thaw the raspberries completely.

Poached Pears with Zinfandel and Five-Spice Syrup

Poached pears are a favorite winter dessert because they aren't too filling after a rich meal. The Asian spice combination of star anise, Szechuan peppercorns, cinnamon, cloves, and fennel is a delightful addition to the typical wine-poaching mixture. You'll need whole spices, as five-spice powder will give the wine syrup a gritty, dusty texture. Bosc pears hold their shape best after poaching, and Zinfandel wine has a peppery edge that is complemented by the spices. Serve the pears with crisp cookies (the Moravian Spice Wafers on page 120 are my favorite, but buttery plain cookies are fine, too, even high-quality store-bought ones).

● You may have to go to an Asian market to find star anise and rust-colored Szechuan peppercorns, where they will be very reasonably priced. An Asian market is also the place to find cinnamon sticks and fennel seeds at bargain prices, too. You will have plenty of spices left over.

Star anise makes a fine addition to mulled wine, or it can be ground in a spice grinder and used with ground cinnamon in cookies and apple pies.

Szechuan peppercorns have an aromatic menthol scent; add a few of them to poultry or meat broths or crush and use to season roasts. They were outlawed briefly in the United States because the peppercorns (actually berries of a bush) were thought to carry a plant disease, but that proved to be incorrect and they are now available again.

The cinnamon in Asian markets is often soft-bark cassia, which has more flavor than the typical hard cinnamon sticks, but it can be used in the same way.

Fennel seeds, which have a mild licorice flavor, are frequently required in Mediterranean recipes.

Store the spices in tightly sealed containers in a cool, dark place. If you don't use them in a year, toss them out, as they will have lost much of their flavor.

Makes 8 pears

Make Ahead: The pears can be made up to 1 day ahead.

Eight 8-ounce firm-ripe Bosc pears
1 lemon, cut in half
One 750-milliliter bottle Zinfandel wine
¾ cup packed light brown sugar
2 star anise
2 cinnamon or cassia sticks
½ teaspoon Szechuan peppercorns
6 whole cloves
¼ teaspoon fennel seeds

1. To peel and partially core the pears, working one at time, using a vegetable peeler, peel the pears, leaving the stems intact. Using a small, sharp knife, working from the bottom of each pear, remove the bottom third of each core. If necessary, trim the bottom so the pear will stand up. As each pear is peeled and cored, rub the surface with a lemon half and set aside.

2. In a large, nonreactive (nonaluminum) saucepan large enough to hold the pears in a

single layer, bring the wine, brown sugar, star anise, cinnamon, Szechuan peppercorns, cloves, and fennel seeds to a simmer over high heat. Add the pears, on their sides, and reduce the heat to medium-low. Cover tightly and simmer, turning the pears after 20 minutes, until they are tender when pierced with the tip of a sharp knife, about 45 minutes total. Using a slotted spoon, stand the pears upright in a shallow dish.

3. Strain the cooking syrup through a fine-mesh wire sieve into a medium bowl and return to the pot. Boil over high heat until the cooking liquid is thickened and reduced to about 1½ cups, 10 to 15 minutes. Pour the syrup over the pears. Cool completely. Cover and refrigerate until well chilled, at least 2 hours. (The pears can be prepared up to 1 day ahead.)

4. To serve, place a pear in a soup plate and drizzle with the syrup.

Holiday Menu Planner

Here are complete menus and timetables for five different holiday parties. I've included an all-dessert party, an open house that could work as a tree-trimming event or a New Year's celebration, two separate sit-down dinners for moderately large groups, and an intimate New Year's supper for four.

Photocopy the timetable and tape it up in the kitchen so you can mark off the steps as you finish them. Tape up the menu, too.

Before making a recipe, read it thoroughly, checking to ensure that you have the right utensils and any special ingredients. If you don't have a cookbook holder, or you just don't have enough counter space, photocopy the recipe and tape it up at eye level on a kitchen cabinet. This is a real space saver.

Most of the dishes for the buffets are make ahead. Make sure you have enough refrigerator space for storage. Remember that large roasts should sit for 20 minutes before carving (a large turkey can stand for at least 45 minutes). This gives the cook time to finish the side dishes. Take advantage of this window of opportunity!

Nutcracker Sweets Party

The holidays are the time for indulging, and this menu is Indulgence with a capital I. An all-dessert menu can be served as a late-afternoon tea or as an after-dinner party. Be sure to state "A Dessert Party" on the invitation, so no one comes expecting dinner. Choose Marie's Orange-Walnut Cake, Pear and Cranberry Crisp, or Classic Raspberry and Sherry Trifle as the centerpiece of the menu, and make a double or triple batch of the main event. Single batches of the cookies and fudge will suffice.

You can make any cookies you like, but the ones here have been chosen to give a variety of shapes and flavors. Choose either gingerbread or sugar-cookie dough, and cut out cookies for decorating as you prefer. When I make this menu, I bake large cookies and write the name of each guest on each one to have as a party favor. (When baking large cookies, you may want to make a double batch of dough.) Decorating cookies takes time, but the other cookies I've suggested are very easy to make.

Instead of wine, I set out a coffee bar so guests can make their own specialty coffees if they like. Offer bottles of Irish whiskey, coffee-flavored liqueur, brandy, and dark rum with bowls of lightly sweetened whipped cream and sugar cubes, then let people make coffee drinks to their taste. You will need a large-capacity coffeemaker. This menu will serve up to 24 guests.

Marie's Orange-Walnut Cake (page 144), *or*

Pear and Cranberry Crisp (page 148), *or*

Classic Raspberry and Sherry Trifle (page 155)

Gingerbread Cookies 101 (page 116) *or*

Sugar Cookies 101 (page 114)

Chewy Molasses Drops (page 127)

Cranberry Oat Bars (page 134)

Chocolate, Cranberry, and Walnut Fudge (page 100)

Hot Coffee

Cold Apple Cider

Assorted Liqueurs and Brandies

Bowls of Sweetened Whipped Cream and Sugar Cubes

Timetable

5 days ahead:

Make orange-walnut cake; wrap airtight and
store at room temperature

Make fudge; store in airtight container at room
temperature

4 days ahead:

Bake molasses drops; store in airtight container
at room temperature

2 days ahead:

Make gingerbread or sugar cookies; decorate
and store in airtight container at room
temperature

Bake cranberry bars; wrap individually in plastic
and store in airtight containers at room
temperature

1 day ahead:

Make trifle; cover and refrigerate

4 hours ahead:

Make crisp; store covered at room temperature

1 hour ahead:

Make coffee

Whip cream; refrigerate

A Tree-Trimming Open House

This is my kind of holiday party menu. Every dish is cooked ahead of time, and requires just an occasional refilling of bowls and platters as the party progresses. The menu is designed for 24 guests, but you may multiply the yield of these dishes to as many servings as you need. However, prepare and bake the cakes one at a time, as cake recipes don't always work well when extended. Make double batches of the cauliflower and tortellini salads and the bread. You could make a double batch of the chicken cassoulet, but it is rich and most guests won't take much, especially with ham and salads on the table.

If you wish, you can offer plain apple cider and red and white wines with the holiday beverages, but the seasonal drinks will be pretty popular.

Santa Fe Crunch (page 13)

Sicilian Caponata with Garlic Crostini (page 12)

Caesar Dip with Crudités (page 11)

Stilton and Walnut Balls (page 11)

Salami and Cheese Stuffed Bread (page 92)

Baked Smoked Ham with Pineapple and Seeded Mustard Glaze (page 53)

Chicken Cassoulet (page 54)

Cauliflower Salad with Red Pesto Dressing (page 38)

Tortellini Antipasto Salad (page 40)

Assorted Rolls and Mustards for Ham

Deep Dark Stout Gingerbread (page 143)

S'mores Rocky Road (page 102)

Spritz Butter Cookies (page 130)

Old-Fashioned Eggnog (page 20)

Mulled Wine with Honey and Orange (page 25)

Timetable

5 days ahead:
Make caponata; refrigerate
Make cheese balls; refrigerate
Make rocky road; store in airtight container at
room temperature

3 days ahead:
Make crunch; store in airtight container at room
temperature
Make Caesar dip; refrigerate
Bake spritz cookies; store in airtight container at
room temperature

2 days ahead:
Bake gingerbread; wrap tightly and store at
room temperature

1 day ahead:
Prepare crudités for dip; refrigerate
Make chicken cassoulet; refrigerate
Make cauliflower salad; refrigerate
Make eggnog; refrigerate

8 hours ahead:
Make dough for bread; let rise, then bake; cool
and store at room temperature
Bake crostini; store in paper bags at room
temperature

6 hours ahead:
Make tortellini salad; refrigerate

3 hours ahead:
Bake ham

1 hour ahead:
Remove caponata from refrigerator

Just before guests arrive:
Stir broth into cassoulet and add bread crumb
topping; reheat
Make mulled wine; keep warm
Transfer eggnog to punch bowl; add ice cream
to keep chilled
Thinly slice stuffed bread and place on platter

After serving:
Put out gingerbread, rocky road, and cookies

Roast Beef for Dinner

This celebratory meal is extravagant but not hard to make. While the dinner starts out rich, then gets richer, it concludes with refreshing poached pears in a spicy syrup.

If you aren't buying Prime grade meat, and you choose to refrigerate-age your beef (see page 51), allow 3 to 5 days for aging. Time the dinner service from when the roast beef comes out of the oven. Slip the gratin into the oven, increase the heat to 400°F, and serve the soup. By the time the soup is cleared, the *au jus* sauce prepared, and the vegetables heated, the gratin should be hot. If you choose to make the Yorkshire Puddings, the batter is very easy to mix up, but you will need a second oven or plan to reheat the gratin in a microwave oven. Preheat the oven to 400°F before baking the puddings—they need high heat to rise properly. The roast beef will stay perfectly warm, tented loosely with aluminum foil.

This is a meal for very good wines. Serve a crisp Sauvignon Blanc with the soup, then move on to an excellent aged Cabernet Sauvignon. If you wish, serve port with dessert.

Sweet and Spicy Candied Walnuts (page 105)

Parsnip and Leek Soup with Bacon (page 43)

Rib Roast *au Jus* 101 (page 48)

Sour Cream–Horseradish Sauce (page 49)

Potato, Mushroom, and Roquefort Gratin (page 78)

Baby Carrots and Green Beans in Tarragon Butter (page 74)

Herbed Yorkshire Puddings (page 80; optional)

Poached Pears with Zinfandel and Five-Spice Syrup (page 157)

Hot Coffee and Tea

Timetable

3 days ahead:
Make walnuts; store in airtight container at room temperature

Up to 1 day ahead:
Make pears; refrigerate
Make soup; refrigerate
Make horseradish sauce; refrigerate
Blanch baby carrots and green beans; refrigerate

About 2 hours before serving:
Make roast beef
Make gratin; store at room temperature
Cook and crumble bacon for soup; store at room temperature

About 1 hour before serving:
Remove horseradish sauce from refrigerator

15 minutes before roast is done:
Reheat soup; keep warm

When roast is done:
Transfer roast to serving platter
Reheat gratin
Bake puddings, if making
Serve soup

Just before carving roast:
Make *au jus*; transfer to gravy boat
Finish baby carrots and green beans

After serving roast:
Make coffee and tea
Serve pears

A Plantation Turkey Feast

Here's a turkey dinner that features down-home southern flavors. It will serve up to 12 people. I try to keep my turkey menus under control by not serving too many side dishes. If I am already serving stuffing and sweet potatoes, I see no need to add mashed potatoes, even though tradition may dictate it. However, you can if you wish.

The time of the dinner centers around when the turkey is done. Remove the turkey from the oven and serve the crab cakes and salad. The pudding can be reheated in the oven while the turkey stands. Remember that the turkey must rest for at least 20 minutes before carving. While the sugar cakes can be reheated before serving, they are also fine at room temperature. Serve a Chardonnay or a Pinot Noir with this menu.

Spicy Cheese Straws (page 14)

Crab Cakes on Baby Greens with Lemon Vinaigrette (page 31)

Roast Turkey with Bourbon Gravy (page 60)

Cornbread Succotash Stuffing (page 80)

Yam and Pineapple Pudding (page 79)

Long-Simmered Greens (page 74)

Cranberry-Kumquat Chutney (page 83)

Moravian Sugar Cakes (page 88)

The Original Ambrosia (page 41)

Hot Coffee and Tea

Timetable

1 week ahead:
Make chutney; refrigerate
Make turkey stock for gravy; freeze

2 days ahead:
Bake cheese straws; store in airtight container at
room temperature

1 day ahead:
Make cornbread; let stand at room temperature,
uncovered, to stale
Make long-simmered greens; refrigerate
Make sugar cakes; store in self-sealing plastic
bags at room temperature
Make ambrosia; refrigerate
Make lemon vinaigrette; refrigerate
Defrost stock overnight in refrigerator

About 6 hours before serving:
Make stuffing; stuff turkey
Roast turkey

About 4 hours before serving:
Make crab cakes; refrigerate

About 2 hours before serving:
Make yam pudding; store at room temperature

15 minutes before turkey is done:
Cook crab cakes; keep warm
Transfer chutney to serving dish
Finish pudding and bake

When turkey is done:
Transfer turkey to serving platter
Reheat extra stuffing
Reheat cheese straws
Toss baby greens with vinaigrette; serve with
crab cakes

Just before serving turkey:
Make gravy; transfer to gravy boat

After serving turkey:
Make coffee and tea
Reheat sugar cakes; serve
Serve ambrosia

An Intimate New Year's Eve

We enjoy spending New Year's Eve with very close friends and a very special menu. This is a time for treats that you don't have every day of the year, like Champagne and caviar.

There are no tricks to this menu except for timing the potatoes. A second oven comes in handy here, as the potatoes ideally cook at 400°F, and the duck cooks at 450°F. If you wish, cook the potatoes in the same oven as the duck, but reduce the cooking time to about 30 minutes. If the potato skins seem to be browning too much, tent the potatoes with aluminum foil.

Start with a simple selection of your favorite cheeses served with walnuts and ripe pears. I like a blue cheese, such as gorgonzola, with this combination. After serving the first course, it will take about 12 minutes to cook the duck breasts and spinach and reheat the wild rice, so bring your guests into the kitchen with you to chat while you cook if you wish. Serve Champagne with the caviar and a Pinot Noir or French Burgundy with the duck.

For dessert make the entire recipe, even though you will be using only half for this meal. The remaining cream puffs can be frozen for up to 1 month and used for another dessert or filled with savory stuffings and heated as appetizers. The leftover ice cream will keep for 2 days, and the chocolate sauce can be refrigerated for up to 1 week.

Assorted Cheeses, Pears, and Walnuts

Salt-Roasted Yukon Gold Potatoes with Caviar and Crème Fraîche (page 35)

Two-Way Duck with Pecan-Orange Wild Rice (page 55)

Sautéed Spinach (page 57)

Peppermint Profiteroles with Chocolate Sauce (page 149)

Hot Coffee and Tea

Timetable

1 week ahead:
Make crème frâiche (if not purchasing)
Bake cream puffs for profiteroles; freeze

2 days ahead:
Prepare ice cream; freeze
Prepare chocolate sauce; refrigerate

1 day ahead:
Cut up ducks; refrigerate
Render duck fat; refrigerate
Make duck stock; refrigerate
Make duck sauce; refrigerate

2 hours ahead:
Make wild rice; store at room temperature

1½ hours ahead:
Steam duck; store at room temperature
Recrisp and fill profiteroles; freeze until serving

1 hour ahead:
Cook spinach

About 45 minutes before serving:
Roast potatoes

About 30 minutes before serving:
Roast duck

After serving potatoes:
Cook duck breast
Reheat spinach
Reheat wild rice
Reheat duck sauce

After serving duck:
Make coffee and tea
Reheat chocolate sauce
Serve profiteroles

Gifts from the Kitchen

A number of recipes in this book are perfect for holiday gift giving. Kitchenware shops and mail-order catalogues carry empty bottles, cookie tins, and candy boxes to lend your gift a finished, professional look. With cookies or baked items that keep best stored airtight, I often purchase covered plastic containers, and give the container along with the gift. A cake or cooked plum pudding in a tube pan or steamed pudding mold with the recipe attached makes a wonderful present for a fellow cook.

Index